From Nihilism to Possibility

Democratic Transformations for the Inner City

UNDERSTANDING EDUCATION AND POLICY
William T. Pink and George W. Noblit, *series editors*

From Nihilism to Possibility

Democratic Transformations for the Inner City

edited by
Frederick Yeo
Southeast Missouri State University

Barry Kanpol
St. Joseph's University

HAMPTON PRESS, INC.
CRESSKILL, NEW JERSEY

Printed in the United States of America

Library of Congress Cataloging-in-Publication Data

From nihilism to possibility : democratic transformations for the
  inner city / edited by Frederick Yeo, Barry Kanpol
      p. cm. -- (Understanding education and policy)
    Includes bibliographical references and index.
    ISBN 1-57273-212-1. -- ISBN 1-57273-213-X (pbk.)
      1. Education, Urban--United States. 2. Critical pedagogy--United
  States. I. Yeo, Frederick L. II. Kanpol, Barry. III. Series.
  LC5141.F76 1999
  370'9173'2--dc21   99-34379
                                                                     CIP

Hampton Press, Inc.
23 Broadway
Cresskill, NJ 07626

Contents

Series Preface

Books in this series, *Understanding Education and Policy*, will present a variety of perspectives to better understand the aims, practices, content and contexts of schooling, and the meaning of these analyses for educational policy. Our primary intent is to redirect the language used, the voices included in the conversation, and the range of issues addressed in the current debate concerning schools and policy, In doing this, books in this series will explore the differential conceptions and experiences that surface when analysis includes racial, class, gender, ethnic and other key differences. Such a perspective will span the social sciences (anthropology, history, philosophy, psychology, sociology, etc.), and research paradigms.

Books in the series will be grounded in the contextualized lives of the major actors in school (students, teachers, administrators, parents, policymakers, etc.) and address major theoretical issues. The challenge to authors is to fully explore life-in-schools, through the multiple lenses of various actors and within the anticipation that such a range of empirically sound and theoretically challenging work will contribute to a fundamental and needed rethinking of the content, process and context for school reform.

As the evidence mounts about the failure of school reform, there is a tendency to believe nothing is possible and to surrender to despair over the future of education. Fred Yeo and Barry Kanpol, in *From Nihilism to Possibility: Democratic Transformations for Inner City Education*, demonstrate that the reason for the failure of school reform is due to the nature of the reforms proposed. They and the other authors who have contributed to this volume show that reforms which are fundamentally democratic create new possibilities for schools and for our society. To be sure, the possibilities are grounded in critical praxis and pedagogy. With critique, new possibilities can be uncovered. With democracy, new possibilities can be realized. We are glad to have this book as part of the series, *Understanding Education and Policy*.

Introduction: Our Own "Peculiar Institution": Urban Education in 20th-Century America

Fred Yeo
Southeast Missouri State University

Barry Kanpol
St. Joseph's University

In the mid-1800s, the institution of slavery was rendered socially innocuous in this country by referring to it as that "peculiar institution," thereby connoting both legitimacy and a certain quaintness outside of normative society. The legality and social rightness of slavery as an institution was supported by political, social, economic, and religious ideologies that portrayed the "Negro" as being enslaved for his or her own good, for the good of White society as constituting America, and/or because the "Negro" deserved segregation and disenfranchisement due to his or her barbarous and inferior nature. The historical entrenchment of the synergism of White cultural and political entitlement and racial minority disenfranchisement has left us a legacy whereby Black Americans are in general perceived to be at fault for their own social and economic failure, are better off segregated in some manner from White society, and that this somehow constitutes a moral, economic, and political "good." In like fashion, both Hispanic and Native Americans have come to be similarly associated with segregation, less-than-adequate education, and to be perceived as self responsible for both. This U.S. notion of the "common sense" of racialized inequalities has recently come to the political forefront in the so-called "backlash" against affirmative action, immigration, and perceptions of minority entitlements introduced into the electoral process in several states (e.g., California) during the 1996 national elections.

During the latter part of the 19th century and the first half of the 20th, education for minorities in this country varied, not so much in quality, but in its response to geographic, demographic, and legal contexts. Two major developments shaped the nature of schooling for Black Americans during this time period; the evolution of segregated education, both de jure in the south and de facto in the north, which was given the force of law by the Supreme Court decision of Plessey v. Ferguson in the 1880s, and the dramatic demographics of Black relocation to urban areas of the north to escape rural poverty in the South. Beginning in the 1870s, this process has continued right up to the present time, although currently it has been somewhat muted by the return movement of African Americans to semi-rural areas of the midwest and south to escape the harshness and poverty of U.S. center-city life. Both of these trends, socially and economically derived and generated, gave rise to the distinct educational institutions intended and actualized to segregate the majority of Black Americans from the mainstream of U.S. society. By the middle of the 20th century, and continuing into the late 1990s, these trends have culminated in the creation of the stereotypic urban scene in this country, where cities are perceived as repositories of blackness, danger, crime, poverty, and social dissolution (Haymes, 1995).

At the end of the 20th century, the terms and names have changed, the locus of the environment has shifted from rural to urban, Negro has become African American, Mexican has become Hispanic or Latino, Indians has evolved into Native Americans, but 140 plus years after the adoption of the 13th and 14th amendments to the Constitution, 150 years after the *Brown v. Board of Education of Topeka Kansas* decision, the typifications and those synergistic social understandings remain at the heart of U.S. mainstream ideology. The categorization of people of difference, generally referred to as people "of color" for reasons having to do with the U.S. ideology of race (Omi & Winant, 1986), based on assumptions of inferiority, blame, and rationalization of the requisites of segregation, have expanded to include Hispanic/Latino, Native American, and Southeast Asian people within the rubric of what constitutes the "urban." Urban centers have become and are represented as a terrain of black, nightmarish, kaleidoscopic images of burned-out husks of buildings, city streets whose images flash by of wrought-iron bars on store windows and doors, graffiti, bars, roving police cars and helicopters, and knots of blank faces congregating on corner's and in doorways, all combining to form an atmosphere of ugly xenophobia, palpable tension and violence bearing witness to the consequences of the lethal linkage of economic decline, cultural decay, and political lethargy in U.S. life (Bell, 1992).

As noted by Massey and Denton (1993) in *American Apartheid*, most Americans (particularly White Americans) perceive that urban centers are peopled by racial minorities for the most part, but few appreciate the depth of minority segregation or the degree to which it is maintained by ongoing institutional arrangements and contemporary individual actions. The assumption sponsored by mainstream political, economic, and cultural leaders (including educators), and maintained by educational institutions, is that segregation is to be found in only a few places in the south and a few of the larger cities. Even textbooks for educational introduction courses posit that segregation has been cured by busing, civil rights laws, and affirmative action (e.g., Hessong & Weeks, 1991). Massey and Denton (1993) argued that there is little recent data to suggest in fact that racial segregation has been moderated over the 1980s, nor is there anything in the political or social climate of the country to suggest that it will, the recent *Time Magazine* articles notwithstanding (Kunen, 1996).

> Our fundamental argument is that racial segregation—and its characteristic institutional form, the black ghetto—are the key structural factors responsible for the perpetuation of black poverty in the United States. Residential segregation is the principal organizational feature of American society that is responsible for the f creation of the urban underclass. (Massey & Denton, 1993, p. 9)

Segregation (in whatever form, including that of Native American reservations) functions institutionally to link other racialized inequities by the synergistic concentration of effect in an isolated spatial/urban area. Urban areas represent spatially racialized social values in the urban realization of the ideology of apartheid (Haymes, 1995). White mainstream society has defined the issues of urban-ness as technical, negating the issues of race and segregation, and promulgating policies within the mediated image of the city as alien, foreign, a place to fear (i.e., the urban has become a metaphor for racialized locales of less-than-human-others). More pointed, however, is the charge that the maintenance of racial segregation is intrinsic and rooted in U.S. culture. The minority enclaves of the inner city, ghetto, and barrio are part of modern U.S. society. They are maintained by a set of institutions, attitudes, and practices that are deeply embedded in the structure of U.S. life. As conditions in the ghetto have worsened and as poverty-stricken minority communities have struggled socially and culturally with this deteriorating environment, the ghetto has assumed even greater importance as an institutional tool for isolating the by-products of racial oppression: crime, drugs, violence, illiteracy, poverty, despair, and their growing social and economic costs (Massey & Denton, 1993; West, 1993).

This is nowhere more true, and more tragic, immoral, and violative of democratic principles, than in the schools that have come to represent the ill chances of peoples of difference to share in the "American Dream" occasioned by educational opportunity (Weiner, 1993; Yeo, 1996). In this sense, the inner-

4 Yeo & Kanpol

city school has come to be representative in this culture of all that is to blame, to be held as responsible for social failure and personal nihilism, and to constitute the location of those who represent alienation within the U.S. social matrix. Movies, such as *Dangerous Minds, Boyz in the Hood, Dead Presidents, Lean on Me*, and so on, illustrate the personal and sociocultural qualities we as a society have come to associate with those who inhabit the realm of the urban.

Within the geographical and political enclaves of urban zones, inner-city schools, whose dehumanizing conditions should be a national embarrassment except that they exist within a national concord of silence, bear witness to the national response to the increasing diversification and impoverishment of this country's ethnic minority populations. U.S. urban schools are increasingly populated by a clientele that is "of color," predominantly Black and Hispanic, poor, non-English speaking and educationally demarked by profound racialized differences in achievement scores, drop-out rates and illiteracy (Grossman, 1996; Neito, 1995).

These schools almost universally include bankrupt districts, burgeoning populations of minorities and immigrants, classrooms empty of materials but packed with children, pandemic drug and alcohol abuse, gang violence, nonexistent resources, crumbling physical plants, all situated in impoverished communities malignant with anger and frustration. The national drop-out percentile for secondary schools is in the low 20s, but it is 65% to 75% in most urban schools (Fine, 1991). In Chicago's ghetto schools, only 8% of a ninth-grade class will graduate reading at grade level, only 15% will even graduate (Fine, 1991). Many urban children come to school hungry, abused, or poorly clothed. They come to school from communities distinguished by empty buildings, boarded-up shops, proliferating liquor stores, random violence, pent-up anger and dehumanizing marginalization, poverty, and self-inflicted crime. Urban youths who begin their lives at the greatest risks of class, racial, or ethnic or gender exploitation, who have the least to begin with in terms of community and educational resources, attend the most traumatized schools in the country and receive the poorest and most impoverished educations (Fine, 1991).

Their school experience is demarked by often overwhelming educational failure unheeded or addressed by local school or distant state educational administrators. For example, among Black and Hispanic students in the five largest U.S. cities, the drop-out rate exceeds 55%, and for Black males it approximates 75%; nationwide (Comer & Haynes, 1990). Other research reports disclose similar figures representing unprecedented social and educational failure in that 50% to 80% of all inner-city students dropout by the second year of high school; 1 million urban teenagers cannot read above the third-grade level, and almost 25% are functionally illiterate. This same report cites that in New York City alone, 66% of all high school students fail to graduate; for Hispanics the rate is more than 80%; for Blacks, 72%; and for other non-Whites, the statistics are around 70%. Hispanics, the fastest growing minority, have been particularly damaged; 40% of all Hispanic students drop out before grade 10, 35% are systematically tracked into vocational education or special education (Kozol, 1991; Lomotey, 1990; Nieto, 1995).

The tragic result of these kinds of school experiences in the inner city is evident in the continued reproductive cycles of student and school failure and the prophesy-fulfilling dropping out of adolescents they understand that school cannot ensure a job, so they drop out and ensure joblessness. The irrelevance of the curriculum, the turnover in teachers, the burdensome pedagogy, and the discordance of school rhetoric juxtaposed to student experiential knowledge results in large numbers (many times in excess of 50%) of students choosing to make their own way in the more familiar and seemingly affirming world of the streets and gangs (Fine, 1991; Yeo, 1992, 1996).

To put the statistics in more human terms, racial segregation and racialized education of children is bad enough, but when the hellish conditions of inner-city schools are added, travesty and tragedy become the order of the day. Jonathan Kozol (1991) noted not only the remarkable degree of racial segregation in urban schools but that national reports are obsessed with passing and achievement scores, literacy rates and drop-out rates, but not inequality and segregation. Segregation has been reinstituted in this country, both in the cities and in urban schools. For the first time since the Supreme Court's ruling in *Brown v. Board of Education* took effect, racial and ethnic segregation, between cities, suburbs, schools, and classrooms, is growing worse (Kunen, 1996). The statistics of poverty, free lunches, low testing scores, illiteracy, school violence, and the myriad of other reductionistic outpourings of city schools represent the daily school lives of millions of urban children. These places, along with the rest of the urban zones in which they exist, spawn lives cheapened by poverty, violence, and the racism of an uncaring society that blames them for the very conditions it imposes.

> Something violent hits almost every young person living in America's inner cities. The flagrant violence of street crime, the concealed violence within families, and the silent violence of emotional neglect and absence of nurture are commonplace in urban neighborhoods . . . the violence that is part of their lives disables or deflects any positive sense of future or even the conviction that they have a future. . . . "Ain't no makin it" in legitimate or mainstream society becomes the perceived reality of most inner city youngsters. (Heath & McLaughlin, 1993, p. 37)

However, it is not enough to document the numbers, the losses, nor is it enough to simply empathize with the hurt, the failure, the anger that resonates through the corridors and classrooms of urban schools. There are unequivocally reasons, understandings, and choices, as well as groups and individuals that formulate the texture of inner-city education. These connections between people, institutions, and cultural differences do not arise by accident. The actors' beliefs, cultural consciousnesses, and identities (both individual and collective) come together synergistically within urban schools and classrooms to form and drive the particular educational practices of inner-city education.

Urban schools, particularly the inner-city variety, represent the educational portion of a society that, as Heath and McLaughlin (1993) commented, has always had a love-hate relationship with cultural diversity. In what is perhaps one of the most divisive contradictions of our society, the public seems to want on one hand to discern and label any possible source of ethnicity or cultural diversity, whereas on the other hand it wants to claim to promote integration and cultural homogenization to deny differences (Heath & McLauglin, 1993). Thus, urban schools have become pedagogical creatures of assimilation, representative of educational rhetoric frozen in baleful promises of success, and totally irrelevant curriculum.

In order to comprehend the "why" of inner-city schools and in order to offer for discussion any amelioration of their conditions, practices, and failures, we must confront the consummatory social ideology of our culture; the defining of the "Other," the alien stranger, and the subsequent dehumanization of those so labeled on the basis of race, not ethnicity, meritocracy or distorted individualism. To understand what passes for education in urban schools, the state mandates that position the funding, the curriculum or pedagogy, and the ongoing urban travesty against democratic ideals is to confront what Derrick Bell (1992) called the "faces at the bottom of the well; the maintenance in American society of racism" (p. 12), that is deeply and inextricably embedded in the psychology, economics, politics, religion, education, and culture of our society. This is specifically not to argue that economics, other ideologies of the U.S. scene (individualism, competition, elitism, etc.), and extracts of Euro-Western culture and philosophy are not important in forming American society. However, the issue is their synchronicity within the penumbra of racism and the historical development of inner cities.

URBAN EDUCATIONAL RESEARCH

Currently, much of the mainstream educational literature attempts to explain the experiences and structures of urban education in such a way that the schools and their occupants are disconnected from their environment, as if they could be analyzed in absentia from their community, or as if inner-city schools represent suburban schools gone wrong somehow. Or that urban schools represent some focal point for substantive or transformative social change in U.S. society. Much of that literature, particularly in its mainstream educational versions, reflects the pervasive ideologies of this country wherein loss, failure, and personal devastation are seen as the failures of the victim.

Current texts on urban and inner-city schools represent a myriad of approaches to urban education, from moderate texts on teaching minority children and "how to survive" practical guides, to critical and other radical texts on multiculturalism as a transformative curriculum for urban schools, to more liberal and humanistic tracts on bringing cultural sensitivity to curriculum and pedagogy in urban classrooms. One increasing trend in the literature about urban and inner-city schools is the emergence of ethnographic and autobiographical-oriented explorations of the human, social, and cultural side of urban schools and their meaning for the lives of the students who pass through these institutional travesties.

Admittedly, critical theorists and researchers in education have attempted some description and theorizing on the systemics and dehumanization of minority education in a general sort of way; on the need to reconstruct both the social and ideologic paradigms of how we understand what is often referred to as *urban* education; and on the need to incorporate educationally configured postmodern understandings of issues such as difference, identity, borders, marginalization, and so on. Yet, each of these arguments have foundered in the face of the degrading conditions of racial segregation and deracinationalized education that demarks inner-city education.

It is perhaps justifiable, then, that the mood of so many critical theorists is one of increasing despair. Even from within a democratic and critical perspective, it seems that there is really no hope, no transformative possibilities for inner-city schools; nor any way for them to begin to match their more affluent contestors for cultural, economic, or ideological capital, despite the plethora of multicultural or "excellence" panaceas that have gripped educators in recent years in this country. Perhaps that is why much of the critical literature has eschewed directly grappling with inner-city education.

Recently, other Critical educators have begun within the boundaries of mainstream education and suburban schools to argue for a moral or spiritual infusion of issues aimed at reconstitution of democratic values and purposes in education. However, noticeably absent within this discourse of Critical moralism has been the "inner-city" school site where difference, marginalization, spiritual nihilism, and oppression are the norm. Even within the bold efforts framed within the discourse of "border pedagogy" there has been little attention paid to the potential for democratic meanings and pedagogy within inner-city school systems and locations.

It has been our intent to construct this text as a project that includes to some extent these same critical arguments, and moves to specifically and directly apply their respective understandings to education in inner-city schools. While acknowledging that there do exist excellent works describing various facets of inner-city education, they generally fall short of advocating theory and practices for transformation of inner-city education through the development and application of critical principles grounded in the sense of the postmodern, the moral, and possibility. It is our purpose to attempt a combination of postmodern and the democratic.

Within that frame, it is the purpose of this text to investigate and propose in both theory and praxis a democratic educational platform that suggests means and rationales to move beyond the despair and hopelessness that informs inner-city education. Although recognizing that it may seem somewhat contradictory to the postmodern condition, it is the guiding intention here to propose some form of comprehensive educational framework that while paying heed to issues of difference, and so on, also argues for a democratic platform of education for inner-city schools that directly confronts mainstream society's unwillingness to recognize such a platform and the hopelessness and despair evident within even the critical approach that struggles to postulate it.

Within the project's intent, we wanted a text that would not only articulate a somewhat eclectic, albeit grounded in notions of critical democracy, theorizing on the subject of urban schools, but would ground or connect theory building with the practices of inner-city schools as represented by ethnographic or narrative experiences. Additionally, we desired that all contributions, whether theoretical in scope or more praxis oriented, would help formulate an overall scheme of an educational framework that while paying heed to issues of difference, identity, ethnicity, poverty, and educational and community borders would also argue for an unabashedly democratic platform for urban schools. Although the individual chapters represent a broad range of educational understandings and locations, as well as ethnicities and gender, each confronts mainstream education's unwillingness to recognize its own agendas, its blatant refusal to acknowledge its undemocratic ideologies and practices, and the human loss and despair that are too often hidden behind urban school doors.

The collection, although not formally so structured, divides into two parts. The first is essentially theoretical and is represented by chapters 1 through 4. The second part, although equally grounded in the theoretical, is framed in more descriptive, even practical, pieces that tend to include ethnography and similar forms of educational research. All of the chapters, some more prosaically than others, offer arguments and suggestions for the construction of a more democratic praxis for urban curriculum, pedagogy, and educational organization.

CHAPTER DESCRIPTION

In chapter 1, Carlson questions the purposes and assumptions underlying the current "detracking" movement in urban school systems. He argues that couched within transformative and humanistic rhetoric is a "reform" that will act to increasingly dichotomize school tracks, decrease opportunities for a larger group of urban students, and decrease chances for hopes of any democratic notions within urban school structures. At the same time, he notes how an increasing postmodern sensibility in our culture as to identity and difference is being eroded and increasingly truncated into dualistic, oppositional motifs polarizing communities and thought into educational schemes that underwrite increasing separation and inequitable social tracks. Carlson argues that although there are potential benefits for the changes in how the tracks are organized within and among schools, these are being subordinated by corporate and bureaucratic interests into increasingly hardened class structures. In essence, and as to urban education, Carlson points out that urban schools are being relegated in toto to a lower track placement that will condemn their students to irrelevant and service-oriented tasks.

Chapter 2 by Anijar, is powerfully postmodern, aesthetic, and jars the reader by evoking her and a reader's sense of self, angst, and nihilism. Put into the frame of urban education, Anjar's language and imagery can, for a sensitive reader, displace one into the self-symbolism of adolescents who are the citizenry of the margins. In keeping with the spirit of the chapter, we have struggled to find the right music to listen to while becoming entwined within the imagery—but we allow and encourage the readers to do so for themselves. The author moves the reader/participant through a series of intersections with urban adolescents whose lives are struggles with the signifiers of post-Fordist America, where, as she notes, multiculturalism is about places that tourists alone define and ethnicity is imposed from without silencing the within. Education in urban schools is about the children of the cities who are perceived as the leading cultural disease, it is about new metaphors wrapped around old messages of oppression absorbing enduring images and symbols of identity and experience. The chapter is both disquieting and thought-provoking, which is the author's intent as she witnesses her own and "her" children's struggle with an urban sense of despair, hopelessness, and what constitutes truth and meaning.

Lalvani, in Chapter 3, analyzes the nature of the inner city, what he terms an *inner space* that represents the racialized conscious of this society and culture. The chapter examines the nature and truths of the inner city through the lens of popular culture and its inherent, if subliminal, critique and contestation over legitimating middle-class notions of race and the urban poor. Lalvani also argues that it is the very dialectical nature of popular culture, and its importance as a social signifier, that requires its incorporation into critical pedagogy as the significant resource representing the urban disenfranchised. He argues that this means that schooling institutions in the urban centers must take as their primary pedagogical tool and focus, the affective, including the senses and the sense of the body, the spirit, and the multiple loci in which the purveyors of inner-city popular culture live and move. The chapter concludes that it is with popular culture and its inclusion as an index of basal relevance that lies potential democratizing education for urban schools.

Boateng argues in chapter 4 that multicultural education as emplaced in urban schools needs to be disconnected from its continued centering within a European gestalt, and other centralities promulgated (e.g., Black studies, etc.). The chapter delineates what should be a meant by a multicultural curricular program to enhance student engagement and argues that at its heart, multicultural education requires the infusion of non European experiences into educational capital. The author points out that it is often inappropriate teacher behavior based on teachers' own Euro-dominated cultural capital that is one of the major blockages to such an infusion, tangentially implicating teacher education. He follows up by using Black studies as an exemplar of an infusive program designed to change the way Black students (and as an example as to others) are perceived and taught. In the course of such an infusion, the material can and should democratize urban education.

In chapter 5, Pink explores the use of the organizational concept of *school pairing* to energize inner-city elementary schools. Pink argues that in contradiction to conventional wisdom about such models, both inner-city and suburban schools benefited in a number of ways from the collaboration. The chapter is based on a research project involving two such "paired" schools in Chicago, and results in the inescapable conclusion that this kind of organizational restructuring (which Pink notes occurs outside of district bureaucratic auspices and involvement) has tremendous potential for urban schools, teachers, and students. The issue is one of seeking ways to redefine an urban and suburban school's culture through mutual educational and professional development. The chapter describes the project, its operative assumptions, the specific purposes and goals, implementation, and the basal requirement for all parties to enter into reflective dialogues that problematize practices, values, and presumptions about others so as to seek substantive democratic change. It is the need for this kind of dialogue that makes such a project both problematic and potentially rewarding and is the primary interstice of any such pairing. The chapter describes each parties' efforts, stumblings, and how the two schools managed to effect the project.

Chapter 6, by Weiner, looks at two federal programs of the 1960s for the purpose of considering how reforms in teacher education might effect educational outcomes in urban school reform in the 1990s. She notes how these other similar programs are often constructed ahistorically, that is without reference to the successes or failures of prior programs intended to bring some form of educational reform to urban schools. The result, according to the author, is the continued reproduction of additional failure resulting in increasing inertia acting against urban educational reform. One of the significant issues raised in this chapter is the failure of many such reform programs to incorporate and connect with existing teacher cadres in the urban schools, often inculcating in new teachers' minds that these older, experienced teachers are somehow the "enemy." Historically, such programs have alienated the current teachers and in the contested process at school sites have often ended up pitting new versus existing teachers. Additionally, the chapter analyzes the effect that urban school organizations and bureaucracies have had on derailing substantive reform, suggesting another area that urban school reformers need to address in proposing transformational programs. The author notes the pivotal nature of teacher education, both in implementing and sustaining urban school failure and its contemporaneous potential to provide the critical catalyst for change, which teacher education has generally chosen not to do. This leads the chapter into suggestions about realistic possibilities for urban reform.

Chapter 7, by Yeo and Kanpol, argues for specific changes in the goals and assumptions of curriculum and pedagogy currently used and proposed to be used in reform packages within urban schools. Framed initially by Yeo's narrative as an inner-city school teacher, the chapter critiques current curricular schemes for their lack of democratic understandings and basal values, particularly those deriving from current holistic/humanist-oriented multicultural programs. The authors argue that in order to engender democratic educational change, the basic values and overall philosophy must be transformed to a democratic one, in practice as well as in terms of its rhetoric. The chapter ends by detailing how such a democratic formula contrasts with others, how it can substantially change the pedagogical praxis in urban schools, and suggest how such ideals might be used in schools and teacher education to change urban teaching and education.

In chapter 8, Yeo argues that the continued educational failures of inner-city schools are derived of two primary factors; first, the U.S. cultural ideologies as to race and the urban. Second, the actual educational practices utilized in urban schools, which are flawed by the mix of dominant cultural understandings concerning minority communities and students and the misapprehensions and assumptions used to rationalize these practices. The author connects community issues with those of the schools and examines how under the auspices and hegemony of the broader cultural understandings the current reforms of multiculturalism and "skills" packaging of curriculum and pedagogy are antagonistic to community histories, values, and goals, as well as largely irrelevant in the classroom. The chapter examines the manner of the use of multicultural education in urban schools acts to further educators' current notions of learning, which results in increased failure and estrangement of students from schooling and mainstream society, and becomes another rationalization for blaming the victim and the community commensurate with already extant assumptions about minorities in this country. The author argues that possibilities for success in and with urban schools lies in realigning the focus of education in these schools to include the communities themselves, and although he sees problematics with radical Left programs of intervention and social reconstruction, does assert the potential for a critically democratic educational motif in the reinterpretation of urban educational settings and goals.

Flannery, in chapter 9 investigates through an ethnographic research project, the educational meanings and implications of interactions between Puerto Rican women and adult health care educators and providers in New York City. The focus is on adult educational experiences occurring off site from traditional institutionalized educational processes. The author argues that given the high incidence of school disconnection and educational failure in the traditional sense of Latina's, that significant learning experiences however do occur in the arena of health care, as well as in other daily experiential locations. She asserts that much of adult education in the urban environment occurs in such contexts and it is these interactions that need further research by critical educators. The chapter describes her research project, the setting, the women involved, their experiences, their own interpretations of their educational experiences, and the implications for urban communities and urban education in the more traditional sense for adult learners.

In chapter 10, Kanpol and McLaren collaborate in an interview session with one of Kanpol's graduate classes. Many of the students involved are teachers themselves, although they acknowledge their unfamiliarity with issues of urban education and urban school sites. The discussion revolves around the problems of urban education in U.S. society and the potential for a democratizing agenda through the use of critical pedagogy in the reformation of the curriculum and pedagogy used in urban schools. Through the questions put to him, McLaren responds with explanations of the history, use, and potential of critical pedagogy, particularly in terms of urban education. McLaren discusses from his own experiences as an urban teacher, the problems, failures, and successes of inner-city teaching, but also asserts the possibilities inherent within critical pedagogy for democratic change and transformation. He also responds to the question of despair that seems to be the atmosphere for so much of Left critique, and acknowledges the question of public and educator apathy in seeking or understanding such change. The questions and answers are pointed and raise concerns as to teachers' roles in policy, student success, and issues involving the overall culture of U.S. education.

CONCLUSION

It was and is our intent to produce a text that directly confronts the problematics of education in U.S. inner cities, and while acknowledging the despair and hopelessness that suffuses both these schools' efforts and the research that describes and theorizes about them, we want to argue for and pose agendas for hope and transformation grounded in critically democratic educational concerns that are morally, politically, and educationally emancipatory. We believe that this text initiates at least the discussion of those agendas. Each of the chapters looks at different areas and approaches to issues concerning urban education, although all argue for the potential of transformation within a democratic critical pedagogy approach.

The authors, all of whom are educators (many with years of teaching in urban schools), evidence their own struggles with the concerns and experiences of urban education through their willingness to participate in this project. Although we acknowledge that this text in some senses merely scratches the surface of the issues of urban education, we do believe that it is a start. All of the authors in this book have agreed that those who advocate the use and inculcation of critical pedagogy with its potential for democratic change and reform must begin to focus more on the educational margins, that is to begin to argue and advocate on behalf of the students, teachers and communities in America's center cities. It is with heartfelt thanks that editors note the efforts of each of the contributors to take on that task.

REFERENCES

Bell, D. (1992). *Faces at the bottom of the well.* New York: Basic Books.

Comer, J., & Haynes, N. (1990). Helping Black children succeed: The significance of social factors. In K. Lomotey (Ed.), *Going to school: The African American experience* (pp. 103-112). Albany: SUNY Press.

Fine, M. (1991). *Framing drop-outs.* Albany: SUNY Press.

Giroux, H. (1992). *Border crossings: Cultural workers and the politics of education.* New York: Routledge.

Grossman, H. (1995). *Teaching in a diverse society.* Boston: Allyn & Bacon.

Haymes, S. (1995). *Race, culture and the city: A pedagogy for black urban struggle.* Albany: SUNY Press.

Heath, S., & McLaughlin, M. (Eds.). (1993). *Identity & inner-city youth: Beyond ethnicity and gender.* New York: Teachers College Press.

Hessong, R., & Weeks, T. (1991). *Introduction to the foundations of education* (2nd ed.). New York: Prentice Hall.

Kozol, J. (1991). *Savage inequalities: Children in America's schools.* New York: Crown.

Kunen, J.S. (1996, April 29). The end of integration. *Time Magazine,* pp. 39-45.

Lometey, K. (Ed.). (1990). *Going to school: The African American experience.* Albany: SUNY Press.

Massey, D., & Denton, N. (1993). *American apartheid: Segregation and the making of the underclass.* Cambridge, MA: Harvard University Press.

Nieto, S. (1995). *Affirming diversity: The sociopolitical context of multicultural education* (2nd ed.). New York: Longman.

Omi, M., & Winant, H. (1986). *Racial formation in the United States.* New York: Routledge & Kegan Paul.

Weiner, L. (1993). *Preparing teachers for urban schools: Lessons from thirty years of school reform.* New York: Teachers College Press.

West, C. (1993). *Race matters.* Boston, MA Beacon Press.

Yeo, F. (1992). The inner-city school: A conflict in rhetoric. *Critical Pedagogy Networker, 5,* 3.

Yeo, F. (1996). *Classrooms of the inner city: Urban education and teacher education.* New York: Garland Press.

1

The Rules of the Game: Detracking And Retracking the Urban High School

Dennis Carlson
Miami University

A text is not a text unless it hides from the first comer, from the first glance, the law of its composition and the rules of its game.
—Derrida (1981, p. 63)

Much the same thing can be said of the "rules of the game" that govern the current discourse and practice of *detracking* in the urban high school. The discourse of detracking needs to be read suspiciously, against the grain of its intent, interrogating its silences as much as what gets said, and deconstructing the rules that govern its composition and purpose. Tracking discourses and practices have always hidden themselves beyond a language of "meeting student needs" and (at the secondary level) with providing students with curriculum "choice." By *tracking*, at least within the context of the urban high school, I refer to the separation of students and classes into differentiated curriculum programs based on their expected adult statuses and occupational location in the labor force (i.e., college preparatory, general academic, and vocational-technical education tracks) and (in an overlapping manner) the hierarchial ability grouping of students based on their presumed intellectual capacities and development levels. Historically, professional discourse in education has not even acknowledged the existence of tracks as such. To acknowledge that the public schools are tacitly or overtly participating in sorting and tracking young people for inequality would be too unsettling to the rules that govern what can and cannot be said within professional educational discourse. Interestingly, it is only within the past decade or so that many of the major power brokers in educational reform have begun to acknowledge the existence of tracks, and then only within the context of a discourse of reform that claims to be doing away with them, that is, a discourse of detracking. Suddenly it seems that almost everyone is jumping on the detracking bandwagon, including prestigious and influential groups such as the National Governor's Conference and the Carnegie Foundation (Brewer, Rees, & Argys; 1995; Mansnerus, 1992).

This detracking discourse and reform movement may be interpreted, at least partially, as a response to a growing effort among progressives educators to make tracking more visible by naming it and thus bringing it within the parameters of what can be spoken about in professional educational discourse. Perhaps the most influential single text in this regard was Oakes' (1985) *Keeping Track: How Schools Structure Inequality.* Oakes presented new observational and other qualitative research data to support and update an argument that democratic progressives had been making since Dewey (1916) early in the century. The research data, Oakes said, demonstrated that "Classes in the high-track groups consistently had students with the highest aspirations and the most positive views of themselves . . . [and] students in low-track classes reported the lowest levels of aspiration and the most negative feelings about themselves both academically and generally" (p. 202). She concluded that this "may have the effect of maintaining inequalities in the larger society" (p. 202)—inequalities of class, race, and gender. Oakes also argued, however, that because tracking practices have been so pervasive in public education and are closely related to the role public schools have come to play in reproducing class, race, and gender inequality, it will not be easy to detrack the schools—at least without challenging some powerful beliefs and interests.

If detracking is such a radical democratic proposal, how, then, do we make sense of all the recent reform discourse, particularly in urban school districts, that claims to be about detracking? That is the question I take up in what follows here. In very basic terms, I suggest that the detracking movement in urban education has more to do with revising and reconstituting tracking practices than with doing away with them or replacing with a more democratic, egalitarian form of education in which differences among students are not hierarchicalized and distributed according to a disciplining norm. In fact, the dualistic view of student identity historically enacted in tracking practices, namely, that which separates high achievers from low achievers, the success-oriented from the failure-prone, the mental from the manual, and so on, has been strengthened and extended in recent years in America's urban high schools. If, throughout much of the 20th century, it was possible to talk about three major tracks in the urban high school (college-bound, general, and vocational), there has been a gradual but rather dramatic shift over the past several decades toward two major tracks defined in a more dualistic and thus oppositional way.

One of these tracks I refer to as the new *basic skills* track, reconstituted out of the "old" general academic track and closely integrated with remaining vocational and school-to-work programs. The curriculum in this track is (generally) directed toward learning basic "functional literacy" and "occupational literacy" skills, passing a high school proficiency test, and graduating into the new service industry workforce. As students in this broad track are perceived as having very similar or identical skill needs, defined in behavioral, performance-based terms, more use is being made of individualized, computer-based instruction, which facilitates heterogeneous grouping. All of this gets presented in the language of detracking, but it is a detracking that hardly seems consistent with raising expectations for the majority of urban students now enrolled in this track. The other major track—the college preparatory track—has become increasingly differentiated from the new basic skills track in terms of curriculum and expectations for achievement, and it is being spatially distanced from the basic skills track through relocation to specialized "magnet schools" and special school-within-a-school programs. All of this means that the borders between tracks are become more pronounced.

In sketching out these developments and arguments, based on a review of recent reports issued by the U.S. Department of Education as well as private institutes and commissions, I suggest that this *retracking* of the urban high school may be interpreted in terms of several interlocking shifts occurring in postmodern, postindustrial U.S. culture. The first of these I already alluded to. The postmodern cultural landscape is becoming more bifurcated and dualistic rather than less so, and tracking practices at least partially are a reflection of this shift. If postmodern theory in the academy generally is associated with the celebration of difference as diversity, outside of the normalizing gaze that disciplines difference within hierarchies, oppositions, and dualisms, there is little evidence to support the contention that class, race, gender, and sexual identity politics are becoming less dualistic and oppositional in postmodern America. Quite the contrary. Public schools, because they are not "outside" of this dominant culture, but very much a part of its production, for the most part remain highly tracked communities of learners involved in constituting increasingly unequal identities.

This, in turn, is related to economic shifts over the past several decades toward a more two-tiered and inequitable labor force, with the boundaries between the new service industry tier and the new professional and middle-class tier more impenetrable. Not coincidentally, this has impacted most dramatically on urban communities where poverty levels have risen steadily. Although public school tracks are in no way determined by these economic conditions, urban public schools have always been very closely linked to the urban job market and this linkage is being strengthened.

Finally, the retracking of the urban high school may be related to the deepening fiscal crisis of the liberal welfare state. The fiscal crisis of the state has led to an increased concern with finding more cost-effective and efficient means of "delivering" specified educational outcomes. Within this context, vocational programs have been cut as too expensive and as not providing a "good return on investment" in human capital. A basic skills curriculum, in contrast, appears to offer more "bang for the buck." What results is a stripped-down, no-frills education delivered in a cost-effective way. As for the new magnet schools serving primarily the college bound, they provide urban districts with examples of visible, well-funded programs even as the system as a whole is in fiscal crisis.

BUILDING THE NEW BASIC SKILLS TRACK

A good place to begin a discussion of the retracking of secondary education in the United States is by looking at changes in enrollments in various tracks. An examination of data from the U.S. Department of Education reveals that in the decade between 1982 and 1992, some quite dramatic shifts were taking place in tracking practices in urban high schools. The general academic track in urban schools grew very rapidly, from about 32% of high school seniors to about 43%. This rise was even more dramatic, from 40% to 56%, for the lowest socioeconomic quartile of students—most of whom attend inner-city schools. Meanwhile, the proportion of students enrolled in college preparatory courses grew at a moderate pace, from 37% of all seniors to about 45%. Enrollment by students from the lowest socioeconomic quartile in college preparatory courses remained virtually stagnant over the decade, rising only slightly from 21% to 23%. Finally, the big loser among the high school tracks was vocational education. Enrollment in vocational programs in urban high schools plummeted over the decade from 30% to 11%. For the poorest students, enrollment in vocational programs fell from about 40% to slightly over 20%. (U. S. Department of Education, National Center for Education Statistics; 1995; Table 134).

In attempting to make sense of these changes, I begin with a discussion of changes in the general academic track, the growth of which has been the most dramatic. One of the most obvious reasons why this track has grown so rapidly, even though it has been much criticized for lowering academic standards and providing students with a "watered-down" curriculum that prepares them for little after high school, is that the job market for high school graduates keeps growing—particularly in urban communities. Between 1990 and 2005, the service sector of the economy is expected to contribute approximately 50% of all new jobs to the U.S. labor force. By comparison, it contributed about 43% of all new jobs in the 1975 to 1990 period (Kutscher, 1992). By sheer numbers, the largest subdivisions of the service sector are those in which skill requirements and wages are relatively low, employment is often part time, and there are few or no health benefits. These include jobs such as waiters, household workers, janitors and maintenance workers, security guards, food-service workers, along with jobs involving routine data entry and processing on computer terminals. It is estimated that only about 50% of all service industry jobs pay more than the minimum wage (Johnson, 1993). The rapid growth of the general academic track thus is very closely linked to the growth of this new service sector workforce.

In fact, reform discourse over the past decade or so oriented toward the general academic track has quite explicitly been organized around the theme of improving the functional literacy skills of entry-level workers and thus increasing the nation's economic competitiveness (Carlson, 1992). As a result, the general academic track curriculum has been radically reconstituted. Where once courses offered students a watered-down version of a liberal arts college preparatory curriculum, now the curriculum was about teaching students a core set of instrumental basic skills and testing them to see that they were proficient in these skills before they graduated. According to *A Nation at Risk* (National Commission on Excellence in Education, 1983), basic skills were those individuals needed "to secure gainful employment, and to manage their own lives" (p. 8). Functional literacy skills were usually associated with an eighth- or ninth-grade achievement level.

Although basic skills reform discourse has generally not differentiated between schools and school districts, it is clear that its impact has been felt most in urban districts. It is in urban districts where the majority of students have traditionally been oriented toward the high school graduate workforce. Of course, basic literacy skills in English are essential for young people if they hope to advance themselves; but because functional literacy skills have been set at such a low level and linked to the skill needs of entry-level, low-wage workers, they have not been consistent with the development of the kind of critical literacy needed in democratic cultures or the kinds of higher order thinking skills valued in higher tier jobs. Nor have they provided room for students to affirm their own cultural and linguistic backgrounds. As a result, a basic skills curriculum has not helped empower most urban students. Expectations get lowered to basic skills mastery and high school graduation, all in the name of raising standards and holding students accountable. In the meantime, the "drill-'em-and-test-'em" routine has been associated with a very high drop-out rate, so that only about 50% of all inner-city ninth graders stay in the system long enough to graduate (Carlson, 1992).

By the 1990s, the basic skills reform discourse increasingly moved beyond a concern with language and math skills to define functional literacy more broadly. One area of functional literacy that is gaining much more attention is what is often called *technological literacy*. Unfortunately, the kind of technological literacy that has been emphasized in basic skills reform discourse is very similar to that emphasized in lower tier jobs. So far, we lack detailed empirical studies on how students are using computers in basic skills classrooms. But my own observations and work with students in urban high schools suggests that computers are most often used in one of several ways. Students often play interactive "skill-building" games on computers that teach them basic skills within the context of a graphic game for either one or two students. This is usually an activity students are rewarded with after they have completed their regular assigned work. Students are also assigned to computers for individualized remedial instruction, sometimes in special remedial education computer labs. Finally, students often use word processing programs to complete comprehension-level questions about a text they have been reading. Papert (1993), one of the pioneers in the use of computers in education, refers to these as "tightly" programmed usages, with the programmer "cast in the role of a 'knowledge architect' who will specify a plan, a tight program, for the placement of 'knowledge bricks' in children's minds" (p. 207).

Also receiving increasing attention as part of the new basic skills are interpersonal skills related to being a good "team player" and learning how to cooperate with others in accomplishing work tasks (Pullin, 1994; Secretary's Commission on Achieving Necessary Skills, 1991). All of this is very much in tune with the new management discourse in business and reflects shifts in the organization of work in a postindustrial economy. The so-called "new paradigm" in management theory has begun to impact on educational reform discourse in recent years in some important ways. For example, Spady (1992), who developed outcome-based learning, talks of a shift in educational reform from seeing "students as isolated performers" to seeing "students as collaborative performers" He observes: "What some call 'Getting along' and 'Working together for the common good' . . . have within the past decade become issues of urgency within the world of work"(p. 22). Spady maintains that states and school districts should establish outcome goals for students that have to do with demonstrating effectiveness as team members who "can successfully contribute their best efforts to achieve success in collaborative endeavors . . ." (p. 58). Certainly, cooperative learning skills, competencies, or virtues need to be developed within democratic cultures. However, when these concepts and approaches to educational reform are embedded within an economic rather than democratic discourse—one that emphasizes adjusting or "normalizing" young people to the world of work and socializing them to docility—then cooperative learning is more disempowering than empowering.

I have suggested to this point that the growth of the new basic skills track is related to the growth of a new service sector economy and the presumed skill needs of entry-level workers. But economic elites have not only promoted an economic rationale for curriculum reform. They have, at the same time, promoted cost-effective models of organizing instruction and public schools; that is, models that improve performance and reduce costs at the same time. This concern with cost-effective models of instruction has heightened in a time of fiscal cutbacks in the state, and basic skills models of instruction are at least partially a response to this concern. This is based on the rationale that student achievement levels on standardized tests can be raised and costs lowered by spending more "time on task" with basic skills and eliminating almost everything else. A good example of this rationale is provided by the recent report of the National Education Commission on Time and Learning (NECTL, 1994), *Prisoners of Time*. The NECTL was established by Congress as an advisory body. Its nine-member board, selected by Congress and the Department of Education, reads like a "who's who" of power brokers in public school policy, including members representing the conservative think-tank (the Hudson Institute) and the major corporate player in education (the Business Roundtable). The report bemoans the fact that schools are burdened with

> a whole set of requirements for what has been called "the new work of the schools"—education about personal safety, consumer affairs, AIDS, conservation and energy, family life, driver's training—as well as traditional nonacademic activities, such as counseling, gym, study halls, homeroom, lunch and pep rallies. (p. 10)

If these are to be made available to students, according to the report, they should be offered after the regular school day so that during the regular school day the focus can be kept on mastery of basic skills. The report notes:

> Establishing an academic day means, in essence, that the existing school day be devoted among exclusively to core academic instruction. What this means is obvious: many worthwhile student programs—athletics, clubs, and other activities—will have to be sacrificed unless the school day is lengthened. (p. 32)

This can be taken two ways. On the most literal level, the report is recommending the lengthening of the school day so that these "worthwhile" activities can be maintained. But it is also suggesting that if the school day is not lengthened, those activities not narrowly linked to basic skills mastery in the core subject areas will have to go. In most urban districts, lengthening the school day is not a very realistic option financially or otherwise. The implications in this case are, I think, alarming. The report in effect provides a rationale for further cuts in program offerings and staff (such as counselors, music, art, and physical education teachers, and librarians). It is also distressing, I think, that the report lumps together consumer affairs, AIDS education, and conservation education in the same category with driver's training—as subjects that "steal" from time spent on basic skills. The report thus also provides a rationale for eliminating the last vestiges of a progressive, student-centered curriculum within the new basic skills track—all in the name of raising test scores and lowering costs.

The growth of a basic skills curriculum in the general academic track may be related to another element of cost effectiveness—cutting labor costs. A basic skills curriculum can be programmed to make it self-paced, and by bringing more computers into basic skill classes, fewer teachers may be needed. Such is the hope expressed in a recent report by the conservative Brookings Institute, *Making Schools Work* (Hanushek, 1994). The report speaks of the "advantages to using certain kinds of technology for instructional purposes—including drill and practice activities on computers" Among the major advantages, according to the report, would be "the substitution of capital [i.e., technology] for labor in schools," an advantage that the report fears teachers will resist without the right mix of incentives, because "they are unlikely to advocate the adoption of technologies that will . . . threaten them as a group with decreased employment possibilities"(p. 78). We are likely to hear more in the years ahead about bringing computers into the classroom to replace teachers and thereby reduce the single largest cost in public education as in industry—that of labor. This also suggests that a battle may be looming between teacher unions and certain uses of computer technology in the classroom.

Ironically, all of these developments associated with the shift to a basic skills curriculum, which are having a very damaging impact on urban schools in particular, are being represented in the language of detracking and better meeting the needs of students. Detracking in this case is associated with a movement away from homogeneous grouping of students in ability groups towards the heterogeneous grouping of students working at their own pace, "mastering" one skill at a time. According to *Prisoners of Time*, mastery learning

> makes it possible for today's schools to escape the assembly-line mentality of the "factory model" school. . . . Instead of the lock-step of lecture and laboratory, computers and other new telecommunications make it possible for students to move at their own pace. (NECTL, 1994, p. 37)

Heterogeneous grouping, in this case, is related to the pacing of a predetermined learning process rather than the personalization of the learning process, which would be more progressive. It is a form of detracking that replaces the assembly-line metaphor of instruction with one equally reductionistic and disempowering—that of computer-guided instruction. Unfortunately, this means that the movement to heterogeneous grouping of students is not necessarily progressive in the democratic sense. This also reminds us that slogans like "detracking" have no fixed or stable meaning, and that they can take on quite different meanings within the context of different reform discourses. Despite all the talk of raised expectations, the identity of the new basic skills urban student is still understood in professional discourse to be fundamentally defined by deficits and deficiencies, and by below normal skill levels. Such a deficit theory can only participate in constructing subordinated identities and thus in keeping marginalized youth disempowered.

THE NEW VOCATIONALISM

I indicated earlier that one reason the general academic track has grown so rapidly in the past decade or so is that enrollments in vocational education programs—once quite high in most urban districts—have fallen off rapidly. Nationally, the numbers enrolled in vocational education programs peaked in 1984. Then, in the decade between 1984 and 1994, enrollments began to fall off sharply (Gray, 1991). A number of prestigious foundations even began suggesting by the mid-1980s that vocational education be eliminated entirely (Claus, 1990). The collapse of vocational education in recent years may be attributed to a complex set of interrelated factors. One obvious problem was that in a deindustrializing economy, where the most substantial growth has been in the low-pay, low-skill service sector, vocational education programs have had an increasingly difficult time placing graduates in jobs they are trained for and at wages significantly above minimum wage. Most employers in the expanding service sector of the labor force prefer that their new workers have generalizable literacy and math skills more than specialized, technical training that is often too narrow and quickly outdated.

Other factors contributed to the decline of vocational education. For example, the vocational programs offered to students in the 1970s and 1980s in many cases continued to be linked to a gendered division of labor at a time when the women's movement was pushing schools do more to promote gender equity and when adolescent girls where beginning to challenge traditional gender roles. From the 1920s through the 1970s, the vocational educational programs with the largest enrollments were trade and industry programs designed to train boys in the use of heavy industrial equipment, and home economics programs designed to prepare girls to be "good" homemakers and mothers (U. S. Department of Education, National Center for Education Statistics; 1980, Table 144). With the passage of Title IX in the early 1970s, which outlawed discrimination in educational programs receiving federal funds, many vocational education programs were unable, or unwilling, to change rapidly enough. But vocational education suffered from an "image problem" more generally. Over the years it had developed an image as a track for "low ability" or "low achievement" students. This image or representation of vocational education not only kept many students away from vocational programs, it also provided a rationale for closing vocational programs, because policymakers could claim that by eliminating such programs they were promoting higher standards for students. Finally, budgetary considerations played a big part in the decline of vocational education in the 1980s. As student enrollment in vocational education dropped off sharply, already high per pupil costs skyrocketed, state funding of vocational education programs continued to decline, and local school officials found that shutting down vocational programs offered a "quick fix" way to cut costs.

Gray (1991), a leading scholar in the field of vocational education, posed the question of whether vocationalism might, like the Phoenix, rise from its own ashes in the years ahead. The jury is still out on that question, although there are indeed signs that vocational education is staging something of a comeback, often under a different name, such as occupational education. Behind these changes, however, there are continuities between the "old" and the "new" vocationalism—including a tendency among both to emphasis an overconforming conception of work roles and an overly utilitarian conception of education. To the extent that the new vocationalism can be distinguished from the old vocationalism—that vocationalism that reigned before the dramatic collapse of vocational education programs over the past decade—it is primarily because newer models call for a much closer integration of academic and applied occupational education so that the distinction between the vocational track and the general academic track is blurred.

So far, the new vocationalism or occupational education is still in embryonic form, and a number of factors may limit its further development. However, there are clear signs of change. For one thing, students in the new occupational education programs typically take most of their classes with general academic track students and take occupationally related courses only as electives for several hours a day. This is a dramatic change from the completely separate courses that were typically offered to vocational and academic students in the "old days"—along with completely separate sets of teachers on separate campuses. But if advocates of the new vocationalism have their way—and they represent powerful interest groups in school reform—we are likely to see other changes. One of these changes is likely to be that general academic classes will become more occupationally oriented, thus completing the detracking of vocational and general academic track students. According to a recent report by the U.S. Department of Education entitled *Goals 2000: Building Bridges From School to Work* (1993), many communities are rethinking the practice of tracking and eliminating or phasing out outdated vocational programs along with general track courses. It concludes that students in "general" programs "take a random selection of courses that lead nowhere, exiting high school with a diploma that is practically worthless"(p. 6). The report recommends that all or most all general academic track students learn work skills and gain work experiences. To do this it suggests organizing core academic courses around occupational or work themes and linking students more closely with the "real" world of work outside the school.

Building Bridges endorses a variety of different types of occupational programs to achieve this end. Youth apprenticeships involve placing students in work sites for part of the school day under the supervision of skilled craft workers, who teach students skills of the trade and serve as mentors. So far, however, very few students are involved in apprenticeship programs, largely because it is hard to find adequate placements and ensure that students are getting an education on the job and not just being exploited as cheap labor (Kantor, 1994).

Another model endorsed in the report is "cooperative education." In these programs, students may spend the morning at school and afternoons working at local businesses. According to the report, about 8% of U.S. 11th and 12th graders participate in cooperative learning programs. Unfortunately, one of the reasons for the relative success of cooperative education may be that such programs are less discriminating in finding placements for students, which also means that many students end up working in service industry sites, including those in the fast food industry. A third model of occupational education endorsed in the report is the "career academy." This, according to the report, is "a school within a larger school, where a group of students and a team of teachers stay together for a several-hour block of time each day. These students and teachers often remain together for 3 years. Instruction is focused on a single industry cluster" (p. 3). A final occupational education model endorsed by the report is "tech prep." Tech-prep programs are sometimes called "2+2" programs because they involve 2 years of high school and 2 years of postsecondary instruction. For example, students may choose between several occupational clusters such as business/management, engineering/mechanical, and health/human services.

According to *Building Bridges*, a major theme in all of these various occupational education programs is "business and industry sitting across from educators as *equal partners* at the table to work toward mutual goals"(p. 5). As one example of a possible partnership between public education and the business community, the report suggests making records on student performance available to prospective employees in a region through a computerized management information system (MIS). This will, according to the report, "send a clear message to students: That their school performance counts"(p. 8). Such systems also send a clear message that education is about job training and learning to be a "good worker" more than a critical citizen.

Reform discourse such as that represented by *Building Bridges* raises serious doubts about the capacity of a "new" vocational education to overcome the limitations of the "old" vocationalism. No matter how appealing its supporters make it sound in terms of motivating students and making learning more relevant to their "real-life" needs, the new vocationalism continues to participate in the channeling of some students toward low-skill, low-wage jobs and sets very low expectations for these students. Programs such as tech prep, which supposedly prepare students for a "middle range" of jobs requiring some postsecondary education, must face the "hard" reality that this middle sector of the labor force has continued to shrink in proportion to the service sector (Grubb, 1992). Finally, the new vocationalism, like the new basic skills, continues to take for granted an economically functional model of education. Dewey (1916), in *Democracy and Education*, warned of the dangers of this kind of economic functionalism in the discourse of vocational education.

He wrote: There is a danger that vocational education will be interpreted in theory and practice as trade education: as a means of securing technical efficiency in specialized future pursuits. Education would then become an instrument of perpetuating unchanged the existing industrial order of society, instead of operating as a means of its transformation. (p. 316)

Certainly, work is a central life experience and students should learn about work in schools. Education in its most engaging and productive sense is a form of work experience. Nevertheless, the new vocationalism does not appear to provide a basis for empowering students, and it will likely continue to participate in the construction of unequal class, race, and gender identities.

MAGNET SCHOOLS AND THE NEW COLLEGE PREPARATORY TRACK

As the general academic track and the new vocation education track are becoming more closely integrated in the urban high school, the college preparatory track is being more sharply differentiated and distanced from them. Curriculum reform within the new college preparatory track, as with the other tracks, has been based primarily on an economic rationale, in this case the one having to do with the skill requirements for new high-wage, high-skilled, high-tech jobs. Whether it is designing a new product or the assembly-line to produce it, and whether it is making decisions about how to meet customer needs or design commercial images to appeal to a new "market niche," the new professional, managerial, and scientific jobs require much more than minimum basic skills. One of the most articulate statements of how the skill needs of the new college-educated labor force are changing can be found in a report by the Carnegie Foundation for the Advancement of Teaching (1986), *A Nation Prepared; Teachers for the Twenty-First Century*. According to the report, the new high-tech and professional-managerial jobs are dependent on people who "have a good intuitive grasp of the ways in which all kinds of physical and social systems work". They must

> possess a feeling for mathematical concepts and the ways in which they can be applied to difficult problems, an ability to see patterns of meaning where others see only confusion, a cultivated creativity that leads them to new problems, new products, and new services before their competitors get to them. . . . (p. 44)

This metaphor of the student as a knowledge-production worker has led to a growing interest in a "constructivist" curriculum for college preparatory students. Constructivism as a curriculum reform movement has been most closely linked to science and mathematics education in recent years, and to "discovery" or inquiry learning. Nevertheless, something very similar—what we might call *social constructionism*—is becoming influential in college preparatory English, social studies, and other disciplines. In this case, the emphasis is on how knowledge is represented in different historical periods and among different cultural and subcultural groupings. Constructivism approaches to curriculum and pedagogy are based on a nonreified conception of knowledge, that is, one that treats knowledge as something that is constructed by individuals and groups as they grapple to solve concrete problems in unique ways (Doll, 1994). All of this suggests that the college preparatory curriculum is becoming more progressive in ways that Dewey would have appreciated. Nevertheless, the limitations of constructivism as a reform discourse and practice are considerable as well, at least from a democratic progressive standpoint. Foremost among these is the fact that constructivism has been primarily linked to an economic rationale in state reform discourse. As with basic skills and occupational education reforms discourse, within constructivist discourse curriculum decisions get reduced to questions about how we prepare young people to be "better" (i.e., more productive) knowledge workers rather than how we should prepare young people for participation in the reconstruction of a democratic culture and community life. Furthermore, as the general academic curriculum has been reorganized around routine "basic skills," the gulf between the curriculum and pedagogy of the general track and the increasingly constructivist curriculum and pedagogy of the college preparatory track is becoming more difficult to bridge.

This widening gulf between the curriculum and pedagogy of the general academic and college preparatory tracks is associated with an increasing spatial separation of the two tracks. Many college preparatory students are now enrolled in magnet schools or separate school-within-a-school programs. Such schools and programs are open to students from throughout a district or a high school attendance area, typically have some admission requirements, and often organize instruction around themes or specialized programs (e.g., performing arts, math–science, communications, the humanities, etc.); Metz, 1988; Young & Clinchy, 1992). They typically are freed up from many central office and state regulations pertaining to class schedules, course offerings, and student evaluation and may be given greater control over hiring of teachers and administrators so that they can attract and retain a qualified, committed staff. Not everyone who attends a magnet school is college bound; and at this point the majority of college-bound students are still being educated in neighborhood high schools. Still, the trend, at least in urban districts, is toward the greater separation of the college track from neighborhood high schools and its relocation in magnet schools.

The emergence of magnet schools since the 1980s in urban districts may also be interpreted as an attempt by dominant power brokers in public education to maintain adequate funding for quality, college preparatory programs in a system that is otherwise being fiscally starved. As budgets have been slashed, magnet schools have continued to flourish. According to one study, school districts spend on the average 10% to 12% more per pupil to operate magnet schools and programs, and a recent study of magnet schools in St. Louis found that the district spent 25% to 42% more on magnet students than on nonmagnet students (Young & Clinchy, 1992). In addition to receiving more aid from the school district, magnet schools and programs are much more likely to be linked up with corporate and foundation "partners" who provide further financial support. Magnet schools, then, are often allowed to become "investment sites" for outside capital, unlike "regular" neighborhood schools. For example, the RJR Nabisco Foundation's "Next Century Schools Program" allocates large grants to individual magnet schools rather than school districts (Jehl & Payzant, 1992). Corporations and business foundations support magnet schools because they allow them to focus their philanthropic efforts on one or several schools, where it is possible to see results. These changes raise disturbing prospects of a two-tiered system of public education, one (for those bound for college and middle-class jobs) well-financed with the help of corporate capital, and one (for those bound for the new working and underclasses) fiscally starved. All of this threatens to override efforts by state supreme courts to equalize per pupil spending.

Ironically, magnet schools also have important democratic potential and often have been supported by democratic progressives. They were originally developed in the 1970s and 1980s in response to court-ordered desegregation of major northern school districts because they provided an appealing way of promoting school desegregation without an overreliance on compulsory school assignments and busing (Metz, 1986). The rationale has been that spaces in magnet schools can be filled to maintain a racial composition very similar to the composition of students in the district as a whole. In order to encourage enough White parents and students to consider enrolling in magnet schools, they offer top-quality education. However, because of the limited number of magnet schools available, magnet schools have not replaced busing to achieve racial balance so much as supplemented it. Young and Clinchy (1992) noted that there has been "no instance where a major school system has achieved noticeable desegregation in its public schools by using a voluntary magnet program"(p. 24). At the same time, there is abundant evidence indicating that magnet schools have contributed to class segregation, something the courts and school districts did not recognize (or care to recognize) in their narrow focus on achieving racial balance. According to Metz (1988), author of one of the most influential studies of magnet schools in the 1980s:

> Magnet schools are often designed for students who achieve best and are
> organized around curricular emphases more likely to appeal to elites than to
> a cross section of citizens. In many communities, all or most magnets
> developed are schools for the gifted and talented, or high schools stressing
> math and science, or at best schools for the performing arts. (p. 57)

Metz noted the irony in school policy that declares all schools officially equal, "even as middle-class parents and alert working-class parents diligently strive to place their children in schools where the education will be more than equal. . [and] where merit is far more likely to blossom . . ." (pp. 58-59).

Magnet schools, for all of their faults and elitist tendencies, have in some instances provided space for groups of teachers along with progressive groups in the community to "reinvent" education in democratic ways. For example, although they are the exception rather than the rule, some magnet schools have explicitly sought to serve low-income students, have an open admissions policy, and are governed by boards composed of teachers, students, and community groups. Magnet schools are also worth supporting in principle at least because they provide students and parents with some choices regarding students' education. Although choice in education has most often been associated with conservative voucher plans to privatize public education, choice is also a basic democratic value. Finally, because students have to apply to be admitted to magnet schools and typically go through some admission process, they are likely to be more committed to the school and to their own education—something often lacking when students are assigned to a school and told what to learn. Thus, the magnet school movement at this point in time is deeply contradictory, and democratic educational policy will need to carve out a middle ground, seeking to maintain the desirable features of magnet schools while working to overcome their current limitations.

The recent expansion of magnet schools in New York City provides a good case study of the contradictory character of the magnet school movement in the mid-1990s (Henderson & Raywid, 1994). Between 1993 and 1995, the New York City school system established 48 experimental magnet high schools, 46 with enrollments between 110 and 600 students. The new magnet schools have been started by an unlikely coalition of very diverse groups under the banner of the Network for School Renewal, including the Fund for New York City Public Education (a private philanthropic group that channels corporate funds to public schools), the Center for Collaborative Education (an umbrella urban reform coalition affiliated with the Coalition of Essential Schools), the Manhattan Institute (a conservative research group that supports school choice plans), Acorn (a community organization of low-income residents), and the Annenburg Foundation (a corporate foundation). The latter group donated $25 million to the project and has agreed to support 50 more small magnet high schools by the year 2000 (Dillon & Berger, 1995; Henderson & Raywid, 1994). By that time, magnet schools in the city are expected to serve about 50,000 students or approximately 5% of the city's projected 1.3 million students (Dillon & Berger, 1995). Although this may still be a relatively small proportion of the total, if current growth rates were to continue over the next decade or two, magnet schools could enroll a substantial proportion of students in the system. In order to allow magnet schools to innovate and provide top quality education, the coalition is attempting to gain special status for the schools as a type of "educational free-trade zone," known formally as a "learning zone," that is unencumbered by bureaucratic regulations and red tape (Dillon, 1995).

A special *New York Times* series on the new magnet schools in 1995 was full of praise for the constructivist, student-centered learning going on in the schools. According to one article:

> Within many schools, there has been a radical break with the traditional disciplines. . . . In a course whose theme is water, classes may be taught some biology as they study fish, chemistry as they look at river pollution and a smattering of physics as they examine ocean currents. . . . Many experimental school directors criticize traditional tests. Students at only 13 of the 30 new high schools . . . took even one state Regents test in 1993–1994. (Dillon & Berger, 1995, p. 2)

Another article in the series featured a magnet school named the El Puente Academy for Peace and Justice, which trains young people on Williamsburg's predominantly Hispanic south side to become community activists. On a typical day at the school, the article noted:

> Jennifer [a student] was documenting traffic flow for a 10th grade science lesson on how pollution affects the respiratory system. Marilyn and her friends in the ninth grade surveyed neighborhood advertising, the first step in a lobbying campaign against local merchants to reduce the barrage of cigarette and beer ads. Nytopia was helping build a community garden. . . . A discussion about environmental racism . . . arose out of the areas's coexistence with several waste-collection businesses, legal and illegal, and its designation as the proposed site for an incinerator. (Gonzalez, 1995, pp. 1-2)

Yet another article featured a school named Renaissance, run entirely by teachers. It observed: "Teachers in Renaissance do not have to use ancient textbooks and rigid school-wide lesson plans; they can pick and choose from a variety of texts, workbooks, novels, and newspapers, or write their own curriculum" (Firestone, 1995, p. A12).

These would appear to be promising sites for the reinvention of the public high school in ways that effectively empower teachers, students, and progressive community groups and relate education to students' real-life concerns and interests. As such, they potentially provide some limited space for moving beyond the "rules of the game" that govern tracking practices. But as I noted earlier, the fact that magnet schools are in most cases privileged educational sites for college preparatory students places severe restrictions on their current democratic potential. It will be hard to challenge this privilege, for part of what currently gives magnet schools their identity and appeal among the middle class is this privilege. The high expectations set for magnet schools students are the opposite side of the coin of the low expectations set for general track students in neighborhood high schools. The high per pupil costs in magnet schools are offset by low per pupil costs in other schools. If magnet schools are a mechanism for "saving" some students at the expense of the vast majority of others in urban school systems, then support for them has to be very limited and qualified. The challenge is to reconstruct the idea of specialized, small schools within the context of a more democratic discourse and practice.

BEYOND THE DILEMMAS OF DETRACKING AND RETRACKING

Although the developments I explored here are complex and dynamic, one thing is clear: Curricular tracks are not disappearing in public high schools, despite all the talk of detracking. Tracks are also still very much implicated in the production and reproduction of unequal identities. The rules of the game that organize tracking structures and practices have been altered and rewritten a bit, but not substantially altered. As we face a new century and millennium, the democratic promise of a society in which inequalities of opportunity are expanded, real inequalities of wealth, status, and power are greatly reduced, and individuals and groups are free to develop their full potentials and engage in the process of making themselves an culture within the context of a caring community, has not yet come to fruition. In fact, we risk becoming a formally democratic nation, but a nation in which the democratic spirit, as part of the living culture of everyday life, is slipping away. Democracy cannot long survive or prosper in a two-tiered, two-tracked society. Public schools cannot, on their own, effectively undo the inequalities students bring with them to school. But public schools can, I believe, serve as sites that affirm an alternative, democratic vision.

How might democratic progressive educators (including teachers, administrators, teacher educators, involved parents, and members of the community) respond to all of this, given that the problem of tracking is so deeply engrained in the rules of the game and in various interlocking sets of cultural developments? There are no easy answers to this question and many other questions faced by democratic societies and communities. All ways of proceeding, to at least some degree, involve dilemmas and contradictions. Democratic progressives need to be willing to get engaged in numerous, specific struggles going on over the course of educational reform and renewal in communities across the nation; and they will need to be prepared to strike accords or settlements with dominant power brokers in education, and then seek to extend our gains and strike better bargains (Carlson, 1995). The important thing is that the vision of a more democratic society is somehow driving our pragmatic, here-and-now work in the schools.

Perhaps the most pragmatic response to tracking—one that works within the framework of modifying existing practices—is to make current tracking practices less discriminatory by class, race, and gender. In this regard, Page (1991) suggested that track and ability group placement decisions be regularly revisited and reviewed. Beyond that, we might also seek to make each of the existing tracks in secondary education less unequal in terms of the kinds of educational experiences to which students are exposed. All young people have a right to a curriculum that develops their critical thinking capacities and expands rather than limits their potentials. All need to be active rather than passive learners. As for vocational or occupational education, if they are to have any place in a democratic education, a greater effort will need to be made to ensure that they move beyond narrow job preparation and "workplace literacy" to focus on critical, democratic forms of literacy. Kincheloe (1995), for example, suggested that vocationalism be replaced with a critical "work education," the purpose of which would be "to restore the knowledge of the work process and the overview of the relation of the job to the larger economic processes . . ." (p. 61). According to Kincheloe, "the critical dimension of work education involves the skill to interrogate the democratic limits of both work and the capitalist economy" (p. 322). In a similar vein, Simon, Dippo, and Schenke (1991) advocated what they call "critical work pedagogy," the aim of which is "to encourage students to: question taken-for-granted assumptions about work; comprehend workplaces as sites where identities are produced; see this production as a struggle over competing claims to truth and to correctness; and envisage ways in which the quality of their working lives can be improved" (p. 15).

What about magnet schools? Is there a place in a democratic progressive agenda to support magnet schools? The answer must be, "it depends." It depends very much on how magnet schools are institutionalized within local districts. Young and Clinchy (1992), in their examination of choice plans in education, suggested that "the best approach is to make all district schools alternative or magnets and allow students to choose the school or program they prefer" (p. 26). In such a system, access to a school would not be restricted by admission requirements, inadequate dissemination of information to parents and students, or lack of transportation. Continual efforts also would be needed to counter tendencies for magnet schools to become segregated by class, race, or gender. Finally, in order to promote dialogue and community by students across their differences, several magnet schools might be located on a common campus, with some courses and projects designed to bring students from different magnets together to explore common concerns and develop a more inclusive sense of community.

Another idea that is worth pursuing, that embodies some of the advantages of a magnet school system but overcomes some of its limitations, is to divide comprehensive neighborhood high schools into school-within-a-school units. Each of these schools-within-a-school may have its own identity and curricular focus, and even an admissions process, but also maintain a heterogeneous grouping of students. A good example of this is the "charter" school reform movement in Philadelphia in the 1990s, where old comprehensive high schools were broken up into smaller, heterogeneously grouped schools, organized around shared decision making (Fine, 1994). In charter schools, anywhere from 200 to 400 students work with a group of 10 to 12 core subject teachers over the course of the 4 years of high school. Charter school teachers enjoy a common preparation period daily, and it is the responsibility of teachers in each charter to invent curriculum, pedagogies, and "substantive themes" that give that charter its unique character. Charter schools are, in fact, an attempt to create semi-autonomous communities of learners in public high schools and overcome one of the major impediments to providing personalized instruction in the "old" comprehensive high school—the great and ever-changing number of students teachers interacted with daily. Among the payoffs of the switch to charter schools has been better attendance records and lower drop-out rates. Similar school-within-a-school programs are cropping up in school districts across the country and are proving to be particularly effective in improving achievement levels and lowering drop-out rates among low-achieving inner-city youths.

Unfortunately, all of these reforms are only palliatives so long as the underlying forces that perpetuate tracking practices remain unaddressed. It is naive to believe that urban high schools can be "detracked" outside of a broad-based movement for democratic renewal in the culture, including a movement toward a more equitable economy and an improvement in the quality of people's working lives (Johnson, 1993). A democratic progressive discourse that is serious about detracking will need to be integrated with a new economic policy discourse that begins to talk seriously about countering the growing inequalities that divide us as a society and as a people. Ultimately, to move away from tracking is to move toward recognizing difference among students and tailoring the curriculum to the different needs of students, but within a system where difference does not get normalized or marginalized, which is to say does not get categorized, hierarchically ordered, and positioned within dualisms. This has always been the promise of a democratic education. To participate in rewriting the rules of the game, to reinvent ourselves, and to detrack our lives.

REFERENCES

Brewer, D., Rees, D., & Argys, L. (1995). Detracking America's schools. The reform without costs? *Phi Delta Kappan, 77*, 210-215.

Carlson, D. (1992). *Teachers and crisis: Urban school reform and teachers' work culture.* New York: Routledge.

Carlson, D. (1995). Constructing the margins: Of multicultural education and curriculum settlements. *Curriculum Inquiry, 25*, 407-432.

Carnegie Foundation for the Advancement of Teaching. (1986). *A nation prepared; teachers for the twenty-first century.* New York: Carnegie Foundation for the Advancement of Teaching.

Claus, J. (1990). Opportunity or inequality in vocational education? A qualitative investigation. *Curriculum Inquiry, 20,* 7-39.

Derrida, J. (1981). *Plato's pharmacy.* Chicago: University of Chicago Press.

Dewey, J. (1916). *Democracy and education.* New York: The Free Press.

Dillon, S. (1995, May 25). Islands of change create friction. *The New York Times,* pp. A1, A15.

Dillon, S., & Berger, J. (1995, May 22). New schools seeking small miracles. *The New York Times,* pp. A1, B11.

Doll, W. (1994). *A postmodern curriculum.* New York: Teachers College Press.

Fine, M. (Ed.). (1994). *Chartering urban school reform: Reflections on public high schools in the midst of change.* New York: Teachers College Press.

Firestone, D. (1995, May 24). When teachers unite to run schools. *The New York Times,* p. 1+.

Gonzalez, D. (1995, May 23). A bridge from hope to social action. *The New York Times,* pp. A1, A14.

Gray, K. (1991). Vocational education in high school: A modern phoenix? *Phi Delta Kappan, 72,* 437-445.

Grubb, W. (1992). Postsecondary vocational education and the sub-baccalaureate labor market: New evidence on economic returns. *Economics of Education Review, 11,* 225-248.

Hanushek, E. (1994). *Making schools work; improving performance and controlling costs.* Washington, DC: The Brookings Institution.

Henderson, H., & Raywid, M. (1994). "Small" revolution in New York City. *Journal of Negro Education, 63,* 28-45.

Jehl, J., & Payzant, T. (1992). Philanthropy and public school reform: A view from San Diego. *Teachers College Record, 93,* 472-487.

Johnson, B. (1993). The transformation of work and educational reform policy. *American Educational Research Journal, 30,* 39-65.

Kantor, H. (1994). Managing the transition from school to work: The false promise of youth apprenticeship. *Teachers College Record, 95,* 442-461.

Kincheloe, J. (1995). *Toil and trouble: Good work, smart workers, and the integration of academic and vocational education.* New York: Peter Lang.

Kutscher, R. (1992). Outlook 1990-2005: Major trends and issues. *Occupational Outlook Quarterly, 36,* 2-5.

Mansnerus, L. (1992, November 1). Should tracking be derailed? *The New York Times,* Section 4A ("Education Life"), pp. 14-16.

Metz, M. (1986). *Different by design: The context and character of three magnet schools.* New York: Routledge.

Metz, M. (1988, January). In education, magnets attract controversy. *Today's Education,* pp. 54-60.

National Commission on Excellence in Education. (1983). *A nation at risk.* Washington, DC: U.S. Government Printing Office.

National Education Commission on Time and Learning. (1994). *Prisoners of time.* Washington, DC: U.S. Government Printing Office.

Oakes, J. (1985). *Keeping track: How schools structure inequality*. New Haven: Yale University Press.

Page, R. (1991). *Lower-track classrooms: A curricular and cultural perspective*. New York: Teachers College Press.

Papert, S. (1993) *The children's machine; rethinking school in the age of the computer*. New York: HarperCollins.

Pullin, D. (1994). Learning to work: The impact of curriculum and assessment standards on educational opportunity. *Harvard Educational Review, 64*(1), 31-54.

Secretary's Commission on Achieving Necessary Skills (SCANS). (1991). *What work requires of schools: A SCANS report for America 2000*. Washington, DC: U.S. Department of Labor.

Simon, R., Dippo, D., & Schenke, A. (1991). *Learning work: A critical pedagogy of work education*. Toronto: Ontario Institute for Studies in Education (OISE) Press.

Spady, W. (1992). *Outcome-based restructuring presentation*. Eagle, CO: The High Success Network.

U.S. Department of Education. (1993) *Goals 2000: Building bridges from school to work*. Washington, DC: U.S. Government Printing Office.

U. S. Department of Education, National Center for Education Statistics. (1980). *Digest of education statistics, 1979*. Washington, DC: U.S. Government Printing Office.

U.S. Department of Education, National Center for Education Statistics. (1995). *Digest of education statistics, 1994*. Washington, DC: U.S. Government Printing Office.

Young, T., & Clinchy, E. (1992). *Choice in public education*. New York: Teachers College Press.

2

The Rubber Band Club and Other Fables of the Urban Place

Karen Anijar
Arizona State University

THE PROSAIC

*Old certainties—never certainties for everyone in any case are
wearing thin.*
—Lavie and Sweedenburg (1996, p. 1)

I have been floundering for weeks trying to figure out how to begin this chapter.
It seems that all that I have ever wanted to say (and more) has been written by
both myself and others. It seems whenever I play Voltaire and say: "Well it just
can not get much worse"—something else transpires, and I am pulled further into
a wallowing vortex filled with protrusions and monoliths that I cannot negotiate
my way around. Sometimes I feel as if I am standing precariously teetering on
the edge of the existential abyss, waiting for the Earth to swallow me up.

> And someone in me takes matters into our own hands, and eventually takes
> dominion over serpents—over my body, my sexual activity, my soul, my
> mind, my weaknesses and my strength. Mine. Ours. Not the heterosexual
> white man's or the colored man's or the state's or the culture's or the reli-
> gion's or the parents'—just ours mine. . . . And suddenly I feel everything
> rushing to a center, a nucleus. All the lost pieces of myself coming flying
> from the deserts and the mountains and the valleys, magnetized towards
> that center. Completa. (Anzulda, 1987, p. 51, cited in Alarcon, 1996, p. 50)

37

Completa, sin embargo: en proceso! I have been living in southern California for almost 3 years now. I have learned so much. Some of the lessons were unanticipated, some were painful. Given the opportunity to change the circumstances of my existence would I have come here? No, never. But having been here, the experiences have forever transformed my being, I am forever branded by what I have seen here, I can never look for hope or possibility or transformation in the same manner.

Branded people look for others who carry the (in)signifier, and find ways to decenter, and resignify as strategies for coping.

> Chela Sandoval, writing of third world women in the United States, explains that differential consciousness which she labels "equal rights" consciousness, "revolutionary" consciousness, "supremacist" consciousness and separatist consciousness. Mobilizing this oppositional strategy involves the refusal to privilege any one of these four tactics but, rather, opting situationally for the most effective strategy at any given moment. (Lavie & Sweedenburg, 1996, p. 5)

Indeed, although the dominant forces seem to panoptically police, I have found myself in a position to hear different marginalized people communicating with one another, without the "center as an interlocutor between them" (Lavie & Sweedenburg, 1996, p.4). So we find in ourselves,

> A self that becomes a crossroads, a collision course, a clearinghouse, an endless alterity who once she emerges into language and self-inscription so belatedly, appears a tireless pegrine collecting all the parts that will never make her whole. Such a hunger forces her to recollect in excess, and produce a text layered with inversions and disproportions, which are functions of experienced dislocations, vis-a-vis the Name of the Father and the Place of the Law. (Alarcon, 1996, p. 53)

Gabriel Garcia Marquez (1967), wrote in his most famous book (*Cien Anos de Soledad*) "everything written on them was unrepeatable because races since time immemorial and forever more because races condemned to one hundred years of solitude do not have a second opportunity on earth" (p. 422). I feel like Aureliano Babilonia sometimes watching the "fearful whirlwind of dust and rubble being spun by the wrath of the biblical hurricane" (p. 422). I, too, am living and deciphering and sensing that I may never leave this place of mirages and illusions. Yet, in the prosaic of the total lack of possibility comes new formations and new ways of configuring the universe. Trying to gather the pieces of an ever so slippery self, that will never make me whole *ni aqui ni alla* (see Perez-Firmat, 1994) but, *siempre en* process.

> When hybrids delve into their past, it need not be essentialized nostalgia or
> salvaging an uncontaminated precolonial past. On the contrary, reworking
> the past exposes its hybridity, and to recognize and acknowledge this
> hybrid past in terms of present empowers and gives it agency. . . . A self
> that fractures into multiple subjectivities that are unable to mend by form-
> ing seams, so the hybrids refuse a Cartesian linear narration. The hybrids'
> refusal of individuation empowers them to agency as a group, to resist the
> hegemony of the Eurocenter, not only to reacting to it but also by opening a
> new creative space in the borderzone. The group's creative action can
> implode the Euro-USA center. Therefore the borderzone is not just a dan-
> gerous space but a festive one, because of the energy liberated by the com-
> mon struggle for resistance. (Lavie, 1996, p. 68)

My colleague named Carlos tells me he has come to terms with his
own violence, he acknowledges, he embraces it, it is the Aztec within. I look at
my friend Ron Gonzales in whose eyes I often see possibility. I see him with the
children. We joke about Aztec-centric gods, and Ron's Aztec-centric curricu-
lums. I look at my friend Lana Krievis who has an empathy that gets so close to
Buber's I-Thou, in that she can feel the children's pain and take the pain as her
own, she embraces it, and stands steadfast letting it come toward her, without
fear. I may be fragmented but I am not alone. Knowing that you are not alone,
however, does not ameliorate the conditions of the personal pangs of vexation
when looking out my window at an uncaring world. I stand in solidarity with
my colleagues. Huitzilopochti must have placed them here for me to understand.

> And when Huitzilopochti had killed them, when he had expressed his
> anger, he took from them their finery and adornments their destiny, put
> them on, appropriated them incorporated them into his destiny, made them
> of his own insignia. (Root, 1996, p. 187)

I read a wonderful paper the other day by a woman named Ann
Berlack, although it is a paper in process and I cannot quote her, the idea of tes-
timonials and bearing witness resounds throughout the paper. Sometimes, I do
feel as if I am bearing witness to a tragedy just beginning to unfold. Hopefully,
we incorporate, and appropriate into our destinies, ultimately creating our own
insignias, without the definer to name our struggle. We may be displaced, but,
we shall struggle with our last breathe not to be replaced. "Signification makes
meaning tremble." So, we must appropriate meanings for ourselves! For, "what
is displaced—dispersed, deferred, repressed, pushed aside, is significantly still
there" (Bammer, 1994, p. xxiii), there is a murmur in the air and a trail of
smoke that obscures our tears.

The (in)signia, the emblematic, the signifiers, that we carry with us
comes from the sheer weight of the tragedy, in the shadow of something almost

foretold. The apparition envelops me and surrounds me not so much in the sense of Hegel's pure being, but more like the polluted air, and the smog that blankets this space like a licentious landscape of an aberrant Brigadoon.

STATIC LOCATIONS ON THE IDENTITY TERRAIN

I know I should start this with situating myself, and my "identity" but I have become rather bored with static location politics that seek to name me. People resist categories. Yet, invariably the categorical is always imposed. We seem to festishize identity. We are so concerned with situating people that we cannot see how frightfully reductionist this is. If "differentiated age grades are a product of modern industrial life" (Luker, 1996, p. 25), then perhaps static differentiated identifies as absolute objective markers are part of the prosaic of the postmodern. We always seem to need to find a beacon in a tempestuous sea to cling to. But identity much like culture, like history, and narrative are not monoliths, are not things, but are processes, constantly transforming shifting, swirling, transmutating, transforming expressions. We are not puppets that are inscribed on, we all consistently (re)articulate any and all subjects.

I went to several conferences this past year, and at each conference everyone was busy situating themselves, grounding themselves, cementing their beings into the ground. You must grout mosaics, even metropolitan ones. They must be firmly braced just in case the earth moves. The only way to change a mosaic is to break the tile. Ricky Ricardo had no name, he was a double diminutive (see Perez-Firmat, 1994). But, of course anything that is foreign is dimunitized. If I cannot be grateful, I cannot be. If I am part of more than one mosaic, I must be broken a part. Identity cannot be slippery in Los(t) Angeles, you must choose sides. Welcome to the world of the walking dead. Undoubtedly, California is the boldest leap of all into the ontological void. "Nothing Theory"—(a post-Newtonian idea) "the universe is one of those things that happen from time to time," please pass the sun-dried radicchio, do you want a latte or a double espresso It is all image (and I do despise that word). La-de-dah. Perhaps, it is as Tennessee Williams' said—(I admit paraphrasing) "a vacuum is a hell of a lot better than some of the stuff nature replaces it with." So, if the world exists merely because it is superior to nullity, then California really is the dream. It surrounds us, it is in us, it is Hegel's pure being having no qualities, it remains a vacant void (again I am paraphrasing an article from *Harpers* magazine).

> Staring into the void of history, filled with mirages, I have stepped behind the Orange Curtain. If I close my eyes and click my heels three times, can I ever go home again? Gregor Samsa holds nothing over me, sorry Kafka. I may be an insect, but I am not a gusayno. Somewhere over the rainbow

coalition, high above the heights of Hollywood, the screams of the children still can not be heard. (Anijar, in press)

Does situating oneself mitigate past, current, and future injustices? You cannot move anything or change anything if it is super-glued into the ground. I think it was James Baldwin who said (and I am paraphrasing) you cannot know who a person is until you hear them speak. Will you at least let me listen? Concurrently, will you allow me to speak. Or are our frames and markers so cumbersome that it is part of the already known? Are we already dead, and does our silence come as a specter? I still walk, I still cry, I still bleed, so I am here.

As an undergraduate I read a lot of Octavio Paz, his contention: Silence was stoicism. I don't think so, I just think you refuse to hear. Like Munch's painting "The Scream" forever frozen in time, but unheard. But, because we have a linear progressive mode of time, time does not stand still, time cannot be placed in a bottle. Dory Previn wrote in a song once about "doing it alone, screaming in her car in a twenty mile zone," but, I am not alone. Yet, the isolation of our cars, our cubicles, and fears, relegate us to an agoraphobia of the soul. We are afraid. We become stolidly stoic. And we wear masks, revealing our anguish and sadness only among the closest of friends. *Nelson Ned y Sus Estrellas*, way back in the late 1960s or early 1970s (about the same time as Dory Previn screamed in her car) wrote a song about the Payaso: the clown, who sent his mask to/for his love (the record melted on our way through the Mojave, so, I can't remember the precise words). The clown sent his mask to those he trusted, I however, reveal myself carefully, recalcitrantly only to those I trust, for, to do otherwise is just too risky, too dangerous. Yet, even in partially dissipating the smokescreen, I leave myself vulnerable and open to pain. And, I would, as did the speechless slave in Villaverde's Cecilia, "prefer to swallow my tongue before entering any over determined spaces" (Ramos, 1994, p. 33).

Vulnerability is a border crossing. California is a border crossing, the land mines are the demarcations, the children are the debris. So we swallow our tongues, and work ever so cautiously. In ballet school I learned that there must be the appearance of movement even through stillness. In philosophy I learned that if I was immortal I would be like a rock. When nothing moves it is static. When something is so situated it becomes stuck, movement and change gives way to stasis.

Identities are about questions of using the resources of history, language and culture in the process of becoming rather than being: not who we are or where we came from, so much as what we might become, how we have been represented and how that bears on how we might represent ourselves. (Hall & DuGuy, 1996, p. 4)

There are competing interpretations about what our identities and our spaces, locations, cultures, ethnicities, races and genders signify. The meaning of citizenship, who are to be counted as the true bearers of America's destiny and promise, undergoes revision as society and the state fail to make good on the complex, and also evolving fantasy of what America is. (Patton, 1996, p. 7)

In the Odyssey, or was it the Iliad (I did read the Cliff Notes), the hero needed to slay the monster. Typifying fairy tales, the hero (and we are all the heroes in our own stories) needed to vanquish the monster before continuing on the bridge. There may not be real monsters or dragons to slay, there may be no holy grails to acquire, but we are still consumed, and swallowed whole. I recognize that I am not swallowed or devoured alone. I am consumed in a Gargantuan feast. I made my choices I stand with my brothers and sisters, I will not sell out love, and life, and be what I can not be (even though the U.S. Army tells us we can be all we can be, because we can do "it" whatever it may be, in the Army. And I saw the Army in Vietnam composed of the poor. During the Gulf War I saw the boys in my town march off to the pied piper of multinationals). Like Luke Skywalker in the lair of Jabba the Hutt, Gargantua will not let go, and we do not have lasers, or foils, and we cannot conjure the magic, in a world that has forced us to forget that the magic was ours!

Rabelais Gargantua, of course, a massive heir to the throne whose wants are awesome and unbridled. He is an animated fantasy about greed, strength, and sheer unstoppable corporeality. Whatever Gargantua is or does, in his guzzling and pissing, in his stupidity and violence, he outdoes everyone else. . . . We can recognize in the old giant's size, ubiquity, gluttony, vast knowledge, and warlike nature qualities of our contemporary culture. Like, the celebrated commodities which now strut across the entire globe. Gargantua is more and less than human. His authority is based on sheer force since the very excess of his consumption inspires fear. At the same time his omniscience and lack of failings make him predictable in his actions. After a time . . . the visitor . . . must be reminded that behind it lies a system of wheels and gears which reproduce it from moment to moment, and which needs continual power and maintenance, and which might at any time go wrong. (Stallabrass, 1996, p. 3)

We wait for reprieve, hoping beyond hope, that the political indelibly etched on our bodies, without the benefit of anaesthesia, will stop aching. When will Gargantua realize that it was a mistake, sometimes surgical mistakes do happen. But, the brandishing irons make their stamp, and the smoke rises from our skins, and from our burning bodies, a pyre of the political.

Waiting with masks on in silence, nobody sees or hears. Gargantua has shown his monster face. He cannot hide any longer.

Depressing, nihilistic, NO! You see we are like the arcade game of beaver, you keep bopping us down with your paddle, and, we keep popping up.

Alas, you can never know where we will pop up next. You can't see us anymore for you have made us invisible.

> We're building a bridge to the 21st century? Yeah, the Puerto Ricans and blacks are the stones you're building it on. You ask me what I think revolution is? My revolution is making sure the Latino people cross the 21st-century bridge with everybody else. Back in the church, the nearly two-hour ceremony is coming to an end. King Mission, a 17-year-old Brooklyn Tech student who is also chair of Aspira, a major Puerto Rican youth organization, reads a poem he's written for King Tone. "Every act of love is a miracle," says Mission. "The onyx warrior, Blood, is passing on mythic power to the gold warrior. There was a time when pain was so intense that it was mistaken for pleasure." But when the Kings and Queens speak, they're saying that time has passed. King Tone has taken on the burden of healing his nation. "Yes, I'm at war," he intones. "But it's a war of peace. Bullets can't harm me. If I die, I multiply." And the throng chants, again and again. "Amor de rey!" (http:www.villagevoice.com)

When we no longer see people as subjective beings involved in the process of daily living. When people become the stones upon which we build, that is when people become the most dangerous. You don't see it coming. It is erased in a feel good–do good embrace, much like a snake, the embrace grows tighter and tighter a noose around our necks that extinguishes the light. Embraces are not always caring. But people always struggle!

TOURISMO: PASSPORTS TO VOYEURISM

I don't know what it is that we are looking for when we play location-ethnicity-racial-jeopardy and 20 questions (and we don't even have Alex Trebeck to remind us to reframe our answers in terms of questions). We are all enmeshed in circuits that are not fixed, of social, economic, and cultural ties encompassing no singular space. There is a danger zone in the creation of homogenous groups. There is a danger zone in speaking *for* rather than speaking *with*. There is a danger zone when there is description without thinking of people as active subjects in the creation of their own lives. There is danger, there is erasure in the creation of opaque identifiers. We tend to mystify ethnicity and race in terms of genetic inheritance

> "it is in our blood" . . . while this racial insiderism may go unchallenged ("its a black thing, you wouldn't understand"), it is easy to see how a simple substitution would provoke feminist outcry: "And now I also see what part of me is female it is in our blood." (Bow, 1995, p. 30)

The fetish of identity as absolute: The identifier, the marker, the stamp, the brand, gives way and (re)creates a eugenic entree on Gargantua's platter. We have seen it before and make no doubt that it is happening again.

> Just as the gap between the white and black communities has widened according to Andrew Hacker, into two nations; so too has the gap between the middle and working classes on one hand and the underclass on the other. It is not surprising therefore, that Murray and Herenstien's thesis emerges at this point in our history—a point which emphasis on the behavioral causes of poverty are called upon for the repeating structures of black impoverishment, and second, when the costs of expanding the size of the black middle class seems to have dampened the enthusiasm of liberals in congress for the equivalent of a Marshall Plan for our cities, a commitment of resources sufficient to shift the bell curve of class so it conforms to that society as a whole. If differences of intelligence and therefore, attainment are natural, are genetic why bother? It won't matter anyway. And, this seems to me to be the most pernicious aspect of Murray and Herenstien's dismissal of the role of environment in the performance of blacks on standardized tests: the gap between the haves and the have nots is a reflection of natural variation within the group, and not a function of the cutbacks in the very federal programs that helped create the new black middle class in the first place. As Frederick Douglas might say the crimes of discrimination have become discriminations best defense. (Gates, 1995, pp. 95–96)

> Today's Sunbelt represents a confluence of Social Darwinism, entrepreneurealism, high technology, nationalism, nostalgia and fundamentalist religion, and any Sun Belt hegemony over our politics has a unique potential . . . to accommodate a drift towards apple-pie authoritarianism. So wrote conservative strategist Kevin Phillips in his 1982 book, *Post-Conservative America*. The failed American dream can give way to a new American fairness or a neo-fascist nightmare. It can happen in Europe, it can happen here. (Sklar, 1995, p. 131)

The point is, it is happening here! There is no polite way to word this. At a certain point words became transpositioned, words are always complex, words are always contingent. There is so much complex contradiction abounding on the Western Front (where all seems quiet—but it is simmering waiting to boil over), that you cannot know who to trust. "You need to develop the skill of cynicism" (southern California teacher).

No wonder people feel nihilistic; they are being killed! Gargantua is hungry. The monster must be appeased. His voracious unrepentant appetite will eventually make him ill.

Sometimes, some of the students in my classes and I sneak into my office and we speak our particular version of "Spanglish." We have all gotten so paranoid at a certain level, that we do not speak English any longer, it is an issue of trust. We do not have any. How can we?

I do not want to be cannibalized, exoticized, or touristized. We are not Kachinka dolls, or totem polls, I will not allow my children (and I mean all of our children) to be exoticized and cannibalized by being defined under the neo-colonial embrace of western benevolence.

I saw a famous academic one day who, demonstrating his quasi solidarity with the gente, spoke in a perverse pidgin Spanish with Latino colleagues when everyone there spoke English, it felt oddly quite patronizing. I am reminded of another professor I know who takes teacher education candidates on the train down to Olivera Street. How will this enrich concentric circles of understanding? It is nothing more than turismo. This is not to say that Tijuana, or Olivera Street, or Cancun are less authentic than anywhere else. The issue of authenticity is moot anyway. It is all part of the food fest, the exoticized other fest, the *vive la difference* fest. It is to say that border locales are often constructed in relation to the economy that has the capital to take the tour. It should come as no surprise, then, given the plethora of travel literature written about imperialism during the colonizing 19th and early 20th centuries (which gave rise to some of Francis Galton's eugenicist fantasies) that our preoccupation with static identities, and authenticity, and things, has given rise to a new eugenicism.

In Fritz Lang's (1929) movie *Megapolis* the people who danced in the utopia above ground did not see those who toiled beneath the surface, they were invisible—at least—until—we start collectively singing together!

> Do you hear the people sing? Singing the songs of angry men,
> It is the music of a people who will not be slaves again.
> When the beating of your heart echoes the beating of the drum
> There is a light about to start when tomorrow comes . . .
> . . . The blood of the martyr's will water the meadows of France . . .
> . . . There is a light about to start when tomorrow comes . . .
> (from Les Miserables, Alain Boubill, Claude Michel Schonberg, Herbert Kretzmer, Alain Boubill Overseas Limited)

So, come on baby light my fire (e.g., Jose Feliciano and Jim Morrison) I am waiting. But, Gargantua with his greedy and voracious appetite is too overburdened to move. I can still hide in the woods. With each new measure, with each new proposition, with each new lie and retro-reformist package, comes an anger that will catch on like a fire. And like the brush fires in the state where I reside, a wildfire in a desert is hard to put out!

You may name, and categorize, and ghettoize, be careful where you walk the land mines are everywhere. It is hard to see behind the camouflage the illusion it is far easier to think of the "happy face." The other, the anger, may be too powerful to endure. You can't expunge your guilt by pretending that history no longer exists. You can't walk through life like a racehorse with blinders on seeing only the finish line and nothing on the sides.

I notice the pictures of flowers, window shades and curtains and interiors of pretty-looking rooms, that have been painted on these buildings, on the sides that face the highway. It's a strange sight, and the pictures have been done so well that when you look the first time you imagine that you're seeing into peoples homes—pleasant looking homes, in fact that have a distinctly middle class appearance. I ask her if people who live here did these pictures. "Nobody lives here" she replies. "those buildings are all empty."

The city had these murals painted on the walls, she says not for the people in the neighborhood—because they're facing the wrong way—but for tourists and commuters. The idea is that they mustn't be upset by knowing too much about the population here. It isn't enough that these people are sequestered. It is also important that their presence be disguised or sweetened. The city did not repair the buildings so that the kids who live around here in fact could *have* pretty rooms like those. Instead they *painted* pretty rooms on the facades. It's an illusion.

Well, what a dirty thing to do! Really, it is far beyond racism. It's just—in your face! Take that! We don't clean up the neighborhood, don't fix your buildings, fix your schools or give you decent hospitals or banks. Instead we paint the sides of the buildings so that people driving to the suburbs will have something nice to look at.

. . . The city, she says, denies unkind intentions and insists it's simply decoration. Decoration for whom? (Kozol, 1995, p. 31)

Tourism is not the answer. I am reminded of the multiculturalism that deculturalizes because it is owned and shaped by those who have the privilege to name and define people's situations. Olivera Street, for whom? I am tired of picture postcard pastorals depicting the happy dancing natives. It all reminds me of the border between South and North Korea. There is a Hollywood movie set on the North Korean side, of lovely homes. However, it is merely illusion, it is mirage, it was constructed for the U.S. military to see. We often see through, the Three Monkeys: Hear No Evil, Speak No Evil, and See No Evil, a mythological and foolish maxim. Evil is prosaic, and the earth seems so stable (like a static rock) until you sense the earth shaking underneath your feet, unless you are out in the country you don't hear the sounds of the city. Like a crescendo building to the climax of a play "When the beating of your hearts echo the beating of the drums. . . ."

Although, illusions often become the images that transform reality. Because *tourismo* is always set in relation to home. However, many do not have a home. *Ni aqui, ni alla* (Perez-Firmat) and that is where the land mines are hidden in the spatialization of the historic.

You do not see the discontent underneath. I am reminded of a student one quarter who still haunts me in my nightmares. A Black woman who went to

Mexico and said she thinks "the people are happier being poor, for their lives are so much simpler." In the *mundo* multicultural that abhors history, I was told by the academic powers that be that my answer, which was "and yes the American Blacks were much happier on the plantation, life was much simpler," was too angry, to political, and a personal attack on her being. We invoke the words "Never forget" but they have become as vacuous as most politically engineered sound bytes. How can people who have suffered such indignities comfortably sit by while children are being killed? As educators, we need to recognize our duplicity and complicity emanating from our meliorist routes, with technological fixes, that mask the underpinnings tied to ideas of doing and wanting as substitutes for reflection and action (see Popkewitz, 1995A). We cannot continue to play the name-game–blame-game (mother mother fo fother banana fana bo bother fi fi fo mother . . .). Political exigencies are erased in the process. This is not a game. This is not a test. We only get one life! Whom do we serve?

Because, people are constructed underneath the comfort of somebody else's "paradigmatic understanding," under the whitewashed sheets of multiculturalism, under the diversity embrace that remains a killer.

One of my favorite movies in the world is called *Poppi*. Poppi was a Puerto Rican janitor in New York City. He was a widow who worked three jobs, but could not "save" his children from the streets. One night while busing tables he happened to find himself clearing tables amidst a "Cuba Libre" banquet. The light went off in Poppi's head. He will rescue his children by passing them off as Cuban. So, he set about teaching his children and subsequently sent them out on a boat from Miami Beach (my beautiful hometown, the sun and fun capital of the world, so said Jackie Gleason). The children were painted as heroes of *la patria*. Trucks from FAO Schwartz arrived with toys, the president was going to meet with the children. Until it was found out they were really Puerto Rican. Stripped of their privilege, the children and the father were sent back to the South Bronx. Don't we get it: Each child must be seen as our own child!

I do not want to be set as an exemplar for anything, for I am not. I am tired of checking off the boxes. I am tired of people asking "The Question". I respond that I am a metropolitan mongrel, which obscures and confuses even more, and tends to get people angry. Good! And, that is my point. It doesn't matter what I am. What matters is that there are children out there on the streets, and in the countryside, who do not have the opportunity to make their statements, to name their conditions, it was already assumed. We all know the axiom about assume. When do the people get to speak and indeed when do we begin to listen (see Casey, 1995)? All I want is to find where the hope is, where the possibility is. The past may seem bleak but the future is a heck of a lot bleaker.

I was told in graduate school to begin with the autobiographical, except, that I think I lost mine along one paradigm or another. Perhaps the problem resides in historical transition. I am not talking about a paradigm shift, believe me, I have no use whatsoever for the paradigmatic. But, I am talking about a postmodern universe of slippery signifiers. I am also speaking from an economic framework. We have moved into the post-Fordist Era, where images are purchased. Because nothing is ever ahistorical because nothing emerges out a vacuum and even a vacuum is a force to be reckoned with, it may be tied to the fossil-like notions of a dialectic universe filled with either–or's but not and–boths (see Clark & Holquist, 1984). We have not entered into a dialogical frame of meaning for we are so tied to dualities (indeed, it is almost impossible for me to escape the frame of Cartesian dualism). Discourse can never be a hypostatized "thing" that in its stasis produces the "dead thing like shell" "the naked corpse" (see Clark & Holquist, 1984; Morson, 1990). Meaning is unstable, it is polysemic. Life is unstable, it is polysemic. What Bakhtin termed *centrifugal forces* "compel movement, becoming and history; they long for change and new life" (Clark & Holquist, 1984, p. 7), as opposed to centripetal forces that "urge stasis, resist becoming, abhor history, and desire the seamless quiet of death" (Clark & Holquist, 1984, p. 8), should be considered. Centripetal forces reduce "cultural life to a static system of categorical relationships which leave untouched many critical factors involved in the construction of cultural exchanges" (Quantz & O'Conner 1988, p. 95). Recognizing that nothing can ever be reduced to the categorical may "provide the only meaningful escape from an endless oscillation between dead abstractions" (Morson, 1990, p. xi).

Some of the people I care about most in the world (the students in my classes) write so forcefully and articulately about the conundrum I am trying to express:

I was often told that I needed to be a role model . . . in . . . a graduate program I felt like the focus of intense scrutiny people were placing an uncontrollable amount of pressure on me to study Chicano/a literature. . . . .(student paper, 1996)

My suspicions are confirmed that I can never go back because education has irreversibly changed me. My relatives see it. Old family friends feel it. I know it. Every time I walk into a local meat market I am reminded. My presence is a rupture; the needle on the record player screeches and halts. Eyes pass over me, and most look away because I represent something painfully diluted. (student paper, 1996)

Personally I ache for an American community, but the election that has just passed that the country is becoming increasingly polarized. As I enter the middle class, I see family members situations worsen. The neighborhood in which I grew up is becoming more economically depressed, and the number of people who are displaced grows each time I visit.

It has all been a snow job! For centuries, the white man has fed their white lies to a gullible and unsuspecting youth of America. So far I have written a lot of generalities, thoughts and ideas about how I feel living in American

and being helpless, useless, voiceless and powerless as a person of color for
years I have been angry at the plight of my people. Words lit a fuse in me
that will forever alter my perception oppression and inferiority
I am that fantasy which race has wrought
Of mundane chance material. I am time
Paened by the senses five like bells that chime
I am cramped and crumbing house of clay
Where mansoul weaves the secret webs of thought
Venturer—automation—I cannot tell
What powers and instincts animate and betray
And do their dreamwork in me. Seed and star,
Sown by the wind, in spirit I am far
From self, the dull control with whom I dwell
Also I am ancestral. Aeons ahead
and ages back, both sone and sire I live
Mote—like between the unquickened and the dead
From whom I take and unto whom I give (Siegfried Sasson)

The words speak of a chance existence felt only through weak and mistrust-
ed senses. A vision of a cramped and crumbling metropolis filled with
blind, ghostlike figures. . . . With their eyes closed the people move through
a maze of obstacles created to confuse and inflict despair. Mote-like we are
alone, we are all alone, surrounded by a sea of carefully wrapped and sugar
coated lies. . . . (student paper, 1996)

We look to our caretakers to show us what is right and wrong, what is truth
and what is fiction" (Hall, 1996, p. 9). We look outside . . . Tezcatipola is
commonly called the smoking mirror, but a more accurate translation
would be the "smoke that mirrors.: Doesn't smoke usually hide the truth?
What's the difference? Tezcatipola uses the smoke, its his home front
advantage . . . We can not bear to see ourselves and so we create an
unreachable, unknowable other to take the blame for our distaste. "We can
not see the self, the image in the mirror is constantly shifting, but it continues to make us nervous." (Root, 1996, p. 197)

We need a big fan! (student paper, 1996)

We need a big fan that can blow away the smoke of the hypocrisy and
the lies that have chained and gagged us, set us out to wander in a biblical
wilderness, searching for a home that cannot be, for it may never have been there
in the first place. We ache in our constant wanderings. We ache as Gargantua
consumes our homes, consumes our definitions, consumes our possibilities. But,
knowing the pain, we begin to build a new world from the fragments.

ANOTHER YUCKY DAY IN PARADISE

I went to my car on Monday evening, someone had smashed the windows in, stolen the hubcaps, and bent my antenna. The policeman came out, and was so haughty and supercilious, I wonder if his attitude would be different had I had an Anglo last name? I was attacked last year by a student who came out from behind the dempsey dumpsters angered by a grade he received in class, he asserted his White right to vanquish me (and sarcastically I point out that my size makes me a really formidable opponent). But, can we recapture whiteness for the left? Can we adopt an ethical and moral language for the left and stop giving it over to the (r)white-wing? I have often written about another student my first quarter in California who had a solution to the immigrant problem— "Zyclon B" gas. This young man was an immigrant too, from a more Aryan sort of nation.

And how do I respond to all of this anger, to all of these calls. How can I? I too lost my trust when I crossed over the border and not for Taco Bell. You see,

> The next day I was invited to a theater performance in East Jerusalem. An actor of my acquaintance, a Palestinian citizen of Israel who had done most of his acting in Hebrew, told me for a change he was going to act in Arabic. I could have walked the ten minutes to get there, but being from California and in a hurry I drove my rented car . . . Emerging from the theater, I found my car firebombed—a charred skeleton of buckled metal and soot.
>
> Sympathetic theater goers gathered around and tried to comfort me. From a lit-up window across the dark street, a man poked his head out, and called, in English. "yeah, they fired bombed your car. They knew from the car that you were the only Israeli here—and if you came to this play you must be OK. But you crossed the border. (Lavie, 1996, p. 91)

A PEACE CORPS PEDAGOGY AS PLANTATION PATERNALISM

> The Joke: I talk a lot right? And when I get very tired I interrupt people; and I am making a joke, but in fact it is never perceived as a joke unless I tell them. I will quite often say, "You know, in my culture it shows interest and respect if someone interrupts"; and immediately there are very pious faces, and people allow me to interrupt. (Gayatri Chakravorty Spivak, *Questions of Multiculturalism,* cited in Sawhney, 1995, p. 208)

Little Red Riding Hood, upon her arrival at Grandma's house, met the wolf disguised as granny. That is the way I read the politics of the 1990s that has produced a profound sense of nihilism.

How can I blame the kids? How can I tell them it is going to be better? How can I tell the kids work hard, and you too. It doesn't work that way. The window of opportunity, well actually it was just a crack, was slammed shut. (southern California teacher).

This is truly problematic. We are working within an essentialist framework, that much like a natural disaster, huffs and puffs and blows the house a part. (Anijar, in press)

The house was never well put together to begin with. Little Red Riding Hood is also a profound political parable for the 1990s. Beware of those who want to embrace you. Sometimes, embraces are annihilating. Is it any wonder that multiculturalism emerged as a powerful force in the schools at the same time that (re)actionary forces (re)articulated and (re)named the conditions of poverty.

Alas, *aqui* the only instrument we can play are primitive ones, very valuable hand made objects, demonstrating a peace corps of neo-benevolence. We are "folk," which means less than civilized. The further we move from the epicenter of the Anglo vortex, the more savage we become, the more quaint we become. I feel a mariachi band blossoming from my being, it is an alien feeling. For it is not in people's definitions of themselves, but, who has the authority to define who and what they are. I was invited to a Cinco de Mayo festival, where the students performed a cumbia to the sounds of that great Mexican songbird Gloria Esteban. To paraphrase Shakespeare: "something isn't kosher in Denmark." At one school I learned about Swedish Christmas customs (we ate Swedish meatballs). The teacher had a flag of Israel up because during the next week the children were going to be exposed to the "Israeli Christmas: Hanukkah" (Hanukkah?) I tried to politely explain that Hanukkah had nothing to do with Christmas, and the holiday did not emerge in Israel. But, she told me I was wrong, she showed me her multicultural workbook (I guess I was just suffering from false consciousness). What could I possibly know about the holiday? I didn't write the workbook. And am only Jewish.

The celebration of the multicultural, and calls for diversity merely create a "Museum of Natural History" tour, for the emphasis of otherness comes under the benevolent plantation embrace of the satin sheets of the Hollywood movie set. It isn't a melting pot, it is a melted pot. It is a Velveeta cheese curriculum. A professor I know told me that acknowledging the categories is better than ignoring them, a little bit is better than nothing. I resist, I know that I cannot be a little bit pregnant.

Multiculturalism has produced if anything an even greater rush towards utopian thinking. (Chicago Cultural Studies Group, 1994, p. 114)

Utopianizing is a conservative impulse understood as "reactionary on the grounds that it sought to impose an ideal plan upon reality rather than seeking in that reality the means of social change" (Levitas, 1990, p. 59). An impulse that *vive la difference*, and diversity arguments tend to inculcate particularly when instrumented in schools.

Within these colonized terms (for example) bilingualism and biculturalism make those of us who fall in between the hyphens' bisected entities. Bilingual, bifurcate, bi-sect, dis-sect, and we are dying. You are embracing us to death. Ni-culturalized in a balkanized metaphor (see Perez-Firmat, 1994; Regalado, 1995). People are not collocations of objective characteristics. Nothing is fixed. We are all in the process of changes and exchanges. There remains a blurry netherworld between "description and prescription . . . reality does not match the theory" (Anijar, 1997; Gillborn, 1995, p. 10).

CONSPIRACY THEORIZING AND POPULAR LEGENDS

Karen: There is a rubber band club in your school?
Jake: Yes!
Karen: I don't want to sound stupid but why do you collect rubber bands?
Jake: Cause, they're there.
Karen: Why? What?
Jake: They're there. We are gonna have the worlds largest rubber band collection in the world!
Karen: Everyone has ambitions I guess
Jake: I have no ambitions, I have rubber bands!

Jake has no ambitions, but he does have rubber bands. As innocuous and off the cuff as this narrative fragment may seem, it reveals so much more than it conceals. "Why don't you have ambitions," I inquired? Jake answered, his voice creaking with pubescent crackles and changes, "You really don't get it do you?" "No, I guess I don't." "Well," he said "you see there is a conspiracy. The government is conspiring with aliens and like have you ever heard of Roswell? Well they are housed there." "Who is housed there?" "The aliens, silly! Everyone knows about the aliens. Everyone knows about the aliens so much that they show it on the *X-Files!*"

Jonathan, who was born in Korea, and moved here at the age of 2 (you see I can play identity and location politics too, but it tells you nothing at all about Jonathan) has no rubber bands, but he does have paranoia, he does engage in conspiratorial theorizing.

Jonathan: There are aliens. To quote the great writers who write the Simpsons, when they were taken aboard the space ship. "We invented space travel, we go through time and distances and if we say pong is an advanced game, it is!" If

they travel here they are more advanced than us!" Look,
do you know about Peru?

Karen: Nope

Jonathan: You know they found this stuff up there. Space material
that doesn't come from the Earth, the Mayans buried it a
long time ago, and the Mayan's had landing strips.
The Bermuda Triangle is another dimension. You know
the Druids all left for another dimension too. Emilio
Earhart [sic—and note: I just loved the mispronunciation
so much I had to share it] even though she got lost, she
really didn't she went to another dimension, probably captured by the aliens in retaliation for our actions. She's
dead now, cause she got really old.

Karen: So are the aliens bad guys?

Jonathan: No, they just think we are stupid like fleas. Remember
ID4. That is what it is like. They are going to kill us cause
they feel like it, and, they can!

Joshua   (Karen's son) What about ET? (laughing)

Jonathan: Dead.

MEDIA CULT-URES

A media culture has emerged in which images, sounds, and spectacles help
produce the fabric of everyday life, dominating leisure time, shaping political views and social behavior and providing the materials out of which people forge their identities. (Kellner, 1995, p. 1)

I was really depressed by the idea of the rubber band club. When I got home, I
asked my son about the club (he is also a member). He elucidated in a rather cir-
cuitous word collage, a hermeneutic circle of impossibility (a.k.a: Herman's circle
of nihilism) the benign absurdity of it all, while shooting down enemies in Mortal
Kombat. The rubber band club was founded because of a bet, which eventually up
ended in an escalating barrage of sophomoric pranks. The club's sponsor (my
son's favorite teacher) ultimately stole a rubber band collection from a friend's
dorm room while in college, over a six pack of beer and some MD 20/20. "I see,
sort of," I said (with a sigh of exasperation). Joshua continued speaking while
defending the universe from mutant monsters, "He really kicks! He is the best! He
has a big mouth like Jose (Joshua's godfather), and he tells the best jokes!" "But,
what do you do at the club meetings?" "We count rubber bands!" "Why?" "Why
not? They're there, there is nothing else to do, there is nothing else we can do!"
      Later that day we drove to the desert to get Joshua new jeans at the dis-
count mall. He could not be seen at school and be taken seriously if his pants were

not three sizes too big. "I am going to ask my dad for some foreign rubber bands. I want to get into multicultural rubber band collecting. Some of my friends have started antique rubber band collections. Mr C—has one really old rubber band and he keeps it in a plastic box, he says it is worth a penny. That is just so great."

Okay, so multiculturalism may as well be reduced to rubber bands. It is usually enacted in the most superficial of manners. It is usually a Chinese restaurant curriculum, pick a group from Column A and let's learn effective strategies to deal with them on Column B. It is a small world after all. Why not? Crayola has multicultural crayons, and there are multicultural Barbie dolls. And of course, because I reside in Southern California, I cannot forget the awe-inspiring ride of all possibility (and saccharin reductionism): "It's a Small World." Let's all hail Disney as a (re) visionary.

I told him I thought a multicultural condom collection would be better. "That's *dumb*," said my son. I replied articulately as usual: "What?"

Joshua: Didn't you ever have sex-ed?
Karen: No! Nobody ever had to teach me about how to have sex!
Joshua: For a doctor your stupid and demented! I am going to stay a virgin for a very long time! At least until I really fall in love!
Karen: That is what they all say. Cyber-sex doesn't count?
Joshua: Gross, grow up! If you have sex, you can get an STD or Aids and die!
Karen: What about condoms?
Joshua: Mother, they can break, and you can still get it. I learned it is better to abstain, if you don't you're gonna die!

I knew where I was going with the conversation. I knew what I really wanted to ask him. I needed to cut to the chase so he wouldn't loose patience with my behavioral breach.

"Joshua, do you think there is a government conspiracy, do you think we are hiding aliens, do you think the world is hopeless?" "Yes, mom, yes mom, and yes! You would have to be dense not to know that!" "Did your teacher teach you that too?" "No mom, I know that, and I have known it for a long time!"

"I see!" "No, you don't. When we get back home let me take you to teen chat and to the X-Files room." My beautiful child's eyes seemed both so resigned and so determined to prove to me that "the truth is out there!"

While on line, we found this poem that discloses the rampant nihilism that much like the Chernobyl cloud mutates our progeny into increasingly paranoid, despondent, and nihilistic states. Welcome to the world of overdetermination.

Trust no one
Being cynical is a way of life
Everyone is watching you
There are conspiracies against you
Turn around! It's a government plan
Trust no one!
You don't trust
You can't trust
Humans will invariably let you down
They're sad opportunists
Trust no one . . .

A 13-year-old author wrote the poem for the Internet. She asked that nobody steal her poem. I am and unfortunately I may reconfirm the worst of her fears.

CONSPIRACY THEORY PART 2

LOS ANGELES (AP)—Angry blacks responded with boos and catcalls as CIA Director John Deutch insisted during a town meeting that no evidence had been found to support rumors that agency operatives trafficked in crack cocaine.

Speaking in Watts to a mostly black crowd of about 500 on Friday, Deutch promised a thorough investigation of allegations that drug sales helped finance CIA-backed Nicaraguan Contra guerrillas during the 1980s. "The CIA fights drugs. The CIA does not encourage drugs," he said. "Our employees do not want any Americans to believe the CIA is responsible for this kind of disgusting charge." Many attending the meeting at Locke High School made it clear they didn't believe him. "How are we supposed to trust the CIA officials to investigate themselves?" demanded one questioner who, like most in the audience, refused to give her name, saying she feared reprisals by the government.

The forum was organized by Rep. Juanita Millender-McDonald, a Democrat who represents South Central Los Angeles, to address charges that have spread through the black community since a three-part series was published in August by the San Jose Mercury News. The series alleged a California drug ring sold tons of cocaine to Los Angeles street gangs in the 1980s, and funneled millions in profits to CIA-backed Contras to finance their civil war efforts in Nicaragua.

It did not directly link the CIA with the drug dealers, but people in communities such as South Central expressed outrage, saying the government must have known about the vast amounts of cocaine moving into minority neighborhoods.

That sentiment was echoed by Millender-McDonald.

"We do not have the planes and the ships to bring this over, the tons and tons of cocaine," she said during a news conference before the forum.

The CIA, Justice Department and House Intelligence Committee are conducting separate investigations of the allegations.

Deutch said investigations conducted thus far have produced "no evidence of a conspiracy. But I will not be satisfied, and no one should be satisfied, until a complete and thorough investigation" is finished.

He acknowledged that, in fighting the drug trade, the spy agency sometimes works with unsavory people.

"These are criminals that we must deal with if we are going to stop drugs coming into the country," he said. "(But) we have no evidence of a conspiracy by the CIA to engage and encourage drug traffickers in Nicaragua or elsewhere in Latin America in this or any other periods."

One man, Tarik Ricard, used his turn with the microphone to express his disdain for Deutch's promise.

"You come into this community and insult us," he told Deutch. "You tell us you're going to investigate yourself. You must be crazy. This was a PR move that's not fooling anybody." (Deborah Hastings © 1996 The Associated Press)

On the evening news when the story broke, an ex-policeman stood up and said he knew what the CIA was doing in South Central. The point is not whether this is true or not (truth itself is quite contingent). The point is this, in this a strange "Narcoracy," Los Angeles, is now known as the crack capital of the world. (Knight http:www.aol.channel.html.) Divide and conquer, balkanize and balkanize and balkanize some more: black and browns killing each other off, so international capital can prosper? No, we cannot assume this is just race, this has to do with class as well, this has to do with all sort of peculiar postmodern constructions, and reconstructions.

Does this go back to "The Great White Lie?" Slavery was not an individual enterprise, conducted by unethical people, unable to empathize, but a system, an "all encompassing economic system" (Gratus, 1973, p. 1). Indeed, it can also be demonstrated that the slave trade was one of the great (un)natural catastrophes in the history of the world (see Gratus, 1973). To exonerate systemic spuriousness, history (re)presented a morality of abolition when frankly slavery continued until it outlived its economic utility. I hate to be so cut and dry. But, as we have shifted from an industrial to a postindustrial base, there are people who are just surplus people who may have outlived their economic utility. And, so I ask, and beg the reader to consider the same type of question Kozol asks in Amazing Grace, do we exculpate our own guilt when we speak of test scores because it weighs less heavily on our consciousness than confronting the damage done to children?

Conspiracy theories have abounded in the streets for as long as I can remember. Sometimes I can not dispute their validity. Not when:

I've seen a generation die . . . some of them was killed with guns. Some lost their minds from drugs. Some from disease. Now we have AIDS the great plague, the plague that can not be cured. It's true I've seen it. (Kozol, 1995, p. 169).

Kozol (1995) put it quite eloquently when he wrote about hypersegregated schools:

> Many of the children who attend these schools also suffer the emotional and physical attrition the results from chronic illnesses such as asthma and anxiety, as well as the steady and low level misery of rotting teeth and infected gums, and festering untreated sores. Many like Anthony, have no bedroom of their own but sleep on sofas if they're lucky, mattresses thrown on the floor if they're not.
>
> It is also recognized that many children in poor neighborhoods such as Mott Haven have been neurologically impaired, some because of low weight prematurity at birth, some because of drug ingestion while in utero, and many from lead poison in their homes, and also, shockingly enough within their schools . . . John Rosen a well-known pediatrician and lead-poison specialists at Montefiore Medical Center in the Bronx warned the city as long ago as 1987 that schools in the area were dangerously loaded with lead. . . . The damage done to the brain cells of lead poisoned children is according to researchers, not reversible.
>
> . . . it may seem surprising that scarce research funds should be diverted to investigations of genetic links between the IQ deficits of certain children and their racial origins. There is something wrong with a society where money is available to do this kind of research but not to remove lead poison from the homes and schools of children in the Bronx. (pp. 196-197)

And as we sit debating the benefits of multiculturalism, and pluralism, and, when we remove affirmative action in the name of equality: when we victim blame and label, when, and when and when. So is it any wonder that the poor do not see "innocence in our behavior. They do not think that what is being done to them is a mistake" (Kozol, 1995, p. 182).

WALKMEN, WIGGERS, AND WANNABE'S[1]

The wiggers that I have met are the way they are because of their environment and surroundings. I suppose a better way of saying it is that they have been "blackwashed". . . Most black people that I have spoken to, who see wiggers at first glance, or are meeting them for the first time, take offense to them because they feel as though the white society is trying to steal yet another aspect of the black culture and assimilate it into their own. In a

---

[1]This portion is excerpted from an unpublished paper written by Mary Dalton of Wake Forest University and myself.

sense, they feel it cheapens the message and the pride that goes along with it. (college student from southern California)

I like to sag. It's cool. I like to go to the mall and look for cool clothes. I like clothes. They're cool. Girls like it when you sag. I don't know why the principal doesn't let us sag. I think it's cool. It looks good . . . I guess if you want to call that wiggin', well fine. But, it's just that I know what's cool. (teenage male from south Florida who identifies himself as a wigger)

We first noticed the "wiggers" 3 1/2 years ago; they seemed to suddenly sprout up like the grass on meticulously manicured lawns in Greensboro, North Carolina. Greensboro is a solidly middle-class city where little league is ubiquitous and school children usually have their teachers' home phone numbers. It's a generally tranquil city where families still go on picnics and most attend church on Sunday mornings. Almost every neighborhood, even those within blocks of the downtown area, has the feel of suburbia.

We were getting ready for our mid-morning coffee and cake "fix" when Joshua walked in with his "new neighbor," a kid who had recently moved to Greensboro from South Carolina. He wore no shoes, and his pants sagged somewhere between his knees and shins. His shirt was so large that it hung around his preadolescent frame. At first glance he resembled a little boy playing dressup in a grown man's clothes. His Walkman blared rap music and seemed to be permanently attached to his ear. He greeted us with a resounding, "Yo." Yes, "it" came from somewhere in South Carolina and disturbed our pastoral paradise. As spring turned into summer, we began to notice the presence of several "wiggers" among us. We noticed them in the city, the suburbs, and the rural communities nestled across the Tarheel state. Why would "Southern adolescents" co-opt the culture of inner-city youth in the northeast and southern California?

In much the same way that rock and roll was ultimately (re)articulated back into the center (Grossberg, 1989) in a form of crass, consumer capitalism, we find that "hip-hop" culture has been (re)named and (re)articulated by White adolescent males. Wiggers have translated the experience into entirely different and unanticipated meanings that, on first glance, bear little or no relation to their "inner-city" male counterparts.

This generation, may be the first in history in which "youth" hybridize the other so completely that in hybridization (see Ackland, 1995) there becomes almost a total identification. The "problem of generations" as Bettelheim (1965) suggested, "is what gives us adults so much trouble, and not the problems of adolescence or youth" (p. 77). Bettelheim wrote about the postwar babyboomers: "in many respects youth has turned from being the older generations' greatest economic asset to its greatest economic liability" (p. 88). Indeed, "generation" has no fundamental essence except as a problem, as a crisis of values of economics and of resources. That tension is always played out between two ambiguously defined age groups in a conflict that is only complicated by the particular weight of social demographics. For instance, as culture sways in accord with the hippolike weight of baby-boomers, the overrepresentation of that generation's perspectives becomes a given. In this respect the youth of the 1980's, without the same numbers as their predecessors, could only expect cultural disenfranchisement. (Ackland, 1995, p. 24)

"America" has changed, and as our economic base has transformed from an industrial to a service economy, and there is little work. The nation becomes one "at risk." Hegemonic ideology diverts attention from the root of the problem and "as Foucault would argue the image betrays more than it reveals." (Fine, 1993, p. 105). The collective gaze, in the form of public debate, is redirected. Public discourse avoids the economic difficulties imposed on African Americans and Latinos born in the United States and ignores the collapsing manufacturing sectors and infrastructures, including impoverished urban schools, while our attention is directed toward the individual child (Fine, 1993, p. 105). We must ask who gains by constructing an "enemy" for a "presumed national emergency?" As Fine pointed out:

> The language of risk is upon us, piercing daily consciousness, educational practices, and bureaucratic policy making. It satisfies the desire to isolate children (by the right) and to display them (by the Left). . . . The cultural construction of a group defined through the discourse of risk represents a quite partial image, typically strengthening those institutions and groups that have carved out, severed, denied connection to and then promised to "save" those who will undoubtedly become at risk.
>
> With the image of "youth at risk" comes the litany of threats now saturating the popular, policy and academic literatures. Unless, public education in the United States improves substantially, the Japanese will conquer the international marketplace. Hardworking Anglo-Americans will be swallowed by noneducated nonworkers. As the general population ages, too few will be able or willing to support us through social security. (pp. 92-93)

I am not sure who Gargantua really is, who is swallowing whom? In the glaring gaze of otherness in a Fordist state, we may not have much left to consume (that is why the monster is so hungry, he is a an injured animal blinded by his own wounds, lashing out at anything). The young see a world of diminishing returns, of diminished possibility. Yet, within the somnambulism of nihilism, the carnivalesque rises from the ashes of ruin. The affiliation of youth with other creates possibility in a world where other voices are continually muted into desperate silence. Social ideology is

> real in that it is the way in which people really live their relationship to the social relations which govern their conditions of existence, but imaginary in

that it discourages full understanding of these conditions of existence and the ways in which people are socially constituted within them." (Beasley, 1980, p. 46). As Catherine Beasley would argue, these controversies do, in fact, represent "real" issues (Beasley, 1980). More dangerously, however, they are imaginary, reproducing existing ideologies, shaving off alternative frames, and recommending as "natural" programs of reform that serve to exacerbate class, race, and gender stratifications. (Fine, 1993, pp. 104-105)

There is an exploitation of the other as ideological diversion, to mask the nexus of a national agenda. But notice the words speak to masks. I imagine the smoke again, I think of the clearing of the ashes giving way to new growth after the fire, after the storm. The definitive hegemonic project of the new right affiliates youth with other and fuels the perception that the young are largely responsible for the destruction of the nostalgic and utopian glory days of "America the Beautiful." Possibility is diminished and finally denied our narrators (the children of the "credit-card class"). As one narrator said, "The adults actually just want to see us dead." As one wigger explained, "If you watch the *X-Files*, man, you know that they have a conspiracy. That's what the dude in the FBI is trying to fight unsuccessfully." Or, as another blonde-haired, blue-eyed wigger stalwartly maintained, "Dough boy got smoked. What makes you think that I am so fucking dumb to realize that I won't?"

How does the "social construction" of youth as crime fit into the establishment and reproduce what is referred to as the social order (Ackland, 1995, p. 12) subsequently creating the odd appropriation of otherness by the wiggers? There is, indeed, a perceived "crisis of youth." Childhood may be equated with possibility, but youth is considered a "disease," a threat and a pathology. According to one teacher, "You just know they are up to no good." Ackland (1995) pointed out:

The project of hegemony through crisis is not always a question of massive rallying around single battles; it equally contains numerous debates that infuse the predilections of popular imagination and particular political agendas. Various Others may be present, but at times some are more prominently displayed. Youth—and this is doubly true or African American and Hispanic youth—is increasingly symbolically central as that internal Other defined as a threat to the stability of the social order but central to the composition of that order. As such, the connotative purchase of youth has a profound political stake. (p. 12)

To be a teenager is to be "diseased," to have a condition that can hopefully be "cured" through maturation into adulthood. Ackland (1995) suggested that

[T]he late twentieth century has seen the emergence of a new conception of the period we call youth in extended time, and not only is youth accustomed to its own downward mobility. Where we have a conception of the essential innocence of childhood, we now have another relation: the essential guilt of youth. (p. 146)

The ironic, symptomatic pathology of hormonal instability and violence, for which "society" invariably "seeks a cure," is often rooted within an ideology that names young people as the carrier of the disease, or, in the brave new world of the "Contract on America," young people are named as the disease itself.

> On the occasion of the International Youth Year in 1980, the terms chosen by UNESCO to characterize the youth for the upcoming decade demonstrate a striking prescience: "if the 1960's challenged certain categories of youth in certain parts of the world with a crisis of culture, the 1980's will confront a new generation with as concrete, structural crisis of chronic economic uncertainty and even deprivation." (Ackland, 1995, p. 3)

Similarly,

> the American Medical Association, National Association of State Boards of Education (AMA-NABSE) 1990 report "Code Blue: Uniting for Healthier Youth" concluded that "unlike the past where physical illness was the primary threat to the young, today the problems are primarily behavioral." (Ackland, 1995, p. 6)

Included in the report's litany of symptomatic horrors are crime, sex, and drugs in other words "the unholy Trinity of misguided youth" (Ackland, 1995, p. 6). Within the new right and liberal hegemonic discourses, the causes of the "disease" are debated. Nevertheless, the debilitating socially constructed modernist paradigmatic categories of race, gender, sexuality, class, and age are never brought into the discussion. Amid rhetorical flashpoints, such as "victim blaming," "social meliorism," "lack of family values," and "new construction of family," there is a core belief that constructs youth as a diseased organism, both monolithic and unredeemable.

The violent nature of "American" youth must be understood as a felt crisis (Ackland, 1995, p. 8). Rampaging hoards of frighteningly rabid youth exist in neo-conservative constructions because mothers do not care for them, because there are no strong fathers, and so forth. The implication is that we only have ourselves to blame for allowing the growth of a "welfare state" or for the permissiveness of the 1960s counterculture of problematic morals (as in the widespread diagnosis of attention deficit disorder today is a result of the drug culture).

Within the (re)naming of the new right, conservatism, and quasi-proto-rightist liberalism, Grossberg (1992) described a phenomena known as an "affective epidemic" as "one that consists of a fetishized mobile site that is invested with values disproportionate to their actual worth" (Ackland, 1995, p.

8). This feeds into what Grossberg and Ackland described as "saturated panics." We have had these panics before in the "red scare," and perhaps even in the "War of the Worlds" radio broadcast. But, we have never had a saturated panic in which our young people were named the root cause of "evil."

Yet, the point is that this is a problem that has exceeded the boundaries of the container of the ghetto. It has spilled over into the suburbs, and into the good neighborhoods of the cities (indeed I have seen several school partnerships founded on the notion of diversity, but diversity used in much the same manner as the Dade County Public Schools used the word "Hispanic" to integrate. In Dade County of the 1960s Hispanic was not an oppressed minority. These partnerships often use wealthy communities of Anglos and Asians to articulate a safe rubric of multiculturalism).

Ultimately, there may well indeed be surplus population and much like the smoking mirror of Aztec lore, once the smoke is extinguished you may have even shot your own.

MYOPIA VERSUS MULTIPLICITY

I think we keep missing the point. I am so bored with all of this. I am so angry speaking and writing about all of this, that I am beginning to sound like a broken record. But, we keep missing the point. History is a product of present exigencies. In the movie *Sleeper* (1973) Woody Allen awakens to a world where cigarettes, chocolate, coffee, and sex are good, and nobody remembers Richard Nixon's name. In an anthropology book I have for children, a bathroom motel is mistaken for a temple of sacred points (there is a souvenir stand as well to sell toilet seats as necklaces, and bathtub stoppers as earrings, even in a post-apocalyptic world it seems we can not escape frenzied tumultuous consumerism). As we divert our attention, because we can not see, because we do not want to see, life goes on, the festering sore is now an open wound, that can not be healed with a carrot stick. We can say that the problem is with teenage pregnancy (when actually teenage pregnancy has gone down), we can blame it on welfare mothers, we can blame it on immigrants we can blame and blame and blame. But life goes on.

POVERTY IS POVERTY

Several years ago, while still living in rural North Carolina, I took a student from the school I taught who was also a first grader to Raleigh. He had never been to the city before. His family was poor, lived in a trailer. The manufacturers of evil (see Tiger, 1991)— a.k.a. the testing and measurement industry—had (pre)scribed this lovely child to a life of factory labor (except that the industrial base is drying up in post-Fordism). We arrived in the city and he looked at the skyline with tremendous awe and said "Those buildings are so big that they touch God. Can you imagine touching God? Wouldn't that be wonderful!"

My experiences in North Carolina juxtapose against my experiences here in California. One thing I do know is "poverty is poverty!" It isn't just an urban issue, it is also a rural issue, but make no mistake about it—the question is not in incorporating a plethora of perspectives and hands on cooperative teaching—the question is a question of poverty versus privilege. Although, to be quite frank I find the word hegemony somewhat overused, when poor people band together, when people have nothing left to loose, they will fight back. By extinguishing one voice, by the creation of martyrs, by sacrificing the children at the alter of our contentiousness, we create consciousness that once kindled will in carnivalesque fashion consume the Gargantuan monster. The oxymoronic of Orwellian language is precisely that the language itself is transpositioned, as we speak of saving lives with our missiles. Or as Broughton (1996) exclaimed: "What a PR coup: doctoring the media to portray the bomb as Mother Teresa" (p. 141). What a PR coup to do away with affirmative action to defend equality! What a PR coup to victimize the children at the alter of economic change and transformation! But, as we see the children offered up to the alter, we do not buy the language anymore! You see ultimately, the slippery little monster is finally grasped onto and held firmly in its place, and like the Wizard of Oz, it was all a smokescreen. In the place where "our bodies and minds collide, where our groundedness [and lack of groundedness] in place and time and our capacity for fantasy and invention must come to terms. That collision, phantasmagoric and social is the subject of . . . memoir, including my own" (Kaplan, 1996, p. 64).

AND NOW FOR THE POSSIBILITY—BUT NOT A FAIRY TALE HAPPY ENDING[2]

We need to recognize that the political pedagogy practiced in the public schools is a direct result of the proto-fascism that has emerged in the United States. In a post-209 world we must stop gingerly skirting the issues. We must continuously confront fascism in all of its forms ranging from the ridiculous: "The United States is a Christian nation, the United States is a White nation," to the sublime: "colonization of peace corps neo-liberals who cannibalize and exoticize our

[2]Portions of this section are rewritten from a chapter entitled "Guerrillas in Our Midst Redeux: Kitchen Knowledge" in S. Steinberg (1998) (Ed.), *Students constructing knowledge,* written with Joshua Anijar, Ron Gazales, and Lana Kreivis.

children (for their own oftentimes voyeuristic, feel good, consumption) and who claim ownership of U.S. in terms of my Latinos, my Asians, my Blacks." I am not being alarmist, but I am moved to action by a passion that comes from a historicized morality. I define fascism in terms of the right that celebrates the nation or the race.

> as an organic community transcending all other loyalties. It emphasizes a myth of national rebirth after a period of decline or destruction. To this end fascism calls for a spiritual revolution against signs of moral decay . . . and seeks to purge alien forces and groups that threaten organic community . . . (Lyons, 1995, p. 244)

We need to combat fascism in the schools in every hallway, in every room, in each concombinant (re)form—ranging from the nostalgic: "the resurgence of phonics, back to basics and English only," to the overt: segregation school districting which does exist in Southern California (e.g., San Diego has 43 separate school districts, we have also seen school districts with just one school!) or the incident in Bell Gardens where "a teacher asked students for their immigration papers" (Brugge, 1995, p. 204).

The double-speak that we hear, has nothing to do with celebrating democratic pluralism, and we must respond, no matter what the cost!

> Together we must hold, not only individuals, but governments accountable. The silence of the government equals permission to hate. Local governments must be responsible for the abuse of basic human rights of its citizens. State governments must stand up against intolerance. And the federal government must be the guiding force behind protection of human rights and human dignity in this country in which we claim all are created equal. Local, state, and federal legislation must be enacted and enforced to protect individuals and groups from racial, homophobic, and xenophobic intolerance. (Ross, 1995, p. 180)

But, instead of activism we have atrophy, and silence. *All is Quiet on the Western Front.*

Everything is always mediated by perspective and position. But, it is not a solipsistic relativism, for nothing in the world is ahistorical. Who has the authority to name your conditions? Who defines the guerrilla as a terrorist?

> On Sunday, August 4, 1996, Harry Thomas was winding down from a long hot weekend. He was half asleep watching the eleven o'clock news, when a story came on about the death of General Mohammed Farah Aidid, the self-proclaimed President of Somalia. who had humiliated U.N. and U.S. troops in a series of military skirmishes in 1993. When the newscast flashed a picture of the man who had taken Aidid's place, Thomas laughed and called

out to his wife: "hey, they have gotten the wrong guy! They are showing a picture of Hussien!"
> Thomas was referring to Hussien Mohammed Farah, the soft spoken and impeccably polite part-time clerk who'd worked for him in West Covina's engineering department. (Goodman, 1996, p. 73)

The story in the *Los Angeles Magazine* continues. The adjectives that describe Hussien continually speak of soft-spokenness, and politeness: as if to be a warlord one cannot be soft spoken or polite. Who could have known Mohammed was a terrorist? New right revisionist claims (re)capture the macho, the Rambo, the hard-bodied U.S. male. To paint a terrorist or guerrilla as soft weakens him or her as a formidable or even viable force.

> After all Hussien said "Professionally, I think as an American. . . ." Asked if he was troubled by the fact he had been a Marine in Somalia, he replied "I always wanted to be a marine, he explained. I'm proud of my background and military discipline. With a soft smile, he added "Once a marine always a marine." (p.77)

Why is Hussein a terrorist, and why is Pete Wilson governor? The positions, perspectives, paradigmatics, and prescriptions emerge at a dazzling rate of speed. After all, what is the difference between a religion and a cult? We are peddling as hard as we can just to keep in place. What is needed here, what is necessary to survive is—a bit of *pessimism of the intellect optimism of the will* (a.k.a. Antonio Gramsci)

> What we are aiming for is a period of recolonization. . . . We are already beginning to see it in journals such as Foreign Affairs the notion of "failed states"; that is Third World Nations which have had their experiment with self determination, sovereignty and democracy and failed in it. Now it is up to the United States to re-colonize and re-impose some level of what will be called in the press "civil society." Somalia is only the first example. Paul Johnson makes [this] all too painfully clear in the April 18, 1993 issue of the New York Times magazine. His article is called colonialisms Back—and not a moment too soon. His thesis is simply: "Let's face it: some countries are just not fit to govern themselves." (Merrill, 1993, p. 46)

Therefore, some people are not fit to govern themselves. The macro becomes the micro. Or did the micro inform the macro? What came first? The chicken or the egg? Any way you configure or reconfigure it, it is ultimately racism. Code it, package it or repackage it: If it wags its tail, it is still a dog! "Like paths in an M.C. Escher painting, the data can head off in opposite directions yet invariably lead to the same conclusion" (Tucker, 1994, p. 292).

It is not surprising that long suppressed ideas about heredity racial inequality are now reemerging. Their entry, or rather their return, is made easier by the crumbling of taboos that has accompanied the popular backlash against the excesses of political correctness. (Lind, 1995, p. 173)

But, I do see possibility. I see it in the focus many people are taking that speaks to a morality and ethics in education. I see it when I watch true organic intellectuals operating in their spheres of influence. I see it when the poor people's organization in Greensboro collectively takes action. I see it when I watch my friend and mentor Ron Gonzales work his particular brand of magic in the public schools. I see it when Bill Diaz focuses his anger on the White man and transforms it into a pedagogy of liberation. I see it when Josh Kennerly uses media to teach important historic lessons. I see it when Yvette Wright creates a gospel choir in her school as a mode of resistance. I see it when Lana Krievis dismantles deaf education creating a new curriculum of possibility. I see it because we are all still here. And we are not going to go away. I think back to the revolt in Chiapas. It was a revolt based on "cooperative responsibility among members of grassroots communities" (Simpson & Rapone, 1994, p. 19). What did you think cooperative groupings meant to me—cute methodology?

So, we come back to the concept of ethics and the notion of identity in interpretive community. Cooperative responsibility jells under conditions that can no longer be hidden under a nice veneer. By resigning and consigning many of us to the borderlands of your consciousness, you cannot see us. We are merely things. Everyone was so surprised when the bomb went off in Oklahoma, in the heartland and not on the borders, in the margins. That was a clarion call. So we continue our work, quietly creating a constant buzz that will erupt into a bountiful roar! We are responsible for one another, lines of depending are weaving and being woven everywhere.

I was afforded the privilege of helping out with the Dia de los Muertos ceremony this year at school. The students made a coffin, and placed the sign RIP in front of the coffin. After Carlos Barron harkened the call on his conch shell, I was called to speak to my dead parents. I stand on their shoulders, and I will not forget. Indeed, old certainties—never certainties for everyone in any case are wearing thin (Lavie & Sweedenburg 1996, p. 1). A race condemned to a 100 years of solitude may not get a second chance on earth, so, we take the only chance we have, and I look into the eyes of my child, and all of my children, and know that your condemnation will ultimately become our celebration. My friend Toni Humber went to South Africa last summer. Upon her return, we had the great fortune of hearing Mama Lyndiwae. Here this woman, this small woman who came out of Soweto and into our hearts, spoke with renewed hope and with a sense of potential and possibility. Nothing is ever overdetermined, there are always active and creative means of rearticulating every subject. Our work has just begun. But, I look to Mama Lyndiwae and know in my heart of hearts it can and will be accomplished, not just for mine, but for all our children, for they are all our own.

Wherever people still breathe, there is hope! Several years ago I saw a movie entitled *Testament*. It was a postnuclear Holocaust world, set in California (where else?). Jane Alexander, knowing that she and her children were going to die, chose not to commit suicide, as a testament to their being on the earth. Every action must be a political action. Every theory, every practice is political. We are not puppets. We do rearticulate any and every subject! We are still here! That is a *testimonio*! You see, as Franklin Delano Roosevelt pointed out, "America is not, and never was a matter of race and ancestry." Prior to that statement he said that "America is a matter of the mind and heart." (Norindr, 1996, p. 244). And as the statue says, "give me your tired, your poor," and yet we still yearn. We did not intend to be served up on Gargantua's table.

Somehow, a collective response is beginning to simmer. And, when people have nothing left to loose but themselves they will stand up, waiting, for the opportunity. Think back to Hansel and Gretel. They tricked the witch. Gargantua may be ubiquitous and omnipotent, but in that lies his vulnerability he is just so predictable.

ACKNOWLEDGMENT

I thank my friends and family for helping me complete this chapter: Joshua Asher Anijar, Carlos Barron, Mary Dalton, Toni Humber, Ron Gonzales, and Lana Krievis.

REFERENCES

Ackland, R. (1995). *Youth, spectacle and violence*. Boulder, CO: Westview.

Alarcon, N. (1996). Anzaldua's Frontera: Inscribing genetics. In S. Lavie & T. Sweedenburg (Eds.), *Displacement, diaspora and geographies of identity* (pp. 41-55). Durham, NC: Duke University Press.

Anijar, K. (in press). Once upon a time when we were white—a rather grimm fairy tale. In J. Kincheloe (Ed.), *Whitereign*. New York: St. Martin's Press.

Anijar, K., Anijar, J., Gonzales, R., & Krievis, L. (1998). Guerrillas in our midst part deux: Kitchen knowledge. In S. Steinberg (Ed.), *Students constructing knowledge*. New York: Routledge.

Anzaldua, G. (1987). *Borderlands/La frontera: The new mestiza*. San Francisco: Spinsters/Aunt Lute Foundation.

Bammer, A. (1994). Mother tongues and other strangers. In A. Bammer (Ed.), *Displacements: Cultural identities in question* (pp. 90-109). Bloomington: Indiana University Press.

Bettelheim, B (1965). *When love is not enough: Treatment of emotionally disturbed children.* New York: Collier

Beasley. C. (1980). *Critical practice.* London & New York: Basic Books.

Bow, L. (1995). Asian American criticism. In J. Roof & R. Weigman (Eds.), *Who can speak?: Authority and critical identity* (pp. 30-55). Bloomington: University of Indiana Press.

Broughton, J. (1995). The bombs eye view. In S. Aronowitz, B. Martinson, & S. Menser (Eds.), *Techno science and cyber culture* (pp. 139-157). New York: Routledge.

Brugge, D. (1995). Pulling up the ladder. In C. Berlet (Ed.), *Eyes right: Challenging the right wing backlash* (pp. 191-209). Boston: South End Press.

Casey, K. (1993). *I answer with my life.* New York: Routledge.

Casey, K. (1995). New narrative research in education. *Review of Research in Education, 21,* 211-253

Chicago Cultural Studies Group. (1994). Critical multiculturalism. In *Multiculturalism: A critical reader.* London: Blackwell.

Clark, K., & Holquist, M. (1984). *Mikhail Bakhtin.* Cambridge: Harvard University Press.

Fine, M. (1993) Making controversy: Who's at risk? In C. Wollons (Ed.), *Children at risk in America* (pp. 91-110). Albany: State University of New York Press.

Gates, H. (1995) Why now? In S. Frasher (Ed.), *The bell curve wars* (pp. 94-97). New York: Basic Books.

Gillborn, D. (1995). Racism, identity and modernity: Pluralism, moral anti racism, and plastic ethnicity. *International Studies in Sociology of Education, 5*(1), 3-24.

Goodman, M. (1996). The warlord amongst us. *Los Angeles Magazine, 1*(41), 72-78.

Gratus, J. (1973). *The great white lie: Slavery, emancipation and changing racial attitudes.* New York: Monthly Review Press.

Grossberg, L. (1992). *We gotta get out of this place: Popular conservatism and postmodern culture.* New York: Routledge.

Hall, S., & DuGuy, P. (Eds.). (1996). *Questions of cultural identity.* Beverly Hills: Sage.

Kaplan, A.Y. (1994). On language memoir. In A. Bammer (Ed.), *Displacements: Cultural identities in question* (pp. 59-70). Bloomington: Indiana University Press.

Kellner, D. (1995) *Media cultures.* New York: Routledge.

Kozol, J. (1995). *Amazing grace: The lives of children and the conscience of a nation.* New York: Crown.

Lavie, S. (1996). Blowups in the borderzone: Third world Israeli authors. In S. Lavie & T. Sweedenburg (Eds.), *Displacement, diaspora and geographies of identity* (pp. 55-96). Durham, NC: Duke University Press.

Lavie, S., & Sweedenburg, T. (1996). Introduction: Displacement, diaspora and geographies of identity. In S.Lavie & T. Sweedenburg (Eds.), *Displacement, diaspora and geographies of identity* (pp. 1-26) Durham, NC: Duke University Press.

Levitas, R. (1990). *The concept of utopia.* Syracuse, NY: Syracuse University Press.

Lind, M. (1995). Brave new right. In S. Frasher (Ed.), *The bell curve wars.* New York: Basic Books.

Lyons, M. (1995). What is fascism? In C. Berlet (Ed.), *Eyes right: Challenging the right wing backlash* (pp. 244-245). Boston: South End Press.

Luker, K. (1996). *Dubious conceptions: The politics of teenage pregnancy.* Boston: Harvard University Press.

Marquez, G.G. (1967) *Cien Anos de Soledad* [One hundred years of solitude]. Buenos Aires: Edicionnes SudAmericanos.

Morson, G. (1990). *Bakhtin: Creation of a prosaics.* Stanford, CA: Stanford University Press.

Norindr, P. (1994). Coming home on the fourth of July. In A. Bammer (Ed.), *Displacements: Cultural identities in question* (pp. 233-250). Bloomington: Indiana University Press.

Patton, C. (1996). *Fatal advice: How safe sex education went wrong.* Durham, NC: Duke University Press.

Perez-Firmat, G. (1994). *Life on the hyphen: The Cuban-American way.* Austin: University of Texas Press.

Popkewitz, T. (1995a). *Changing patterns of power.* Albany: State University of New York Press.

Quantz, R., & O'Conner, T. (1988). Writing critical ethnography: Dialogue, multivoicedness and carnival in cultural texts. *Educational Theory, 38*(1), 95-109.

Ramos, J. (1994). Faceless tongues: Language and citizenship in nineteenth century Latin America. In A. Bammer (Ed.), *Displacements: Cultural identities in question* (pp. 25-46). Bloomington: Indiana University Press.

Root, D. (1996) *Cannibal culture: Art appropriation and the commodification of difference.* Boulder, CO: Westview.

Ross, L. (1995). White supremacy in the 1990s. In C. Berlet (Ed.), *Eyes right: Challenging the right wing backlash* (pp. 166-181). Boston: South End Press.

Sawhney, S. (1995). The joke and the hoax: (Not) speaking as other. In J. Roof & R. Weigman (Eds.), *Who can speak?: Authority and critical identity* (pp. 208-220). Bloomington: University of Indiana Press.

Sklar, H. (1995) The dying American dream. In C. Berlet (Ed.) *Eyes right: Challenging the right wing backlash* (pp. 113-134). Boston: South End Press.

Simpson, C., & Rapone, R. (1994, June 3). Why did Chiapas revolt? The making of an explosion *Commenweal*, pp. 16-19.

Stallabrass, J. (1996). *Gargantua: Manufactured mass culture*. London: Verso.

Tiger, L. (1991). *The manufacture of evil*. New York: Marion Boyers.

Tucker, W. (1994). *The science and politics of racial research*. Urbana: University of Illinois Press.

3

Pedagogy and the Politics of Popular Culture in the Inner City

Suren Lalvani
Penn State Harrisburg

We are in the midst of a social and historical crisis; a period marked by the forceful emergence of reactionary forces that have both reversed the previous gains made in social reforms and breached fundamental beliefs about civil rights. What was once hope has succumbed to cynical despair as the conservative New Right crafts a new order in the language of moral fundamentalism, ultra nationalism, and corporate exigencies. These same forces have also issued a determined attack on the democratic impulses enshrined in our schools. Blaming schools for a plethora of ills extending from the moral fiber of the family to the state of the economy, the New Right has demanded that schools function both as hegemonic transmitters of traditional cultural values and as ancillary apparatuses whose sole purpose it is to serve the ever-expanding needs of freewheeling corporate and technical bureaucracies (McLaren, 1989). All this is happening at a time when we most need to revitalize the democratic functioning of our schools, confronted as we are with the increasing presence of racial segregation and the prevalence of a growing underclass in our inner cities. As an inner space delineated by lines of power, the inner city represents the racial unconscious of America and all attempts to transform it, to emancipate it from the grip of power, to make of it a project for the revival of a civic conscience, have met stiff resistance from an established hegemony.

What is the nature of this inner space? What forces operate and conspire to constitute its terrain of forgotteness, throwness, and exile that mark it as both outside and at the same time, central to the dominant ideological project.

71

Inner cities are structurally isolated and racialized spaces marked by a now familiar series of problems—unemployment, high mortality rates, poor medical services, high crime rates, high drug use, and so forth. The consequence of a racist society has been that it functions to create for a non-white male the inevitable fate of death or incarceration; a legally and socially mandated final solution for annihilating difference and otherness in America. The harsh fact is that a non-white male in the United States faces a probability of being murdered that is six times greater than for a white male (Cohen & Rogers, 1983). Although in 1983 Blacks represented only 12% of the population, they comprised 46% of the prison population in the United States (Spenser, 1986). Racism compounds and makes plain the internal contradictions of a capitalist society, for prisons have now become a new growth industry recommended by financial institutions to their clients as a profitable addition to their investment portfolios.

In this context, one of the more powerful stories to make visible the oppressive racial imaginary operating in its concrete effects, to prise open as it were, the racial unconscious of this society and its material geography is Kozol's (1992) *Savage Inequalities.* The book provides us with a brutally honest picture of not only what it is like to live in a culture of silence, violence, and neglect that permeates inner cities like East St. Louis but also what it is like to attend inner-city schools that are characterized by overcrowding; "We have a school in East St. Louis named for Dr. King. The school is full of sewer water and the doors are locked with chains. Every student in that school is black. It's like a terrible joke on history" (Kozol, 1992, p. 35). This cruel irony is not limited to just East St. Louis but includes "landscapes of hopelessness," that extend from New York's South Bronx and Boston's Roxbury, to such low-income housing projects as Cassiano in San Antonio, Texas.

These are the figures and social indices that constitute the contours of a landscape of hopelessness: 50% to 80% of all inner-city students drop out of high school (Bastian et al., 1986). The proportion of 17- to 18-year olds who were high school dropouts increased by 4% in the decade between 1972 and 1982. Among Latinos the drop-out rate is nearly 41%, whereas for Blacks it is slightly more than 23% (Sheridan, 1986). In Chicago itself, the drop-out rate is nearly 50% (Kozol, 1992). The consequence is that 33% of all adults are functionally or marginally illiterate (Bastian et al., 1986). This has been accompanied by a corresponding and dramatic increase in crimes committed by the young. For example, teenage homicide has multiplied by a staggering 200% since 1960. The crisis that affects the children of disempowered groups can be attributed, at least in part, to an educational system that functions to legitimize prevailing class and racial inequities in the social system. Although fostering the illusion of a meritocracy, the much touted use of *tracking* operates to reinforce differences based on class, race, and gender. Tracking institutes a particular set of knowledge–power relations that not only systemically function to lower the aspirations of students lower in the social hierarchy but also provides low-status knowledge to these students, and assist in adjusting and preparing the already underprivileged for low-status jobs (McLaren, 1989). To the extent that schooling functions as a mechanism of social reproduction, it does so on the basis of class-produced differences in cultural capital. The inequalities are further aggravated by resorting to the mechanism of property tax to fund education; so that in effect we have a society, which notwithstanding its protestations regarding equality and freedom, is willing to spend more on the children of the rich and privileged than on its already poor. All this translates into fewer resources and less qualified teachers for the very schools that are in dire need of assistance. It is not surprising then, to discover that the gap between the bottom quintile of the population and the top 5% has nearly doubled since the 1960s (Cohen & Rogers, 1983).

POPULAR CULTURE AND CRITICAL PEDAGOGY

The present conditions of the inner city and its schools illustrates and brings into review the new cultural and social geography of power that has evolved over the last two decades. Schooling functions to funnel the racially poor into low-status service occupations, while advancing myths of racial inferiority that culturally place the blame on those oppressed by a structurally and institutionally organized racism. At the same time, inner-city communities have become the target for the kinds of surveillance and brutality only associated with a police state, seemingly justified by the threat that such groups pose to a racially divided social order. However, it is imperative that we forego the repressive hypothesis that views power as functioning simply as a constraint, as negotiation, and ask ourselves how power functions to elaborate on and support the present matrix of disempowerment and oppression, even as it is productive in providing the repressed with the resources to combat their repression.

In posing the question this way, we are forced to come to terms with the functioning of popular culture, not only in its production of stereotypical representations of minority culture and in its delineation of the inner city as a problem, but in the manner in which it is also enabling, providing subaltern groups with the opportunity to rearticulate their experiences, and in turn to construct oppositional and contradictory subjectivities. This is not to diminish or reduce in significance the real economic and material constraints that operate to marginalize subordinate groups, but instead is an attempt to take into account the intersections between the representational and the material, as it is lived out in relation to the forces of dominance and resistance that characterizes the everyday culture of the oppressed. That popular culture is a field of contestation is evident in the conflicting representations of the dominant media: exemplified by shows such as *Top Cops*, which transform the ills of these communities into a violent spectacle to be consumed by White middle-class audiences, and also by the images and figures of "gangster rap" through which the same discourses and images are struggled over and negotiated. The social paranoia cultivated by shows like *Top Cops*, only further erodes and overrides the slightest desire to empathize and understand the social problems that beset these communities. The result may well mean a legitimizing effect for the political forces that seek to dismantle social assistance programs devoted to the disadvantaged. In contrast, gangster rap, despite the prevailing sexism of its lyrics and its aestheticization of violence, may function in complex ways to stimulate an undercurrent of resistance.

It is against the prevailing hegemony that a critical pedagogy must work to empower the lives of minority students. Crucial to its success is that it takes into account the culture of the everyday lives of the disempowered. A pedagogy that insulates itself from the meanings, pleasures, pains, desires, and concerns of the everyday cultural practices of inner-city students does not attend to the distinctive voices of the oppressed and how that oppression is felt, approached, understood, and translated into practice each day. In this regard, I advocate a critical pedagogy that includes within its curriculum, popular culture texts and practices, for these practices constitute a significant resource in the construction of everyday life and the subjectivities of disadvantaged groups. In proposing such a program, in addition to emphasizing the role of popular culture in any practical resistance project, I develop an understanding of the functioning and effects of popular culture formations in their relation to the fabric of a lived subordinate culture.

The system of popular culture is significant, not only because it represents a central domain through which hegemonic modes of understanding are established, but is simultaneously the site wherein the terms of hegemony are negotiated. Gramsci (1971) understood the significance of popular culture because he directed his own attention to an analysis of popular forms and folklore. As a consequence of the influence of Gramsci's work on cultural studies scholarship, the Frankfurt School legacy of viewing popular culture as simple instances of "manipulation" and "distortion" reducible to the mode of production has been replaced by the understanding that popular culture practices represent an active, ongoing process in the negotiation and construction of a social formation.

What needs to be emphasized is that the utilization of popular culture in a critical pedagogy must not devolve into the simple use of popular culture as an ancillary textual resource for the production of classroom discussions that are issue-oriented, but must be construed as essential to an emancipatory politics that both forces students to examine the manner in which dominant discourses are constructed, and impels them to interrogate the formation of their own contradictory subjectivities. However, a critical pedagogy that seeks to map the popular culture formations of students while providing central importance to questions of manning and representation, must refrain from reducing culture to texts and lived reality in relation to the production of meaning. Although this reduction stems from the understanding that individuals inhabit a meaningful world, it nevertheless privileges the determining power of meaning, with the effect that social and material realities dissolve and collapse into the plane of meaning (Grossberg, 1992).

It is necessary to develop a clear understanding of both the material and cultural realities confronted by students, and the manner in which the particular cultural formations constituted by these practices play a significant role in the construction of daily experience. In the context of inner-city youth, it must be understood that popular culture not only plays a significant role in constructing their experiences, but the materiality of that culture is related to the economic materiality of the conditions of oppression. In this regard, popular culture texts provide a lived texture to the lives of inner-city youth, for they utilize popular culture practices to construct a densely woven map of meaning through which they express and produce their own understandings of the contradictory nature of lived experiences. The material, densely inhabited culture of everyday life, is in turn constituted by the contradictory forces of constraint and creativity, which expresses the tensions between a lived hegemony and the variety of subaltern expressions.

In this context, critical educators must view themselves as critical ethnographers of the oppressed, who engage with and develop an understanding of both the material and representational practices of their students as well as knowledge of the particular dynamics of these practices. How, for example, do gangster rap, fashion practices, and street performances intersect with the material and social practices of gang members? How subordinate groups carve out a representational and material space for the expression and play of identity formation is crucial to any emancipatory program, especially because the inner city constitutes a particular organization of geography and production of cultural place. Spatial politics in turn need to be understood both as a material and a textual practice, a provisioning of practical and practiced space for cultural survival. Subaltern groups are not only involved in the production of particular meanings and representational practices but are also engaging in clearly defined material, spatial, and hence social practices.

In view of the fact that popular practice is creative (Fiske, 1989), educators must comprehend that creativity in relation to how they "poach," construct, and appropriate physical spaces from the places ordered and structured by the dominant order (de Certeau, 1984). The places that carry the meanings and material effects of a dominant order are not only the constructed spaces of school but include the ghetto, as a clearly delineated space of powerful and debilitating effects. As de Certeau argued, space is an indigenously appropriated place and is produced by the creativity of the people using the resources of the dominant system. It is in regard to the emphasis on material practices that I think the term everyday culture has more value than the simple emphasis on the representational uses and deployment of popular culture meanings. I do not wish to slight the significance of representational practices, but rather to situate them within the larger popular culture formation that students inhabit and that is comprised of both the constitutive effects of meaning as well as the effects of social practices.

The critical pedagogist must be aware that as far as representational practices are concerned, what makes a text popular is not ensured in advance. Neither can one simply identify from the formal characteristics of a text the particular effects it will have on an audience (Grossberg, 1992). Contrary to the assumption that a cultural text offers a single, monovalent interpretation regardless of who the reader is, it must be recognized that "the subject's position in the social formation structures his or her range of access to various discourses . . . and correspondingly different readings . . . will be made by subjects 'inhabiting' these different discourses" (Morley, 1980, p. 158). Hence, not only is a discourse formation not without its contradictory elements but the unit of discourse, the sign, is open to contestation and struggle by competing interests. The critical educator is then faced with mapping a discursive struggle of transformations and negotiations, whose shifting points of articulation implicate different texts and provide for a dynamic notion of hegemony in process.

Willis (1977) argued that, "social agents are not passive bearers of ideology, but active appropriators" (p. 175). Similarly, Connell (1979) noted that "Any reading is never simply consumptive, a mere adoption of the subject forms mapped out by the formal operations of a text. Any reading is also and always interrogative" (p. 133). Thus, even though texts can constrain readings, they cannot determine the meanings that will be made from them (Willimen, 1978). In this context, Hall (1988) observed that "there can be no law to ensure that the receiver will 'take' the preferred or dominant reading of a [text] in precisely the way in which it has been encoded" (p. 136). If as Williams (1989) pointed out, no single ideological formation can exhaust the meanings and values in a society, neither can the presence of dominant ideology in a text exhaust the meanings and values that can be produced from it.

Popular readers are not just productive as Jenkins' (1984) study of "Trekkies" indicates but, as Grossberg's (1984) study of rock and roll fans and Radway's (1984) study of romance readers have pointed out, they discriminate between texts too, and are, as Altman (1986) suggested of the television show *Dallas*, selective readers of texts as well. As Fiske (1989) argued, a mass culture text that is popular—offering up the vulnerabilities and contradictions of its preferred meanings, whose meanings exceed its ability to discipline them, and from which those new texts may be created even as it seeks to repress these meanings—is what constitutes the pleasures of a popular practice. Popular culture thus needs to be viewed as a terrain determined by contradictory forces, meanings, and values; and neither the meanings of a cultural practice nor the identity of social groups or the relation between texts and social groups can be fixed in advance. Instead "it is the struggle around popular culture that social identities and groups are constructed" (Grossberg, 1992, p. 77). However, as Grossberg observed, the important question is what people are struggling over and what resources they are deploying in this struggle. This is a significant line of inquiry, for it alludes to not only the types of identities that are desired, but also the range of identities that are available, the availability of cultural resources, and also to why one particular cultural matrix is developed over another.

The significance of one specific cultural formation over another must be viewed in terms of the affective alliances they produce. According to Grossberg, who has given the idea of affect some thought, *affect* may be defined as "a prepersonal intensity corresponding to the passage from one experiential state of the body to another and implying an augmentation or diminution in that body's capacity to act" (p. 80). In other words, affect qualifies the strength of the investment that binds individuals to one set of experiences or practices rather than to another: "the power of the articulation which bonds particular representations and realities" (Grossberg, 1992, p. 83). Affect is not free-flowing energy but is structured and given form by its articulation and disarticulation in relation to cultural formations. Individuals can hence be said to possess "mattering maps" that indicate the extent and degree to which they care and are invested in certain meanings, ideologies, and practices. This is especially pertinent to a critical and popular pedagogy, because popular culture remains the primary terrain for the articulation of affective relationships. Individuals invest popular cultural practices with the power to shape their identity and they do so because these practices "matter" to them, anchor them, and at least temporarily provide them with a sense of belonging. Once positioned within affective alliances, the same individuals are affectively empowered to produce investments in other cultural practices, to expand their investments in what matters, and hence to create new strategies and capacities. This in turn enables them to produce new forms of meanings and identity, to construct new forms of difference, and a renewed basis for coping with despair and pain.

However, as Grossberg (1992) argued, the investment in certain sites and not others by individuals cannot be driven by affect alone but must be justified ideologically. This points to the particular articulations between ideology and affect that are historically constructed by individuals. It is significant that this form of analysis provides us with a basis of understanding how popular culture can offer "the resources which may or may not be mobilized into forms of popular struggle, resistance and opposition." For "the organization of [such a] struggle depends upon its articulation to different affective organizations and empowering investments" (Grossberg, 1992, pp. 85-86). It is then imperative that a critical pedagogy that seeks to empower inner-city students map in relation to the popular culture formations they inhabit, the sites of their affective investments, the forms that these investments take, and the particular articulation between ideology and affect that a popular culture formation represents.

The discussion on affect in turn serves to highlight the significance of the body in any pedagogy of popular culture. Although popular culture is a site of struggle for the articulation of identity, it is always more than the generation of ideological formations, producing effects directly on the lived body. Indeed, what makes a cultural practice popular is the "physical" of its practice. The body has been a significant site of contestation between the forces of power and discipline and the desire of the subordinate to exercise autonomy over the meanings, pleasures, and freedom of the body. Foucault's (1979) genealogy of the body illustrates the manner in which the microtechnologies of power act directly on the body to produce and rank the social differences required by capitalist system. In this case, individuation becomes the consequence of disciplinary mechanisms and surveillance that inhabit schools, offices, and factories. On the other hand, popular practices as exemplified by the carnivalesque body seek to invert the rules of the dominant order (Bakhtin, 1968). If schools silence the body or direct it in organized play, the amusement park is not focused on disciplinary outcomes as it is on the pure expression and release of the body. As Fiske (1992) pointed out, the culture of everyday life "is a site of struggle between the measured individuation that constitute social discipline, and the popularity-produced differences that fill and extend the spaces of the people" (p. 162). In popular culture, the body then becomes a central medium for the negotiation of contradictory meanings and desires. Especially among the young, the struggle for identity is one that is parlayed out in relation to the body. For example, the practices of "attitude" by the young is a significant device for maintaining control over a social world that is inherently outside their control. Drawn from various popular culture sources, "attitude" is an affective state that primarily finds its expression in relation to the body.

The analysis of subcultures and other subordinate groups indicate quite clearly the role that the body plays in the production of popular social differences (Bhaktin, 1968). For racialized bodies whose very difference as a body is marked, proscribed, and inscribed by power relations, resistance through popular culture forms must include the empowering possibility and sensibility of reconstructing that body, of endowing it with dignity and expressive control. In fact, the affective dimension that determines along with ideology and meaning the sites of popular resistance is comprehended, felt, and lived through the body as an expressive whole. Identity is finally a performance wherein the planes of affect, meaning, and subjectivity are construed, coalesce, and expressed finally in relation to the symbol producing capacity of the body. Each popular culture formation and the affective alliances it constructs proposes particular kinds of bodies, forms of subjectivities, and material and social practices.

In identifying the main forms of resistance in schools, McLaren (1989) pointed to the effort of students to oppose to the classroom culture of reason and logical learning, a street corner culture that is libidinally expressive. It is not surprising that schools whose very architecture, rules, procedures, and strategies are designed with the intent of disciplining and monitoring the passion of young bodies in the name of reason and a cultural capital that is alien to them, should elicit such a response from their charges. This illustrates, in turn, the contested nature of schooling where conflicting languages and experiences collide and as a consequence introduce varying degrees of accommodation and resistance

(Giroux, 1983; Willis, 1977). Teachers who possess in general a middle-class cultural capital that valorizes abstraction and reason, must be wary of not devaluing and deprecating the popular culture resources that economically disadvantaged students possess, regardless of the low economic value of this capital.

In addition, a pedagogy that seeks to radicalize the lived space of inner-city youth must come to terms with the "structure of feeling" that determines how popular cultural formations are lived in the interactions of the body's affective alliances and material reality. This analysis may be assisted by the use of Bourdieu's (1984) concept of *habits* that draws attention to the material practices of everyday culture. As a term, it includes notions of habitat, habitant, as well as the habitual practices of engaging the material and social world. As a social environment, it is constituted by social space and the social practices of those who inhabit it. The social space in turn is inscribed by multiple and intersecting vectors of cultural capital, economic capital, class, and historical trajectories, which not only determine in their interactions the social order, but the cultural practices of those who inhabit different positions in it. Does inner-city culture, in representing a particular confluence of the symbolic, the material, and the historical, organize a particular habit, whose material effects and structure a feeling determines how popular culture practices in their affective states are exercised and embodied by its inhabitants?

CONCLUSION

In this context, inner-city youth must be viewed as inhabiting multiple habitudes—traveling between the spaces constructed by dominant regimes of power and their own constructed spaces, between inner city and outer city, between classroom and street corner society, producing social differences that enable them to survive and cope with the everyday culture of racism and deprivation. In turn, educators are by definition ethnographers traveling between spaces— the academic habits and subordinate habits—hence the need for traveling theories, a pedagogy that maps in response, the spaces that the subaltern groups utilize to negotiate their identities (Clifford, 1992). We need to think of the multiple spaces that are occupied by a subordinate culture, the different ways of belonging and not belonging. Because popular culture as the terrain of affective and ideological investments provides the basis for subaltern formations to shape their identities even as it locates them in the circuits and spaces of power, it is crucial that a critical pedagogy that seeks to be emancipatory, take into account these investments, and the manner in which they are deployed by people who navigate the emotional, textual, and physical spaces of the "inner city."

REFERENCES

Altman, R. (1986). Television/sound. In T. Modleski (Ed.), *Studies in entertainment: Critical approaches to mass culture* (pp. 39-54). Bloomington: Indiana University Press.

Bakhtin, M. (1968). *Rabelais and his world.* Cambridge: MIT Press.

Bastian, A. et al. (1986). *Choosing equality: The call for democratic schooling.* Philadelphia: Temple University Press.

Bourdieu, P. (1984). *Distinction: A social critique of the judgement of taste* (R. Nice, Trans.). Cambridge, MA: Harvard University Press.

Clifford, J. (1992). Traveling cultures. In L. Grossberg, C. Nelson, & P. Treichler (Eds.), *Cultural studies* (pp. 96-112). New York: Routledge.

Cohen, J., & Rogers, J. (1983). *On democracy: Toward a transformation of American society.* New York: Penguin.

Connell, I. (1979). Ideology/discourse/institution. *Screen, 19*(4), 125-137.

de Certeau, M. (1984). *The practice of everyday life.* Berkeley: University of California Press.

Fiske J. (1989). *Understanding popular culture.* Boston: Unwin Hyman.

Fiske, J. (1992). The culture of everyday life. In L. Grossberg, C. Nelson, & P. Treichler (Eds.), *Cultural studies* (pp. 154-165). New York: Routledge.

Foucault, M. (1979). *Discipline and punish: The birth of the prison.* New York: Vintage.

Giroux, H. (1983). *Theory and resistance: A pedagogy for the opposition.* South Hadley, MA: Bergin & Garvey.

Gramsci, A. (1971). *Selections from the prison notebooks* (Q. Hoare & G. N. Smith, Eds. & Trans.). London: Lawrence & Wishart.

Grossberg, L. (1984). Another boring day in paradise: Rock and roll and the empowerment of everyday life. *Popular Music, 4,* 225-257.

Grossberg, L. (1992). *We gotta get out of this place.* New York: Routledge.

Hall, S. (1988). The toad in the garden: Thatcherism among the theorists. In C. Nelson & L. Grossberg (Eds.), *Marxism and the interpretation of culture* (pp. 35-57). Urbana: University of Illinois Press.

Jenkins, H. (1984). Star Trek return, reread, rewritten: Fan writing as textual poaching. *Critical Studies in Mass Communication, 5*(2), 85-107.

Kozol, J. (1992). *Savage inequalities.* New York: Harper Perennial.

McLaren, P. (1989). *Life in schools.* New York: Longman.

Morley, D. (1980). *The nationwide audience.* London: British Film Institute.

Radway, J. (1984). *Reading the romance: Feminism and the representation of women in popular culture.* Chapel Hill: University of North Carolina Press.

Sheridan, M. W. (1986). School dropouts in perspective. *The Educational Forum, 51*(1), 57-62.

Spenser, R. (1986). Blacks on the bottom: For an underclass of the poor and alienated, life is only getting worse. *The Washington Post National Weekend Edition, 10.*

Williams, R. (1989). *Marxism and literature.* Oxford: Oxford University Press.

Willimen, P. (1978). Notes on subjectivity. *Screen, 19*(1), 60-68.

Willis, P. (1977). *Learning to labour.* London: Saxon House.

4

Urban Education in a Multicultural Society: The Role of Black Studies

Felix Boateng
Vanderbilt University

This chapter reviews the factors that continue to reinforce and perpetuate multi-cultural education as the logical epistemic foundation for education, and especially urban education, in U.S. society. The discussion focuses on the meaning and importance of multicultural education and calls attention to the need to "decenter" White European consciousness from the multicultural curriculum. This chapter concludes with an analysis of the centrality of Black studies in the development of a sound multicultural education in the urban school curriculum.

THE MULTICULTURAL HERITAGE

Most observers of U.S. society in the 1990s would agree that the conditions or criteria for the application of pluralism or multiculturalism to a society are present and strong in the society. Sociological and several other studies emphasize the existence of ethnic and cultural diversity and the desire and the right of individuals to maintain their ethnic identities within the general U.S. culture (Banks, 1988; Hale-Benson, 1986). All available evidence shows that the melting pot theory of the U.S. society has failed in its application. In fact, it is significant that later in his life, Israel Zangwill, the 1908 writer of the play "melting pot" became very much the antithesis of the melting pot prototype. Later on in his life, Zangwill devoted more of his energy to the Zionist cause and retreated from his earlier position of racial and religious mixture.

Furthermore, it is clear from historical records that the theory of the melting pot was Anglo Conformity notion in disguise. Groups were expected to renounce their ethnic cultures and adopt the ways of the dominant English cultural group (Garcia, 1982). The fallacy in this theory is that although some groups such as African Americans and Native Americans were considered "unmeltable" for a variety of reasons, attempts were made to institute educational programs to deculturalize these groups and to condition them to Anglo-European values. This was another way of colonizing the mind without granting it the privileges of the colonizer. It is the efforts of the Civil Rights Movement and the internal contradictions in the system itself that have, today, spelled the collapse of the melting pot theory.

Gone, therefore, is the concept of the melting pot and the idea that all who come to the U.S. shore can be assimilated by an open society that transforms disparate peoples into Euro-Americans. Instead, there is a new paradigm within the concepts of multiculturalism that emphasizes the racial and ethnic diversity of U.S. citizens, of the many cultures that have conveyed here, each valuable in its own right and deserving of study and respect.

PERSISTENCE OF ETHNICITY

Critics of multiculturalism, such as the National Association of Scholars (NAS) and Arthur Schlesinger Jr. argue that the growing emphasis on the nation's multicultural heritage "threatens the ideal that binds America" (1991, p. 21). These critics who view multiculturalism as divisive are, however, and rather curiously, silent on the politics of exclusion that continues to prevent racial minorities from attaining structural inclusion into the U.S. society.

Discrimination and racism, which are institutionalized and entrenched in the society, prevent individuals and groups with particular ethnic, racial, or cultural characteristics from power sharing. An avenue opened to victims of discrimination is to retreat to their communities and use the communities as sources of sustenance, comfort, renewal, and strength. When this happens, appreciation for the group is heightened, affiliation to the group is strengthened, and consequently the sense of ethnicity is reinforced. To refer to ethnic affiliation as divisive and antisocial where there has been an historic conspiracy to treat ethnic minorities differently is comparable, therefore, to breaking a person's leg and then criticizing that person when he or she limps. Racial discrimination sends a clear message of rejection to its victims and forces them to come together for sustenance and to develop strategies to fight the system.

One outcome of racism and discrimination that resulted in the reinforcement of ethnicity was the Civil Rights Movement of the 1950s and 1960s. During the period between 1950 and 1970, African Americans came together as victims of racism to react against discrimination by embarking on a lifelong struggle to shape a new identity and to shelter old and pervasive stereotypes about their culture and their contributions to U.S. life. The apparent success of the African-American civil rights movement stimulated other ethnic revitalization movements. Chicano-Latinos, Asian Americans, Native Americans, and women also demanded changes in the social, political, and economic institutions and tried to shape new identities. A sense of peoplehood began to emerge among all cultural groups. One can say that the "new pluralism" arrived.

Ethnicity persists also because of other forces that interplay with discrimination and racism in the society. These include immigration, increased birthrate of racial minorities, and the natural inclination for people who share cultural backgrounds to come together.

Immigration to the United States has grown by leaps and bounds since the Immigration Reform Act, enacted in 1965, became effective in 1968. According to the U.S. Bureau of the Census, most of the new immigrants come from Spanish-speaking Latin American nations and from Asia rather than from Europe, the continent from which most U.S. immigrants came in the past. Between 1991 and 1994, 85% of the legal immigrants to the United States came from non-European nations, 15% came from Europe (U.S. Bureau of Census, 1996, p. 11).

In 1996, one out of every three school children in major U.S. cities was a member of a non-European community (American Council on Education, 1988). The Asian American population is expected to double in 2010 and Hispanics, who consisted of 17.7 million people in 1984, will total 30 to 35 million by the year 2,000. (Church, 1985, pp. 36-41).

An increase in birthrates in minority communities is cited as another reason for the persistence of ethnicity. For example, the nation's largest non-White ethnic group, the African Americans, increased from 22.6 million to 30 million between 1970 and 1990. The U.S. Bureau of the Census projects that the African-American population will increase from 11.7% of the U.S. population in 1980 to 15% in the year 2020. African Americans will be nearly one of five school-age children and one of six adults of prime working age 25 to 56 (Jaynes & William, 1989). It is estimated that the African-American population growth during the next few decades will outpace that of Whites because the African-American population is relatively young (The College Board, 1985) It is the interplay of these forces—immigration, increased birthrate, and the naturalness of ethnicity—with discrimination, that begins to explain the growth of ethnic consciousness in the nation.

Discrimination that prevents various ethnic and racial groups from fully participating in the U.S. society, the growth of ethnic minority communities and identities, and continuing immigration will continue to perpetuate ethnic affiliations and the multicultural heritage of the U.S. society. Ethnic and racial variables and issues will continue to influence the lives of all Americans and will have a cogent impact on the process of teaching and learning.

THE MONOCULTURAL-EUROCENTRIC CURRICULUM

Despite the fact that ethnic and cultural diversity has, in the 1990s become an integral part of U.S. society, and almost a condition in urban areas, there are educators who still believe that most cultural groups will and, perhaps, should abandon their unique cultural characteristics and group affiliations and become totally assimilated to European values. Such educators continue to expose students to an academic curriculum that uses one cultural group—the Euro-Americans—as the basis for the evaluation of every activity. There is clear evidence that the traditional monocultural focus of the school curriculum has stubbornly persisted despite the steady shift of U.S. society toward pluralism and despite the remarkable growth of ethnic diversity in the country.

The evidence seems to suggest that cities represent a quantitatively superior expression of such diversity. Consequently, we cannot look at urban schools in isolation from the larger urban milieu where ethnic diversity, non-European cultures, social conflict, and inequality continue to characterize the interrelationships between the school and the communities. The defects and the limitations of the monocultural–Eurocentric model are well documented in the literature (Gollnick & Chinn 1994, White & Johnson, 1991). In the published proceedings of six-head Start research seminars held under the auspices of the U.S. Office of Economic Opportunity, McDavid (1969) stated:

> Our society is a diverse and heterogeneous one, in which we embrace a variety of subcultures delineated by ethnic, linguistic, racial, geographic, educational, and socioeconomic earmarks. Within each of these subcultures, social standards vary, and corresponding socialization practices vary. Yet we plan public education as a single, massive, uniform Procrustean institutionalized system of values, beliefs, and habits defined according to some stereotype rising magically out of the middle-class pillars of society . . . This, then, is the stereotypical target toward which our institutionalized educational system tends to socialize all of its participants, regardless of the adult subculture to which they are bound, and regardless of the relevancy or irrelevancy of these values and habits to each one's own real world. (pp. 5-6)

McDavid's comments are still applicable and illustrate the persistence of the belief in a single exclusive definition of U.S. character. The monocultural—Eurocentric view within the school system assumes that the western structure of knowledge is true, objective, universal, and applicable to all people and circumstances. An unquestioned acceptance of this view, clearly, denies the possibility of looking at reality in a critical cross-cultural perspective and thus ignores the very essence of education that is the liberation of the mind from the shackles of tradition. As White and Johnson (1991) stated in their study of the education of African-American youth, the use of this monocultural–Eurocentric model for "students who come from lifestyles or cultures that significantly differ from the school-valued culture results in the labeling of those students as deficient" (p. 409).

The consequences of this monocultural perspective and labeling of racial minorities are evident in the continued decline in the academic achievement of African-American and other children of color who dominate the urban school population. In the 1990s urban societies are characterized by schools that are mandated to educate failing and unwilling adolescents—failing because they are unwilling and unwilling because they do not see the relevance of their experiences in the school process. In some cases, their cultural experiences might be visible in the school environment but these experiences are marginalized in the learning program. The monocultural—Eurocentric tradition from which the "cultural deprivation" model and "compensatory education" stem, in essence, states that African-American and other culturally different children must reject the culture of their homes in order to succeed in school. The evidence has proven otherwise and shown that academic success has a stronger correlation with a culturally relevant curriculum (Boateng, 1990; Hale-Benson, 1990; McAdoo & McAdoo 1985).

Traditionally, it has been assumed that an understanding of the child is basic to education. More recently, however, research has shown that this understanding must go beyond basic psychological processes and embrace facets of the child's sociocultural world (Maehr & Stallings, 1975). Children bring different historical backgrounds, religious experiences, and day-to-day living experiences to school. These experiences direct the way the child behaves, speaks, thinks, and believes while at school (Boateng, 1990). Educators agree that to work effectively with the heterogeneous student populations found in the urban schools, teachers must acknowledge the cultural backgrounds of their students and the cultural setting in which the school is located. This would enable educators to develop effective instructional strategies that would help students reach their full potential (Gollnick & Chinn, 1986).

Children who come to the teacher are inevitably products of, and are continually influenced by, the cultural world in which they hold membership. According to Maehr and Stallings (1975):

> Not only is this cultural influence reflected in patterns of dress, but more importantly, it is evidenced in motivational patterns, intellectual functioning and communicative skills. As a result, social and cultural factors are among the more important influences on the human development. (p. 1)

This view has been echoed and supported in a number of studies since the 1960s. Previously (Boateng, 1990), I referred to a striking feature of the Coleman Report (Coleman, 1966) that revealed a close tie between African-American academic achievement and the social environment of the classroom. Even though the report limited the definition of social environment to social models, such as sensitive teachers, more recent studies confirm the finding that the environment of the classroom should have some relevance to the child's experience to ensure effective learning (McAdoo & McAdoo, 1985). Most studies reaffirm the long-established conclusion that the sociocultural system of which the child is a product must be clearly emphasized if public education is to be effective (Ramirez & Castaneda, 1982).

Clearly, there is compelling evidence that affirms the need to integrate the multicultural heritage of the U.S. society into the urban school curriculum to ensure that all groups—Black, White, Hispanic, Asian, and Native Americans—are equally valued and presented as fellow human beings in the curriculum. The integration of the diverse experiences would also remove instructional and curriculum inequalities that act as barriers in the academic achievement of African-American and other culturally different children. In other words, what is needed is multicultural education for a multicultural society.

MULTICULTURAL EDUCATION

In an attempt to fulfill the need to integrate the nation's multicultural heritage into the curriculum, and to address the problem of instructional and curricular inequalities, educators have identified multicultural education or pluralistic teaching as a major solution. Even though the term *multicultural education* has acquired no uniform and widely accepted definition, advocates are in agreement about the goals and objectives of this educational program.

Multicultural education seeks to restructure classroom instruction to reflect the diversity of the society and to provide all children the opportunity to participate fully in the learning process. The major goals of multicultural education are to help all students:

1. Reach their potential by drawing on their cultural experiences and by helping them view events from diverse cultural perspectives.
2. Overcome their fear of diversity that leads to cultural misunderstanding and cultural encapsulation.
3. View cultural differences in an egalitarian mode rather than in an inferior–superior mode and expand their conception of what it means to be human in a culturally diverse world. (Banks, 1986)

Multicultural education is, therefore, a demand for inclusion and partnership by historically excluded groups, frames of references, learning styles, and worldviews. It is the intellectual stimulation provoked by the growth of ethnic consciousness and a challenge to the Eurocentric perspective and Western cultural supremacy of the American Academy. It is realistic, fair, practical and perhaps traumatizing only to those with elitist sensibilities and distorted views of our world.

THE ETHNIC ADDITIVE PARADIGM

However, in an effort to implement a multicultural curriculum, many schools have hurriedly put together programs that are basically European-centered with occasional references to African-American and other non-European experiences. Such multicultural education programs come under what has become known as the *ethnic additive paradigm* (Banks, 1986). The ethnic additive paradigm is the inclusion of some information about the cultures and histories of previously omitted ethnic groups in the school curriculum. This usually consists of the infusion of bits and pieces of content about ethnic groups into the curriculum, especially into courses in the humanities, the social studies, and language arts. The teaching about ethnic heroes and the celebration of ethnic holidays are salient characteristics of the ethnic additive paradigm. The major problem with this paradigm is that even though ethnic events are added to the curriculum, the interpretations and perspectives on these events and heroes remain Eurocentric. The limitations of the ethnic additive paradigm are obvious and serious.

When concepts, events, and situations in the curriculum are viewed only or primarily from the European perspective, students obtain a limited view of social reality and a distorted view of the human experience. Because such multicultural educational programs are still grounded in the Euro-American tradition, they result in policies and school practices that require no fundamental changes in the views, assumptions, and institutional practices of teachers and administrators. The evidence seems to suggest that this paradigm also leads to the trivialization of ethnic cultures by well-meaning teachers (Boateng, 1986).

It is important for schools to recognize that, for a long time, our schools have defined knowledge almost exclusively in terms of the dominant White European culture. Any efforts to multiculturalize the curriculum, therefore, should involve more than tacking onto the existing curriculum a handful of stories about ethnic heroes and the occasional celebration of Black History Month. If multicultural education is to remain a challenge or a viable response to the monocultural–Eurocentric tradition in the school system, then it must ensure a fundamental restructuring of the entire curriculum and not some aspects of it.

THE MULTICULTURAL CONCEPTUAL CURRICULUM

The restructuring of the curriculum needs to be done on a conceptual basis with a systematic infusion of the African-American, European, and other non-European experiences. The multicultural conceptual curriculum aims at broadening the base of available knowledge and at providing to a minimum, competing/complementary perspectives. Studying different perspectives on history or on concepts in the arts, humanities, and the sciences expands, not limits, the pursuit of truth. If the school is a place where we search for the truth, it is imperative to have a diversified teaching–learning program because truth often emerges out of the clashing of ideas and perspectives. Truth is not an inherent quality of any single category of people. It is important to note that each person or group's version of truth is conditioned by his or her station in life, past experiences, and future aspirations. Thus, it is the coming together of these perspectives in a multicultural curriculum that provides a distinct, meaningful, educational experience for youngsters in the urban areas.

The multicultural conceptual curriculum is an option that has widespread implications for ensuring the academic success of all children in the urban school system. A conceptual approach would integrate African-American and other cultures into the curriculum and would provide all children with the opportunity to participate fully in the learning process. Unlike the Euro-American-centered curriculum, the multicultural conceptual curriculum and instruction are inclusive, not exclusive. It gives all children—non-European and European alike—the opportunity to see themselves as being members of the human society. For example, one does not wait until Black History Month (February) to teach about the African-American experience. In the conceptual curriculum, concepts are identified from all subject areas and content from various cultural perspectives are selected to explain the concepts throughout the year. Because content has traditionally been drawn from the Euro-American culture to explain almost every concept in the curriculum, there is a need to strive for a balance by selecting content from other cultures and groups. U.S. history, literature, art, music, and so on, should be taught from diverse ethnic and cultural perspectives rather than from only an Euro-American perspective.

Gay (1977) defined such teaching as "cultural context" teaching and suggests that teachers "carefully select illustrations, analogies and allegories from the experiences of different ethnic groups to demonstrate or extricate the meanings of academic concepts and principles" (p. 54). However, it is important to note that these ethnic experiences cannot be fully understood and utilized in the curriculum if they are isolated from the worldviews that shape them. If educators do not understand the worldviews of their students, they may have difficulty developing instructional strategies that can be related to the life experiences of the students in the classroom.

Consequently, from the perspective of educational policy and practice, urban education must seek whatever information the social sciences and humanities can provide concerning the different worldviews and sociocultural systems from which its children come. Teacher education programs must expose student teachers to the unique communication, human relational, learning, and motivational patterns that are produced in African-American and other culturally different children by requiring them to take Black studies and other ethnic studies courses in college. It is after the teachers have been exposed to this knowledge and to these worldviews that they can devise appropriate instructional programs that would be consistent with diversity and the multicultural heritage of the society.

The restructuring of the curriculum and its effectiveness involves and depends on other factors such as proper teacher attitudes, appropriate textbooks, and a supportive school climate. Inappropriate teacher behaviors is a major force that could work against the development of a multicultural conceptual curriculum. Obviously, appropriate curriculum materials are worthless in the hands of teachers who may be insensitive to the needs background and potential of ethnic minority children. A report of the U.S. Commission on Civil Rights (1973) stated:

> The heart of the educational process is in the interaction between teacher and student. It is through this action that the school system makes its major impact upon a child. The way the teacher interacts with the student is a major determinant of the quality of education the child receives.

A great impediment to the development of effective multicultural conceptual curriculum is, therefore, culturally insensitive teachers attempting to teach culturally different children. Teachers who may be culturally insensitive and unconcerned about multicultural education are less likely to encourage students to develop more egalitarian views and to promote respect for all cultures. Appropriate teacher attitudes and behavior may be nurtured through periodic in-service sensitivity training programs organized by the school districts and ethnic studies programs in area colleges and universities.

In some cases, I discovered that the efforts of sensitive teachers may be hampered by a sense of inadequacy and powerlessness to do anything to combat the legacy of years of Eurocentric education. These feelings may be aggravated by the behavior of those colleagues who view their efforts with suspicion or as a threat to their own values. For a multicultural instructional approach to be successful, the element of threat that may come from other teachers and reactionary conservative organizations must be acknowledged and dealt with sensitively. Some successful teachers believe the best approach is to gradually emphasize the positive outcomes of the multicultural approach through campus-and community-wide activities involving cross-cultural experiences (Boateng, 1986).

Sadker and Sadker (1982) also concluded from their research that in order for teachers to maintain a positive multicultural environment in their classrooms, they should make a conscious effort to recognize the subtle and unintentional biases in their own behaviors. In other words, teachers must be encouraged to continuously examine and analyze their own behaviors and classroom interactions. For example, teachers who invite only white professionals to speak to their classes may be sending out messages that contradict the very purpose of the multicultural conceptual curriculum.

Effective restructuring of the curriculum should also involve a critical examination of textbooks and other instructional materials for multicultural content. Teachers who are prepared to introduce multicultural education in their classrooms usually face the problem of inadequate instructional resources. Research shows that many textbooks in the public school system contain biases that encourage the traditional Eurocentric approach. This is a major deterrent because the textbook is one of the most important instructional items in most classrooms.

According to Gollnick and Chinn (1994) who have written extensively about this concern, no matter how biased a textbook may be, the teacher can effectively provide multicultural education by taking time to study the biases in the text and by developing instructional strategies to counteract them. Teachers also have some latitude in bringing supplementary materials to balance the biases they might find in the text.

There is a large number of textbooks in the school systems that contain biases, usually characterized by what Sadker and Sadker (1982) identified as *invisibility* and/or *fragmentation*. The terms are used to describe textbooks in which non-European cultural groups are under represented and in which information about these groups is separated from the regular text. This "add-on" approach drives the ethnic additive paradigm in multicultural education and places non-European cultures outside the mainstream of human activity. The damaging effects of such biases and European-centered textbooks can be reduced when teachers are encouraged to read textbooks critically for multicultural content.

Finally, the success of a multicultural education that is not European-centered but, conceptually structured to embrace a variety of perspectives, depends on a supportive school climate (Gollnick & Chinn, 1986). When respect for cultural differences is reflected in major aspects of the students' educational programs, the goals of the multicultural conceptual curriculum are easier to attain. For example, a school whose choice of speakers, displays, and other extracurricular activities does not reflect the cultural diversity or the multicultural heritage of the society, provides an environment that militates against the success of the multicultural programs in the classroom. A school that has an all-White administration and all African-American custodial staff, for example, has an improper climate for multicultural education.

An institutional change that would enhance the capacity of schools to educate pluralistic urban populations would be the deliberate diversification of administration and teaching personnel, a move that provides a realistic and holistic educational experience beyond the fact that an affirmative action employment requirement is fulfilled.

Teachers who find themselves in environments that contradict what is being taught in the classroom must be encouraged to discuss these contradictions with their students and with colleagues at staff meetings in order to help counter the efforts of such circumstances. Efforts can also be made to invite members of cultural groups that may be under represented in the school to speak at general school functions. In short, a school climate that reflects a commitment to multicultural education reinforces the contributions of teachers who use the multicultural conceptual approaches in their classrooms.

From the foregoing, it can be seen that the ultimate goal of the multi-cultural conceptual curriculum is to enable educators in the urban school systems to meet the individual needs of their students so that they can progress to their fullest potential. In a multicultural society, and especially in urban areas where African-American children are more likely to receive instruction with White and other children in the same classroom, the multicultural conceptual approach provides a needed challenge to the traditional European-centered curriculum that has sustained the deculturalization of African American and other children of color.

The multicultural conceptual curriculum is designed to bring change to the school and not to the child. The traditional approach has been the perpetuation of the other side of the coin—blaming the victim or turning victims into the perpetrators of their victimization. Thus, children who are pushed out of school because schools are not sufficiently creative to accommodate their experience are labeled dropouts. This label places the burden on the child and not on the school. A multicultural conceptual approach would reduce curricular inequalities and would provide African-American and all other children with opportunities to see themselves in the learning program and remove barriers to their academic success. Perhaps the greatest value of the multicultural conceptual curriculum is that it exposes learners to the diverse ways of viewing reality and presents an opportunity for them to appreciate the multicultural heritage of the U.S. society.

BLACK STUDIES AND THE IMPORTANCE OF THE AFRICAN-AMERICAN EXPERIENCE IN THE MULTICULTURAL CURRICULUM

In the multicultural conceptual curriculum, the need for knowledge, understanding, and appreciativeness of diverse worldviews enables the teacher to select appropriate concepts and offer a variety of illustrations and allegories from the worldviews to explain the concepts. For example, the center of a discussion on the "family" as an institution changes from the traditional Eurocentric perspective when the concept is dealt with from the Afrocentric perspective. The European or Euro-American perspective assumes that the nuclear family of man, woman, and children is the only form of family organization. With this Euro-American perspective at the center of the discussion, any community that does not comply fully with this definition of family is labeled *pathological* or *dysfunctional*. When the center of the discussion is shifted to an Afrocentric perspective, for example, the African background and historical experiences begin to show strengths in the African-American extended family. In this discussion, students find out that the strength of the African-American family is centered on qualities other than the absence or presence of a male head. The center of the discussions, therefore, shifts as new perspectives are brought to explain the concept.

However, there are some concepts in most of the subject areas that could not be fully explained without reference to specific worldviews. In other words, there are philosophical/historical characteristics in any given worldview that would make the choice of such a worldview more appropriate for the discussion of certain concepts. The Afrocentric worldview presents a good example. In the social studies curriculum, for example, the understanding of such concepts as freedom, racism, acculturation, assimilation, discrimination, community, and so forth, is basic and paramount. However, as Banner-Haley (1991) pointed out in his study of the state of African-American history, one cannot begin to understand the meaning of such abstract terms or even the constitution, if one fails to study the experience of African Americans, as offered by the discipline of Black studies.

> likewise, recounting the history of slavery, the Civil war, or reconstruction seems incomprehensible without seeing and knowing how Black people participated, thought and lived during those periods. . . . Afro American history, when truly understood as integral to American history, challenges us as historians and citizens to begin to reconceptualize American history. (p. 3)

Looking at the continuing effects of these historical experiences on contemporary America, Banner-Haley concluded eloquently that America would most certainly have been a different place without the presence of African Americans. The study of the African-American experience from the African-American perspective, therefore, becomes critical to the understanding of the U.S. experience. Even though the multicultural conceptual curriculum does not seek to replace Eurocentrism with any other worldview, the importance and centrality of the African-American experience in the general U.S. experience needs to be seriously considered in the planning of the multicultural conceptual curriculum. It is in this respect that Black studies, the Afrocentric study of the African world experience, begins to assume a position of centrality and tremendous importance in the preparation of teachers for the multicultural conceptual curriculum. Black studies as a discipline would expose teachers to the Afrocentric worldview and would provide them with information and perspectives on major concepts that are considered basic to social studies and other subject areas in the multicultural curriculum.

The need to include Black studies in teacher preparation programs in the nation's colleges and universities becomes more critical also when one considers the limitations of present teacher preparation programs. Traditionally, the preparation of teachers for the public schools has been structured under the assumption that the cultural milieu within which the teachers are preparing to teach is European or White. Notwithstanding the multicultural heritage of the nation, teachers are usually taught to melt away ethnic differences and homogenize all students into "model Americans" (Garcia, 1982). Conventional wisdom shows that this orientation is inadequate and highly unrealistic. In view of the centrality of the African-American experience in the general U.S. experience, requiring student teachers to take Black studies courses would sensitize them to the needs, plights, and potentials of African Americans and other oppressed groups.

Third, an understanding of the whole concept of diversity—the basis of multicultural education—requires an acknowledgment of the Civil Rights Movement, which is on record as the most prominent movement for diversity in U.S. history. As Aldridge (1994) aptly stated in her publication *Leadership for Diversity*, Black studies or African-American studies, the intellectual scholastic offshoot of that movement, initiated the first wide-scale effort to broaden racial and social perspectives within the academy. Placing diversity in historical context reveals the importance of Black studies as a field of study that awakened the nation's consciousness of its diverse makeup.

An important concept in the multicultural curriculum are the issues of race and culture. A thorough understanding of these concepts is critical to the effectiveness of a multicultural instructional program. In the words of Aldridge, Black studies "has the platform to address issues of racism and oppression directly from the perspective of its historical victims, within the belly of the beast" (p. 9). Aldridge expanded on the role of Black studies in the multicultural curriculum by providing a cogent, well-grounded example. She stated:

> Traditional social stratification courses too often focus on culturally different behavior and social class without forthrightly dealing with the socially determined role of race and structures of inequality. The role race plays in complicating concepts of culture and class appears less powerful in study than it does in the world of lived experiences. African American Studies has the potential to correct this discrepancy between what is formally taught and what is intuitively known to be true. (pp. 10–11)

Finally, there has always been the contention that the continent of Africa is the birthplace of human societies in all their diversity. Today, there is compelling evidence that supports this contention and makes the study of the African experience critical to the understanding of humanity and the evolution of human institutions (see Allman, 1991). All cultures, and therefore all students, can gain a better understanding of themselves by studying the African world experience and various concepts from an Afrocentric perspective. The discipline of Black studies would provide teacher preparation programs knowledge of the conceptual base and the perspectives needed to develop a curriculum that would have relevance to all cultural groups.

CONCLUSION

In a multicultural society, education should reflect the multicultural heritage of the society. Urban areas manifest the growing diversity, conflicting competing worldviews, and interracial and interethnic conflicts more than other areas in society. Research has shown, clearly, that instructional strategies, learning styles, and curriculum materials operate on assumptions that are embedded in cultural values, attitudes, and beliefs (Hale-Benson, 1986; Shade, 1991). Culturally neutral and culturally free curriculum materials or instructional strategies do not exist. Teaching and learning are influenced by the participants' cultural and ethnic perspectives. "What students learn and what teachers teach are ultimately filtered and strained through their cultural sieves" (Garcia, 1982, p. 6). Rejecting a child's cultural background or centralizing the Euro-American culture exclusively in the curriculum is erecting barriers to the learners' academic achievement and giving them a distorted worldview.

If the educational system is to be in line with the needs of contemporary situations, that is, if schools are to help children fulfill themselves in the urbanized industrial world, schools must educate these children for life in a pluralistic community. Children must learn how to develop a sense of community among heterogeneous and diversified people. In *The Sociology of Urban Education*, Willie (1978) recommended institutional changes in the schools' system to overcome the festering problems of deprivation and alienation that face children in the urban areas. In the spirit of Willie's recommendation, one can conclude that it is time not only to redeem the falling children or the dropouts, but to modify the system that contributed to their downfall.

A multicultural conceptual education would create the environment that would integrate all experiences and perspectives and foster a meaningful learning experience for all. In view of the proven centrality of Africa in the human experience and the importance of the African-American experience in explaining major concepts in the curriculum, Black studies, as a discipline, provides an important intellectual framework and an appropriate beginning for the development of the multicultural conceptual curriculum.

REFERENCES

Aldridge, D. (1994). *Leadership for diversity*. Atlanta, GA: Harold M. Barnette Co.

Allman, W.F. (1991, September 16). Early man: The radical new view. *U.S. News and World Report*, p. 53.

American Council on Education. (1988). *One third of a nation*. Washington DC: Author

Banks, J. A. (1986). *Teaching strategies for ethnic studies* (3rd ed.). Boston: Allyn & Bacon.

Banks, J. A. (1988). Approaches to multicultural curriculum reform. *Multicultural Leader, 1*(2), 1

Banner-Haley, C. P. T. (1991, Summer). Still the long journey: Thoughts concerning the state of Afro-American history. In *Trotter Institute Review* (pp. 3-5). Boston: University of Massachusetts Press.

Boateng, F. (1986). Multicultural education in a mono-cultural classroom. *Viewpoint: Journal on Teaching and Learning, 6*, 2-4

Boateng, F. (1990). Combatting deculturalization of the African-American child in the public school system: A multicultural approach. In K. Lomotey (Ed.), *Going to school: The African-American experience* Albany: SUNY.

Church, G. (1985). A melding of cultures. *Time Magazine*, 36-41.

Coleman, J. (1966). *Equality of educational opportunity.* Washington DC: U.S. Government Printing Office.

The College Board. (1985). *Equality and excellence: The educational status of Black Americans.* New York: Author.

Garcia, R. L. (1982). *Teaching in a pluralistic society.* New York: Harper & Row.

Gay G. (1977). Curriculum design for multicultural education. In G. Grant (Ed.), *Multicultural education: Commitments, issues and applications* Washington DC: Association for Supervision and Curriculum Development.

Gollnick, D., & Chinn, P. (1994). *Multicultural education in a pluralistic society.* Columbus OH: Charles E. Merrill.

Hale-Benson, J. (1986). *Black children, their roots, culture and learning styles.* Baltimore: Johns Hopkins University.

Jaynes, G.D., & Williams, R. M., Jr. (Ed.). (1989). *Blacks and American society.* Washington, DC: National Academy Press.

McAdoo, H.P., & McAdoo, J.W. (Eds.). (1985). *Black children: Social, educational and parental environments.* Beverly Hills: Sage.

McDavid, J. C. (1969). *Equality of educational opportunity.* Washington, DC: U.S. Government Printing Office.

Maehr, M., & Stallings, W. (1975). *Culture, children and school.* Monterey, CA: Brooks/Cole.

Ramirez, M., & Castaneda, A. (1982). *Cultural democracy, bicognitive development and education.* New York: Academic Press.

Ramirez, M., & Stallings, W. (1975). *Culture, democracy, bicognitive development and education.* New York: Academic Press.

Sadker, K.M., & Sadker, M.P. (1982). *Sex equity handbook for schools.* New York: Longmans.

Schlesinger A. Jr. (1991, July 8). The cult of ethnicity, good and bad. *Time Magazine*, p. 21.

Shade, B. (Ed.). (1991). African American patterns of cognition. In R. L. Jones (Ed.), *Black psychology.* Berkeley, CA: Cobb & Henry.

U.S. Bureau of Census. (1996). *Statistical abstract of the United States* (116th ed.). Washington, DC: U.S. Government Printing Office.

U.S. Commission on Civil Rights. (1973). *Teachers and students: Report 5.* Washington, DC: U.S. Government Printing Office.

White, J.L., & Johnson, J. A., Jr. (1991). Awareness, pride and identity: A positive educational strategy for Black youth. In R. C. Jones (Ed.), *Black psychology.* Berkeley, CA: Cobb & Henry.

Willie, C. V. (1978). *The sociology of urban education.* Lexington, MA: D.C. Heath and Co.

5

Critical Dialogue and the Transformation of Schools and Schooling: Urban and Suburban Sister Schools

William T. Pink
Marquette University

In this chapter, I explore a promising strategy for school improvement, namely, *school pairing*. School pairing is not a new idea, and may even strike some as passe. The context in that this specific case is grounded is important because it pairs an elementary school in an affluent Chicago suburb (Copse, a K–5 school) with an inner-city elementary school (Southside, a K–8 school) that sits in the shadow of the Henry Horner Homes (a large public housing project on the south side of Chicago). This case is particularly informative because although conventional wisdom might suggest that the "benefits" of such a pairing would flow primarily from Copse, the ("enriched") suburban school, to Southside, the ("impoverished") urban school, important benefits were also realized by the suburban partner of this pairing. Both schools gained in important ways from the variety of sustained collaborative interactions with the other. In fact, as the case shows, it was the widespread perception of mutual expertise/professional knowledge, together with the shared goal for the superior education of students, that served as the major driving force for the success of this school pairing.

Although the implications of this two-way benefits exchange are important, I focus here on the merits of this union as a school reform strategy for an inner-city school. What this case demonstrates is that a school-pairing

99

strategy that combines the extended involvement of administrators, teachers, students, and parents, and that is centered around the professional development of teachers and the improvement of learning for students, can be a very effective school improvement strategy for an inner-city school. Also important is that such an improvement outcome can be achieved without the benefit of a district-endorsed and sponsored school improvement program. The best strategy for understanding this pairing is to begin at the beginning.

WORKING IN COPSE SCHOOL: TESTING NOTIONS FOR DEVELOPING COMMUNICATIVE COMPETENCE

Elsewhere (Pink & Hyde, 1992), I attempted to articulate a new conception of professional development for school personnel, one that draws together theory, research, and practitioner reflection, tailored for specific school contexts. A primary focus of this new conception is on the successful change or reform of school culture. Here, professional development is seen as the major activity that sustains a range of change strategies. This perspective was subsequently interrogated in some depth through an extended field study in an elementary school on the north shore of Chicago (Pink, 1993). Here, "Ron,"[1] the principal at Copse K–5 elementary school set about reforming the school culture by changing the governance structure, as well as the procedures and expectations for the professional development of teachers. This earlier work explored several systemic "barriers" that emerged to retard the anticipated changes (e.g., resistance to and a fear of change, the discrepant public and private voices, and the district "myth of perfectibility"), and the differential perceptions held by teachers and the administrator of the range of change strategies and their subsequent impact on the culture of the school.

Subsequent analysis of these and additional data have illuminated several key problematics concerned with changing the culture of the school as a means to stimulate and support improved educational practice. Drawing on the theorizing of several researchers working in fields of social construction of knowledge and the sociology of knowledge (Berger & Luckmann, 1967; Bowers, 1984; Schutz, 1962), several assumptions about social reality, truth, and the roles that teachers and schools play in socialization, emerge as a useful way to frame the data concerning cultural change gathered from my extended and ongoing naturalistic investigation of Copse. Specifically, such a perspective suggests the following six points:

1. Through socialization, naturally occurring events often unconsciously experienced, individuals "receive" the functional knowledge that

---

[1]All names have been changed.

permits them to move "without embarrassment" through subsequent events of life. In effect, we learn the normative expectations of the culture. Thus, individuals internalize expectations of significant others—through trial and error our own behavior and thinking are shaped, typically in culturally congruent ways.

2. Language is the carrier of this functional knowledge that is learned and internalized so effectively via socialization. Encoded in this received language, however, are the values, beliefs, and "taken-for-granteds" of the culture. Thus, individuals construct social realities through shared languages, that permit them to both understand (give meaning to) activities around them, and to think. In short, individuals construct realities and truth statements as they learn language.

3. The received nature of this socialization, that results in the taken-for-granteds remaining largely unconscious and unexamined, frequently results in the reification of both cultural beliefs and organizational structures. Both are seen as "the natural order of things" and without human authorship (and therefore difficult if not impossible to alter). What is problematic here is that the language that enables individuals to communicate and think, also constrains how they can think about these things, precisely because the languages they must use to think are amalgams of metaphors, idiomatic phrases, values, beliefs, and so on.

4. Reality, then, is socially constructed. Language is the primary means of representing and defining this reality. Although it is true that the reality is constantly being (re)constructed, individuals develop a stake in maintaining the realities they have constructed to make sense of their world.

5. Such ego investments by individuals in a definition of reality (and, therefore, in the taken-for-granteds that support this reality), work to further reify rather than problematize key aspects of the culture.

6. Schools constitute a major arena in that students are socialized into the dominant worldview. Again, students learn via language acquisition and the prolonged subordination to the teachers' worldview, not only the culturally required functional knowledge (e.g., conduct, expectations, and the ways of presenting self), but also the culturally required symbolic knowledge (e.g., valued ways of thinking about "high status subjects," and the appropriate demonstration of the acquisition of this knowledge through testing etc.). Students learn to define themselves not only through the eyes of significant others, but also against the cultural values, beliefs, and taken-for-granteds that are encoded in the language they must use and that is reinforced through various socialization experiences.

This sociology of knowledge perspective is helpful in a number of ways to an analysis of the problems surfacing when a school attempts to change its culture. The recent school change literature (quite appropriately) talks about such issues as the importance of creating participatory democracy at the school level, the importance of fostering bottom–up rather than top–down change strategies, the importance of creating an organizational structure that facilitates change and rewards improvements, and the importance of moving quickly from organizational concerns to pedagogical reforms (Bullard & Taylor, 1993; Fullan, 1991; Louis & Miles, 1990; Wilson & Corcoran, 1988). Missing from such conceptions, however, is both a recognition of the central importance of socialization and the resultant power of taken-for-granted assumptions, as well as the recognition of the power of the teacher to create and sustain an uninterrogated reality for both students and teachers. Such omissions, I suggest, seriously limit the utility of these conceptions to help us understand and subsequently facilitate school change.

In order to change the culture of school, it is necessary (from a sociology of knowledge perspective) for teachers and administrators to problematize current practices and the taken-for-granted assumptions that undergird those practices. In doing this, they must engage in a sustained reflective dialogue (both with the self and peers) that asks such questions as, "Why do I do this and why do I do it in this way?" "What data and reasoning support this current practice?" "Who benefits (most/least) from my doing this and in doing it this way?" "What (reified) values and taken-for-granteds are undergirding and in turn are transmitted to the students by this practice?" and "In what ways can I think about doing this differently?" Through such personal and group reflective dialogues, school practices can be examined and dysfunctionalities removed.

The problem with this seemingly rational act of problematizing contemporary practices in the schools is twofold. First, teachers and administrators have been socialized through teacher or administrator preparation programs into a social reality that makes the very act of problematizing problematic. Both reification and cultural hegemony work against standing outside of oneself and questioning fundamental personal acts and beliefs—"making the familiar strange" is frequently so difficult because these fundamental acts and personal beliefs are often only tacitly understood, thus problematizing them requires a very conscious and often painful and sustained personal intellectual effort. Simply put, without the ability to understand the power that acquired language has to shape both our constructed reality and how we can think (differently) about commonplace practices, teachers, and administrators frequently experience difficulties in problematizing beyond the selection of preexisting "fix-it" alternative practices (e.g., replacing the basal reader with whole language instruction, or replacing whole group instruction with cooperative learning).

The second problem is the degree of personal ego investment that teachers and administrators have in sustaining both the existing practices and the shared cultural reality of the school that is congruent with those practices. Bowers (1984) succinctly stated the following:

Abraham Maslow and others have pointed out that persons who are insecure in terms of identity tend to distort their perception in order to retain the
prefigured beliefs that provide the basis of the limited psychological security they possess. The individual who has a more maturely developed self-
concept, on the other hand, possesses the strength to move into the zones of
luminality that occur when taken-for-granted dimensions of culture are
problematized. (p. 42)

What this means in practice is that not only will teachers and administrators differ in their abilities to problematize successfully, but they will also
differ in their "psychological maturity" resulting in differential resistance to
attempts to change the school culture via an interrogation of values, beliefs, and
taken-for-granted assumptions.

My work with teachers at Copse centered around a voluntary "dialogue
group" that met about every 3 weeks throughout two school years (Pink, 1992).
This activity was seen by the principal as one of four professional development
choices for teachers—teachers were expected to engage in at least one activity
for the school year (the others being to pursue an individual staff development
program, engage in developing the "sister-school" activity, or explore the integration of technology into classroom instruction). Conceptually, we saw the dialogue group as a place to generate "good/stimulating talk" without the typical
burden of "producing a product" (such as a new curriculum guide, or an integrated set of lesson plans). As a facilitator of the dialogue group, my own intellectual interest centered on constantly problematizing the range of issues raised
by the teachers in ways that surfaced and made explicit fundamental values,
beliefs, and taken-for-granted assumptions. My primary intent was to raise the
communicative competence of teachers—by working alongside them to
enhance their ability to analyze the "language game"/reifications/cultural hegemony, and subsequently play an active role in rethinking and restructuring practices considered dysfunctional (Bowers, 1984). Although this was considered a
very successful activity (by teachers, the principal, and me) it was not without
its problems. As difficult issues were raised by teachers with different levels of
ego involvement in the existing practices and organization of the school (e.g.,
the nature of democratic classrooms, the continued relevance of the districts
much touted philosophy, the place of issues like race, equality, equity, and
social justice in the formal and informal curriculum of the school), teachers
engaged in interactions that ranged from wonderfully supportive and light-
hearted conversations, to very heated confrontational exchanges. To their credit,
teachers who were very comfortable with each other socially, took seriously the
realization that, in some cases, they knew very little about their peers at a professional level (even though they had taught for years in the same school), and
perhaps more importantly were willing to stay engaged with a difficult experience that caused them much personal angst because it required them to problematize their own values, beliefs, and taken-for-granted assumptions. This vol-

untary dialogue group began with about 14 teachers and retained at least 10 of those teachers across the two years.

The dialogue group meetings served as a venue for the discussion of issues that were seen as "much too risky" to bring up at other places in the school (e.g., faculty meetings, and grade-level planning meetings). The problematizing orientation of the dialogue group subsequently served to "set the ground rules" for other "conversations at Copse School." Berry, one of my informants at Copse was excited about the transformative potential of this activity. She talked at great length about the "conversational tone" and the "intellectual precedence for talk and reason laid out by our group," and how this functioned to "legitimate voices of dissent" in conversations. This expectation of and even comfort with diverse ideas is important because the very act of problematizing requires a critical conversation rather than a consensus building conversation. Developing a greater tolerance for diverse views, along with the suspension of the typical rush to closure (the fix-it orientation of the educational professional), appear to be two critical components for the development of communicative competence. As the dialogue group built and sustained a supportive and safe environment for teachers to engage in critical reflection about themselves and their practice, teachers became more willing to "try out new ideas and different ways of thinking [about] alternative ways of doing things around here."

THE PAIRING OF COPSE AND SOUTHSIDE: SISTER SCHOOLS AND THE DEVELOPMENT OF COMMUNITY

Several teachers attending the dialogue group were also prime movers in the pairing of Copse School with the K–8 Southside Elementary. It began initially with the two principals exploring some personal issues. At Copse, Ron looks to his own boyhood and experiences with an "unjust society" as his motivation for wanting his students to "enjoy a variety of perspectives . . . not just their own middle-class values." According to Ron, this motivation "was based upon a powerful experience as a kid. Some serendipitous experiences, but really my best friend's cross-racial barriers. I was observant of inequalities going on. . . ."

This personal story, as Ron describes it, connected to the story told by "Abby," the principal of Southside School, at a professional development meeting he attended. As Ron describes it, Abby presents herself as follows:

> I want you to know I was Black, I was poor, I never experienced a White family in my whole life and I was in Operation WingSpread. I participated actually as a kid. I got tied up into a [White Jewish] family in Oak Park. We became friends, it was the most powerful experience for me and I think the reason why I ended up with my doctorate, this family supported me through this experience.

It is interesting to note how Ron, a White male, has a personal history that involves individuals of color making deep formative impressions on his construction of reality. He is very committed to removing injustices in society. Ron frames the pairing with Southside as an opportunity for "(his) students at Copse to experience firsthand" children from "different life circumstances." Similarly, Abby, an African-American female, has a personal life history that involves experiences with a White family that profoundly impacted her life. Such experiences functioned to draw them together to design and support a pairing plan that would provide their students, teachers, and parents the opportunities they themselves had enjoyed to interact with and "get to know" individuals from different racial groups. This personal connection between them developed as Copse school was creating a "theme for the year." Ron describes it as "Let's think about a theme this year which involved a whole group of people coming together. It was a concept of looking at what's happening in the city and seemed to say, OK, is this school reform a possibility." Ron called Abby. They set up a meeting ("half way between the two schools . . . on neutral ground") involving the two principals and a small select number of teachers and parents. Abby described this initial activity as follows:

> I think basically when the relationship started between Copse and Southside, I wasn't on to anything to be honest with you. I was a very new principal and I was really just open to working with other educators. And so when Ron called me, I was at the end of my first year, and at the very beginning of my second year. And so when he talked about setting up a relationship with Copse and Southside, I think the only thing that came to my mind at that particular time was the fact that this culture was so isolated. It wasn't a multicultural environment and here was another culture. So that's about as far as my thought went at the time when he said it. And I wasn't even sure what the relationship was going to be about. So you know I want to be quite honest; I sort of fell into this you know, not really on to anything with the initial visit. And so I think when he called back and we decided to meet, we met halfway. That sort of set the stage, because then I had done a little bit of research on it—and I knew economically we were way apart. I knew culturally we were apart on both ends of the spectrum. And I knew racially they were 100% one thing and we were 98.9% another. And so, I felt that his saying, "Well let's meet halfway" sort of bridged the gap because I didn't want to get in to an economic thing. I didn't want to get in a thing where one had more to give than the other. . . . So, when we met for the first time, I think it also had a lot to do with—and I don't know if this is good or bad—but it was good for us, but I don't know how you transfer this to other people. It had a lot to do with the fact that our personalities really clicked.

The meeting was a success and Abby was very enthusiastic about the potential for extended professional development for her teachers. A critical element for her, one that validated her own perceptions about Southside, was the acceptance of her school by the parents from Copse School. She was proud of the recent changes made at Southside (i.e., obtaining an academy status, initiating a dress code through uniforms, and instituting a firm yet humane disciplinary code). She describes this as follows:

> As a result of that meeting we decided that we would like to go further. We didn't know where we were going, or how we were going about it. But one thing we did know is that it had to evolve naturally. That it could not be anything that could be forced. And we also felt because of his parents more so than mine, that it had to start with the parents—not even teachers—it had to start with the parents. And so what we did, one of the very first activities we had, was a parent potluck. Where they got to meet each other and feel comfortable and then we could go from there. It's ironic that the idea was to provide a cultural experience for children. But we ended up doing more work with the adults. Before we had the potluck, his parents wanted to come down and visit. And during that time, we were in I guess what you call the honeymoon stage—so they didn't tell me it was to see the environment, or the safety of the school, but we knew. You know—we knew what it was for. They were very pleasantly, I think, surprised and later they let me know that. So I don't think that they really didn't know that there would be order, that kids would not be hanging from the windows, that people would not be shooting all around. So as a result of that visit, they went back and told other parents—other parents would visit also. And to make a long story short . . . they began to feel safe about it. So then we start to get teachers together who also came to the potluck. So it was on a social basis that we actually get together. So after that, many of the teachers at both schools wanted to be involved, but it was strictly voluntary. It was not everyone at both schools.

I was interested in the way in that Abby presented the idea of the pairing to her teachers. I wondered what her thinking and expectations were, if it was voluntary. She answered as follows:

> Well, I told them that we were getting together socially so that they could see if they saw anyone they thought they would like to work with in the sister school. Any teacher that they would like to pair up with. And what I told them was they did not have to be involved in this project if they did not want to, but that those that wanted to would be supported. And the objectives that were in mind were: (1) to expose children to students of other cultures, (2) the other objective that we had in mind, was that we could share resources. By that we meant that if a person was to come who was doing a workshop at Copse or Southside, you could invite your teacher-mate. So that would serve, we could use them for both schools and that would save resources. Also (3) we saw visiting and getting out of your building and your own school, was a professional development within itself. So that you

could see other teachers. And my objective, that I did not tell them, also was the fact that this was less threatening. That they could talk about what they were doing educationally or instructionally in their classrooms with another teacher who wasn't in the school. Because . . . teachers are still threatened by each other, when they work with them. But they seem to be less threatened when it's someone from outside.

Across the initial year, two kinds of activities developed. Teachers began to pair and team for an increasing variety of collaborative activities. Both principals developed closer professional and personal relationships. Abby talks about the pairing of schools as the major professional development/school improvement strategy for Southside school:

> So as a result of that, several teachers sort of paired themselves up. And they started to do things like, they did video penpals. They did nature projects together. We did a project for the city that dealt with the Christmas tree decorating—that kind of thing. So, as a result many instructional projects began to build after that. But meanwhile going on was the building of the relationships of the adults . . . many of the teachers who were not on board initially, wanted to get on board later—at both schools—because they began to feel that they were being left out. Now that may have been because of the situation. May have been sometimes people don't get on new things right away and then they want to be a part of it. So whatever it was . . . I had teachers actually calling me more than him. So that was getting to be really, really something. And it was never an objective for us to become supports to each other, but we became very close and supportive of each other because he was also in a situation, that I hadn't thought of, where the other principals in his area—it was competitive among them. And so there was no competition with me and so a natural relationship grew out of it that I think principals don't normally have. Because in addition to the support, I had a mirror for my administrative development. Because he could say, "You know Abby, I saw you doing this, did you think about trying to handle it this way?" That might be good—might be something I would try. We had many conversations at night at 11 and 12 o'clock, finding out that we had so many of the same issues when it came to dealing with the teachers on our staff and things. He was a lot of help for me in resolving some of these issues because he had more experience. And then I was probably, I think I was, a lot of help for him because I had a different experience.

Clearly, several discourse communities were forged as a result of this pairing: First, teachers were developing a variety of conversational groups across schools (much more so than within their own districts). Second, the two principals were developing a much needed professional relationship that was built on trust and a recognition of (a different) expertise. Finally teachers were talking privately to the principal of the other school. Each of these networks contributes to building a community grounded on shared professional, as well as on personal and social interests (i.e., good education for all students, continuing professional development for teachers, integration of parents into the education of their children, etc.). Each network also contributed to the continuing development of the communicative competence of all the adults in both schools.

It is not the detailing of this range of activities that is most important here (although there is clearly a need for such work to illuminate our understanding of how schools do these activities that are perceived as central to school improvement). Rather, what is important is the realization that this pairing enables the teachers to think about education and engage in doing education in ways that would not have been possible without the pairing. I must also emphasize the growing importance of the development of communicative competence in some teachers at Copse school (the dialogue group participants) because this problematizing orientation was brought to two kinds of conversations in the pairing activities. The first example concerns the kind of questioning and "tolerance for divergent thinking" that became a routine expectation in faculty discussions. For example, the issue was never pairing to seek out the "one best solution to teaching fourth-grade math." Rather, questions centered around issues such as "What is mathematics?" "In what ways might we integrate different ways of conceptualizing math into all subject areas?" "What kinds of difficulties do students have understanding mathematics and what range of instructional strategies might address such difficulties." In this way, teachers challenged each other to think reflectively about their current practices and their taken-for-granted assumptions about mathematics. The second example concerns the involvement of teachers at both schools in team-teaching "methods courses" to student teachers who spent half a year student teaching in each school. This provided a forum for grade-level teachers to talk on a continuing basis, both about their own practice and the fundamentals needed to instruct/guide a novice teacher through their practice teaching experience. Abby sees this sharing of student teachers as an important turning point in the evolution of the pairing plan. She talks about the initial year or so being a "honeymoon stage," that was "grown out of" by the difficulties that surfaced from interactions with student teachers:

> . . . in that honeymoon stage, where no one wanted to step on anybody's toes and they talked instruction but not any really serious issues . . . talked at each other I think instead of with each other. I think that when the children started exchanging some issues came up that they addressed still from an instructional standpoint. I don't think they really got to talk about their feelings until we started sharing student teachers.

She talks with considerable pride, however, of a key meeting of supervising teachers and student teachers in that both she and Ron were asked to leave:

. . . they actually asked that Ron and I leave so that they could talk between the two groups, amongst themselves. Out of that conversation, we don't know what went on, but they grew much closer. I think that they actually discussed some of the things they felt, and they did tell us that they reminded them that, you took on this without discussing it. And we feel that it's 'cause you felt you knew more—you could do. So out of that I think real growth started to develop and relationships really strengthened.

KEY LESSONS TO BE LEARNED FROM THE PAIRING AT COPSE AND SOUTHSIDE

I have avoided detailing the range of pairing activities developed between the two schools (e.g., teacher exchanges, joint student trips and programs, administrator and parent interactions, and a range of student projects such as video pen pals, journaling, e-mail correspondence, etc.) to emphasize the point that it is not the adoption of a school improvement model or package of activities that is the lesson to be learned from this case. Rather, the primary lesson to be learned is that the improvement of an inner-city school is grounded in the development of a range of improvement activities that are both particularistic to their own human needs, and context sensitive. In short, other inner-city schools should design their own improvement plan, rather than expend energy seeking out a blueprint for improvement designed by others. This finding that an inner-city school can improve itself in the face of the many liabilities documented by Kozol (1991) and others, is significant because it provides an exemplar for others to learn from.

A second lesson to be learned from this case is the importance of a focus on the development of the communicative competence of administrators, teachers, and parents—again communicative competence is enhanced by a problematizing orientation to "making the familiar strange" through a sustained interrogation of values, beliefs, and taken-for-granted assumptions. It is evident from this pairing that the pursuit of communicative competence was the sustaining force of the improvement strategy. Without it, teachers would in all probability be reduced to the more traditional activity of learning how to deliver the most recent pedagogical fad.

A third lesson to be learned is the importance of maintaining the sustained involvement of all the adults in the school improvement activities. Both Abby and Ron talk about the importance of parent involvement (e.g., "sharing their dreams for their children," "visiting the other school . . . that validated their belief in the quality of education their own child was receiving . . . as well as, pointing-up areas for improvement," "the PTA chairs calling each other to arrange visitations and field trips"). Teachers talk about the important professional friendships they have forged as a result of the (extended) opportunities they have enjoyed to "simply talk about any issue that interests . . . [us] . . . in an informal and safe setting." Both principals note with considerable warmth the importance of the other's counsel and support to their own professional development. What should not be overlooked here is the power of engaging all of the adults in a serious interrogation of the education received by students, and the ways in that this education might be improved. This case also illustrates the point that school improvement is far more complex than providing teachers with limited in-service days devoted to presentations by "experts" of the latest best practice instructional fad.

A fourth lesson to be learned from this case is that school improvement is a long-term strategy that requires both the support of administrators and the sustained attention of teachers. Both Abby and Ron talk about their deep felt commitment to quality education and the importance of children experiencing "life through the eyes of others positioned differently from them." To facilitate this, both encouraged teachers to conceptualize "different ways of doing things" while they subsequently provided resources for teachers to make these concep-tualizations real—teacher exchange days is a good example, paired student reports following a zoo visit is another example. Teachers also talked about the importance of "getting to know" each other socially before shared classroom projects had meaning beyond ". . . an activity that made us look good because we were quote, 'reaching out to a city school'"—in one instance a teacher from Copse talked about the importance of an early social event in that Copse teach-ers were referred to as "too tight assed" to dance and enjoy themselves. Thankfully, they worked through these early impressions that were "racially and culturally bound." Several teachers have subsequently become good friends— friendships that involve ". . . many long evening conversations that include per-sonal as well as professional issues." In one case, a request has been made to change schools so that teachers might team together in multiage classrooms.

A fifth lesson to be learned from this case is that placing teachers in charge of their own professional development is a powerful catalyst for school improvement. Pairing was a voluntary activity at both schools. Thus, those ini-tially involved had a real commitment to "good talk" (conceptually grounded in enhancing communicative competence), and to interrogating their own practice. What is interesting to note is the difference between a school improvement plan where all the teachers are expected to engage in learning about and implement-ing the same things (e.g., math manipulatives, or portfolios), compared to an improvement plan that both encourages and supports teachers to explore their own intellectual interests within the parameters of a master school improvement plan that is developed by the school community. At Southside, this latter strate-gy was both enthusiastically embraced by teachers (and by an increasing num-ber of teachers as the initial successes surfaced), and resulted in the develop-ment of a faculty who were highly committed to their students, the school, and the quality of the education received by their students.

A final lesson to be learned from this case is that fundamental school improvement can be achieved in an inner-city school when that school enjoys decision-making authority within a decentralized system. The Chicago public schools have a long history dominated by a large centralized bureaucracy. The 1988 Reform Act created localized decision making (through the creation of a local school council at each school), and gave each school discretionary monies. As a consequence of this major shift in decision making, schools have enjoyed much greater latitude to plan for and subsequently fund school improvement initiatives driven by local rather than subdistrict or systemwide directives. Although I am not suggesting that schools have benefited equally as a consequence of the passage of the Reform Act, the Southside case does provide a powerful example of what can be achieved when schools are free to reconceptualize themselves, and when this reconceptualization is grounded in an interrogation of values, beliefs, and taken-for-granted assumptions about "doing education" in inner-city schools.

I began this chapter with the task of exploring a promising strategy for improving inner-city schools. I want to emphasize, again, that although the Southside case is informative, it should not be viewed as a blueprint to be adopted by other inner-city schools—the recognition that the cast of characters and building cultures differs from school to school, makes the concept of such a direct transfer highly questionable. Rather, the case should be viewed as illustrative of the possibility for school improvement in inner-city schools. Thus, the answer to the question, "Can it be done?" is clearly "yes." Perhaps the urgency for doing it in many other schools is best stated by Abby: "I think that one of the most important things is for them to be exposed as young people to people of other cultures . . . I think the future of the United States is going to depend on it . . . I think that what you do with children is everlasting."

REFERENCES

Berger, P. L., & Luckmann, T. (1967). *The social construction of reality*. New York: Anchor Books.

Bowers, C. A. (1984). *The promise of theory*. New York: Teachers College Press.

Bullard, P., & Taylor, B. O. (1993). *Making school reform happen*. Boston: Allyn & Bacon.

Fullan, M. G. (1991). *The new meaning of educational change*. New York: Teachers College Press.

Kozol, J. (1991). *Savage inequalities*. New York: Crown.

Louis, K. S., & Miles, M. B. (1990). *Improving the urban high school*. New York: Teachers College Press.

Pink, W. T. (1992, December 2-6). *Restructuring suburbia: Using multiple strategies to re-form schools*. Paper presented at AAA annual meetings, San Francisco, California.

Pink, W. T. (1993, April 12-16). *Elementary school reform: A case study of governance and collegiality.* Paper presented at AERA annual meeting, Atlanta, Georgia.

Pink, W. T., & Hyde, A. A. (Eds.). (1992). *Effective staff development for school change.* Norwood, NJ: Ablex.

Schutz, A. (1962). *Collected papers* (Vol. 1). The Hague: Nijhoff.

Wilson, B. L., & Corcoran, T. B. (1988). *Successful secondary schools.* New York: The Falmer Press.

6

Preparing Urban Teachers to be Change Agents: A Critical Perspective

Lois Weiner
Jersey City State College

What role can we expect the individual teacher to play in improving education in the cities? How should teacher preparation programs educate prospective urban teachers to assume these responsibilities? Because the Civil Rights Movement galvanized concern about the educational needs of poor, minority children in the 1960s, hundreds of programs sponsored by private and public institutions have been developed to use teacher preparation as a vehicle to improve urban schooling. Yet, characteristically, each new wave of reforms, like the latest effort to restructure schools, has been "unencumbered by a sense of history," ignoring valuable lessons from preceding efforts (Hawley, 1990).

In this chapter I analyze two specific federal programs developed in the 1960s. This slice of educational history is especially worth examining because the initiatives were based on persistent but contradictory ways of thinking about how teachers and teacher preparation might alter the educational prospects for "disadvantaged" children. These opposing paradigms still underlay creation of programs to address urban school failure, so comparing them reveals as much about contemporary strategies as it does educational policymaking in the 1960s. I have discussed both programs elsewhere in some detail (Weiner, 1993), so here I amplify a summary of those findings with discussion of how research conducted in the last several years illuminates the usefulness of each approach, clarifying what we should expect from urban teachers and programs that prepare them.

URBAN TEACHER PREPARATION: TWO HISTORICAL PRECEDENTS

Trainers of Teacher Trainers (TTT) as it was called, and the National Teacher Corps both targeted teacher preparation as an appropriate policy vehicle for improving urban schools but differed in their strategies for achieving this common purpose. The Teacher Corps aimed to educate a "new breed" of urban teacher, one who would teach differently and serve as a change agent to spark schoolwide reform. On the other hand, TTT focused on the relationship between teacher education faculty and other educational constituencies, usually defined as liberal arts faculty, parents, and community groups. The Teacher Corps stressed the characteristics and responsibilities of the individual teacher; TTT emphasized the obligation of teacher educators to share authority in preparing prospective urban teachers.

The Teacher Corps succeeded in recruiting and training thousands of dedicated, idealistic teachers who wanted to improve schooling for poor, minority youth. Although the program could vary in its pedagogical approach from one project site to another and drastically changed its orientation in its last years, the organizational structure was for the most part uniform. Teacher Corps interns enrolled for 2 years of training and teaching, steadily increasing their teaching load over time. This format differed from the traditional program of teacher preparation in emphasizing fieldwork and shifting the locus of teacher preparation from college campuses to school sites.

Most evaluations of the project's ability to prepare effective classroom teachers showed that the Teacher Corps succeeded in this goal, although in some important ways their performance did not vary from that of their older, experienced colleagues. For example, one study comparing Teacher Corps graduates of Grades 2 through 6 with teachers in the same district revealed that Teacher Corps graduates were better at developing classroom materials that were ethnically relevant, tapping community resources, and initiating parent contact. However, they did not differ significantly from other teachers in the affective tone they maintained in their classes, nor in the degree of attention they gave to problem behavior. Although students who had been in classes of Teacher Corps graduates scored much higher on tests that measured self-concept, tests of reading achievement did not show any difference (Marsh, 1975).

The Teacher Corps also expected its graduates to promote schoolwide change. Not only did the project fail in this aim, the strategy caused serious repercussions for individual interns and entire project sites. After the first few years, the Teacher Corps dropped its goal of preparing interns to be change agents. Interns and project directors learned that despite enthusiasm and dedication, Teacher Corps graduates could not lead school reform while fulfilling their classroom responsibilities. When a director of the national program observed that urban school reform was a more intractable problem than interns imagined it would be, he indirectly acknowledged that the program's change agent strategy had been misguided ("The Teacher Corps Concept," 1975).

By imbuing participants with the expectation that as a cadre of newcomers they could improve a school community, the Teacher Corps encouraged interns to view veteran teachers as intractable opponents of reform. Not surprisingly, school personnel frequently clashed with interns, and friction regularly escalated to the point that school sites required interns to leave. Underlying these tensions at the school site were the more profound institutional rivalries between school districts, universities, and the Teacher Corps, all of which had a stake in teacher preparation. For the most part, faculty involved with Teacher Corps projects were isolated within universities and faced substantial resistance in their attempts to alter the teacher education curriculum. Eventually, local directors of Teacher Corps sites learned that they had to collaborate with school personnel and community groups, sharing power with other constituencies.

Although TTT participants had heated political disagreements, the projects seem to have escaped the Teacher Corps' pyrrhic operational conflicts. This stands to reason because the idea of "parity," of sharing responsibility for planning and conducting teacher preparation with students, community groups, school personnel, and liberal arts faculty, was TTT's guiding principle. TTT participants were encouraged to develop new approaches to promote parity, and teacher education faculty at several dozen universities throughout the nation translated the concept into a wide range of programs. For example, Hunter College in New York City focused on curriculum change, involving representatives from the Hunter student body, community groups, and Harlem public schools in the process. At City College of New York, the TTT project headed by Vivian Windley implemented parity by using community members as volunteers in open classrooms and training them as paraprofessionals. Additionally, liberal arts faculty were recruited to teach public school classes directly, as part of an inservice component.

Examining the formal curricula of TTT and Teacher Corps projects reveals that both programs assumed that urban teachers should be familiar with their students' culture and communities, drawing on them as resources. In this respect, they implicitly rejected the popular "culture of poverty" theory that placed responsibility for academic failure on minority children and their families. However, in stressing the individual teacher's pivotal role in improving urban education, the Teacher Corps blamed another party—the veteran instructors that Teacher Corps interns were to replace. The simple, straightforward view that a fresh, new breed of teacher could reform schooling substituted for a more complex understanding of the tangled web of social relations and institutional practices that constrain teaching and learning. Conversely, by emphasizing parity, TTT drew attention to the importance of changing institutional arrangements, to what researchers now describe as micro- and macro–factors in social context of schooling. Thus, TTT's approach shifted the spotlight from the individual teacher to institutional arrangements.

The contrast between TTT's emphasis on institutional change and the Teacher Corps' strategy of replacing old teachers with a new, improved variety illustrates two contradictory conceptualizations of the appropriate roles for classroom teachers and programs that prepare them to teach. The history of these two initiatives demonstrates that the political role of teacher preparation programs—and teacher educators—in altering institutional arrangements among education's constituencies should not be confused with the pedagogical task of preparing teachers with the understanding and knowledge of practices that enable them to fulfill their moral responsibility to help each child receive a high quality education. I discuss these three distinctions more fully later.

USING RESEARCH TO UNDERSTAND THE CLASSROOM TEACHER'S ROLE IN SCHOOL REFORM

Research by educational sociologists, psychologists, and anthropologists about the schools and schooling of poor children of color helps to explain, in retrospect, why the two paradigms represented by TTT and the Teacher Corps' produced their respective results. Research on school restructuring and site-based management is particularly helpful in explaining why individual teachers cannot be expected to spark, plan, and carry out reform of the urban schools that most need improvement.

First, urban school reform is extraordinarily difficult because of the diversity of the communities served by urban school systems and the flaws of "sick" bureaucracies responsible for regulation (Rogers, 1968; Seashore Louis & Miles, 1990). Even under optimal conditions in suburban schools, the "process of change is slow, the casualties many, and the payoff modest" in school restructuring (Marantz Cohen, 1994, p. 267).

Another way to understand what is asked of teachers when they are expected to be change agents is to envision exemplary schools. We have data that permit us to sketch a picture of the organizational environment that seems most effective in helping adolescents to graduate from an urban high school: a small school with substantial opportunities for informal interactions between adults and students, one in which teachers want to work with students, and students pursue similar courses of study in a safe, orderly setting (Bryk & Thum, 1989). Only one of these conditions, teachers' interest in their students, depends on the composition of the faculty. All of the other characteristics are structural in nature and are influenced, if not directly regulated by, urban school bureaucracies and state policies. The school faculty, no matter how dedicated or committed to school change, is hostage to these controls. Indeed, one of the most destructive aspects of life in urban schools for teachers and students is their symbiotic sense of powerlessness in the face of bureaucratic control (LeCompte & Dworkin, 1991). One instructional result of alienation is that the most demoralized urban teachers mirror their own sense of powerlessness with a pessimistic view of students' potential (Fine, 1991).

Reform is a complex undertaking because several diverse, overlapping contexts influence how teachers act, as well as think, and school reform must address all of these contexts for significant change to occur. In high schools these contexts include the school as a formal organization, the culture of the greater community and society, the educational policy system, networks and professional organizations, and subject area divisions (McLaughlin & Talbert, 1990). Presumably the Teacher Corps' conception of change agentry involved one of these spheres, reform of school structures. But teachers are influenced to behave as they do by all of these contexts, so a singular focus on reforming the school's organizational features will not succeed in changing instruction. Because current research on teaching practice is not, for the most part, linked to examination of school organization, we still have little documentation about the specific transformations in school organization that produce changes in teaching (Elmore, 1992).

TEACHER PREPARATION'S INSTITUTIONAL ROLE

As policy analysts begin to examine what happens in classrooms when curricular reforms are mandated at the school, district, state, or federal levels, evidence accumulates to explain why urban school reform requires altering relations among all of education's constituencies (Ball, Cohen, Peterson, & Wilson, 1994a, 1994b), which was TTT's goal. Teacher preparation programs have a pivotal role in renegotiating relations between communities, schools, and universities because their responsibility of educating prospective teachers situates them in a key position in the educational cycle: Communities rely on schools to prepare their children, and schools rely on programs of teacher preparation for well-prepared teachers; liberal arts faculty in colleges expect teachers to educate their prospective students appropriately; teacher education faculty rely on liberal arts faculty to provide prospective teachers with their subject matter knowledge. Institutionally speaking, teacher preparation has the easiest access to all of the constituencies in education's circle.

Much of the recent discussion about the importance of school–university collaborations, especially the material on professional development schools, seems at first glance to follow in TTT's tradition. In reality, most of these collaborations distort TTT's most essential contribution, the notion that all of education's constituencies, including communities, should share in teacher preparation. Although the universities and school districts that establish professional development schools herald them as beacons of collaboration, in actuality they give teachers and teacher educators greater control over education (Weiner, 1993), buttressing educators' professional authority and excluding education's other constituencies, most notably, parents (Labaree, 1992). The ideology of professionalism deserves a fuller discussion than my purposes here allow, but its deleteriousness needs to be noted. As a cohort of teachers who studied effects of the institutional structure of schools concluded,

> the concept of "burnout" is the natural result of the ideology of profession-alism which encourages teachers to see themselves as more powerful than they actually are and, therefore, more responsible alone to correct complex societal and institutional dilemmas. (Freedman, Jackson, & Boles, 1982)

Significantly, the most valuable research to come out of the current interest in school–university partnerships examines the difficulty of establishing authentic collaborations, because of differentials in power, prestige, and working conditions. As two researchers note, one of the most popular methods of linking schools and universities is to invite classroom teachers to serve as supervisors of student teachers. However, classroom teachers enter this role from a lower status organization and without benefit of organizational support; their knowledge is seen as supplementary to university-generated knowledge, and gender relations reinforce these status differences. The status of the education schools within the universities is a function of their distance from the field, a factor that further discourages close ties to schools and equal relations with classroom teachers serving as clinical faculty (Cornbleth & Ellsworth, 1994).

Recognizing teacher preparation's political obligation to alter institutional relationships in the educational cycle acknowledges the wealth of material social scientists have produced about the interplay between social and economic conditions outside the school walls and students' attitudes about formal education and their academic performance (Fine, 1986; LeCompte & Dworkin, 1991; Ogbu, 1989); about the reasons and methods young people have for crossing the cultural borders that impede academic success (Fordham & Ogbu, 1986; Phelan & Davidson, 1993); about changes in family life and student performance (RAND Institute on Education and Training, 1995).

RESPONSIBILITIES OF URBAN TEACHERS AND THE PROGRAMS THAT PREPARE THEM TO TEACH

Two shifts in teacher preparation flow from a systemic perspective on educational reform, like TTT's orientation suggested. One is redefining teacher education's political role, as I explained earlier; the other is reconceptualizing its pedagogical orientation. Assigning teachers the task of school reform and demanding that teacher preparation educate them in this role implies that teaching by itself is less than a full-time occupation, and that learning to teach is not so complex an undertaking as to require in-depth study. Fullan's (1993) call for teacher preparation to help students link their moral purpose in teaching to "the skills of change agentry" (Fullan, 1993) illustrates both assumptions about teaching. Fullan argues that accomplishing this charge entails developing the novice teacher's "knowledge base for effective teaching" and for "changing the conditions that affect teaching".

When Fullan characterizes teacher preparation's pedagogical task as developing the prospective teacher's "knowledge base for effective teaching," he reduces the process of learning to teach to acquiring a knowledge base. Even the researcher whose work was key to generating the knowledge base for effective teaching now acknowledges the limitations of the research, in particular its focus on "very basic" aspects of teaching and the reliance on standardized tests as outcome measures, which failed to assess students' knowledge of interrelationships or application of ideas (Brophy, 1992). Assuming that learning to teach is synonymous with mastering a knowledge base, as Fullan does, misses the need for critical study of the context of teaching and attention to the "personal and idiosyncratic nature" of teaching (Bullough, Knowles, & Crown, 1989, p. 231).

The tendency in teacher preparation to emphasize technical mastery of skills is a shortcoming, not the ideal condition that Fullan's assertion has it, and for prospective urban teachers, this error is destructive. Preparation that emphasizes acquisition of techniques miseducates teacher candidates about the astounding flexibility and range of strategies they must tap to fulfill the moral purpose Fullan sets before them, reaching each student. Urban schools were structured to be impersonal environments, insulated from parents and communities (Kaestle, 1973), and these characteristics sabotage the urban teacher's task of engaging with students as individuals, drawing on their lives and interests outside of school for instructional purposes. The social diversity of the student body in urban classrooms further complicates the process of choosing appropriate materials and teaching strategies; urban teachers who are not educated to be inventive and flexible will not be able to address the heterogeneity in their classrooms.

The view that learning to teach consists of acquiring a knowledge base ignores significant findings on how teachers learn to teach (Kennedy, 1991), including research about the powerful influence of prospective and beginning teachers' beliefs and values on their development as teachers (Cole, 1992; Zeichner, Tabachnick, & Densmore, 1987). Precisely because prospective teachers' initial beliefs are so influential and teaching, as Fullan correctly asserts, is a moral enterprise, teachers should be able to articulate and inspect their educational beliefs, critiquing them in light of other viewpoints. This aspect of teacher preparation is essential for teachers to educate students who are culturally different from themselves. Teacher education has a political and moral responsibility to prepare teachers

> who, wherever they teach, are dedicated to the realization of a top quality education for everyone's children, and who recognize the importance and value of the diverse cultures and traditions that make up our own nation. (Liston & Zeichner, 1991, p. 35)

The moral and political imperatives of preparing teachers who can educate students culturally different from themselves is, in addition, an urgent practicality in urban teacher preparation. The great majority of urban teachers will be different in race and class from the students they teach (Grant, 1989). Most new teachers are young, White, monolingual females raised in suburbs and small towns (Zimpher, 1989), but the students they will be responsible for educating in cities will be poor children of color, with life experiences vastly different from those of their teachers.

Teacher candidates need to learn that their perceptions of schooling are not universally held, and that minority groups differ from one another in their "cultural models" of education (Ogbu, 1989). This is especially critical for teachers who are White and middle class, because their own cultural model underlies school structures and procedures, although they may not realize it. Students who are "involuntary minorities" bring to schooling an oppositional social identity and oppositional cultural frame of reference that have developed in response to racism (Ogbu, 1989). These cultural attitudes influence academic performance in ways teachers must understand when they work with students who feel that academic achievement may subtract from their cultural identity (Fordham & Ogbu, 1986).

When prospective urban teachers are themselves involuntary minorities they are more likely than other teacher candidates to appreciate how the experiences of racism can forge an oppositional social attitude and ambivalence about school success. As Foster (1992) learned when interviewing several expert African-American teachers, their own experiences help them to see how social conditions sabotage students' achievement, yet they do not feel overwhelmed by these factors. Helping prospective teachers grasp how racism affects their students' school behavior is decisive; this insight enables them to learn how to acknowledge the validity of students' cultural frames without allowing cultural differences to limit school achievement. Foster's sample of expert African-American teachers articulate a similar method, noting that they urge their students "to invest in learning" and to explain "the political reasons for doing so" while asserting "their connectedness to and identification with black students and the larger Black community" (Foster, 1992).

When teachers are knowledgeable about students' lives outside of school and feel a connection to the greater community, they have access to an invaluable resource. Because most traditional teacher candidates lack this knowledge, or even a perception of its usefulness, Haberman (1995) suggests that teacher "selection is more important than training" to improve the quality of teaching in urban schools. He argues that the ideology needed to be a successful urban teacher results from life experiences and cannot be "readily or easily taught in traditional programs of teacher preparation." Haberman is probably correct that when teacher preparation emphasizes the acquisition of a knowledge base, as it too often does, and places students for their practice teaching in school sites that have little in common with urban schools, as is common practice, the traditional teacher candidate will be one of the 50% of newcomers to urban schools who quit or leave in 5 years or less.

Haberman's strategy, now being used in several school systems including Chicago, consists of screening candidates for teacher preparation according to a list of behaviors and ideologies he identified as characterizing "star" urban teachers. This plan revises the Teacher Corps idea of putting a "new breed" of urban teacher in classroom; instead of replacing the existing teaching force with young, idealistic liberal arts graduates, Haberman aims to use a cadre of mature adults of color who are themselves parents and inner-city residents (Haberman, 1994). Haberman observes that adults who have encountered and overcome the kinds of life experiences urban students confront bring with them to urban teaching insights that no academic preparation can match. This population has a contribution none other can make, and Haberman is absolutely correct that adults of color who live in cities need to be recruited actively to teaching.

However, his plan goes well beyond this idea and is conceptually flawed in several aspects, chief among them the fact that he simply ignores the importance of altering school structures. When he states that "the surest and best way to improve the schooling of the 12 million children and youth in poverty is to get better teachers for them" (Haberman, 1995, p. 777) he dismisses without mention all of the evidence social scientists have accumulated about the ways institutional arrangements affect teacher and student performance. Foster's investigations, which support Haberman's reasoning about the special contribution minority adults can make, also illustrate why an exclusive concentration on improving urban education by recruiting a different kind of teacher is misguided. Few of the exemplary African-American teachers she interviewed became involved in school reform, explaining that they had insufficient time, had made a decision to focus on helping students directly, or had little faith in reforms' staying power. They critically examined the results of desegregation and wistfully regarded earlier years when "schools and community were closer and political activity in the black community" served as a galvanizing force for academic excellence among African-American students (Foster, 1994, p. 22).

The sentiments expressed by these dedicated teachers, who are like the "stars" Haberman predicts can improve schooling, reveal that even "superteachers" are constrained in what they can accomplish by structural factors, like school and community estrangement. Most urban teachers, including those who are closely attuned to their students' perceptions and needs, toil in schools whose structures, curricula, and procedures are based on "obsolete conceptions of student characteristics, life experiences, family structure, labor market experience, and customary ways of learning . . . not real assessments of what students think and are like and how schools and society are linked" (LeCompte & Dworkin, 1991).

Additionally, Foster's teachers noted that successfully teaching African-American students requires mastering subject matter and pedagogical skills, whereas Haberman is silent about the need for these abilities. One of the most powerful ways schools restrict teachers' range of pedagogical options is by mandating curricula (Carlson, 1992). In order to maximize their teaching options and to create intellectual breathing space in their classrooms, urban teachers need to be especially insightful about their subject matter. An urban teacher's insight about his or her students' lives is the starting point not the end (as Haberman's description of an ideal urban teacher has it) to developing intellectually challenging instruction.

Perhaps the most salient political characteristic of Haberman's approach, which has been publicized in two of education's most widely circulated magazines, is that it is based on an ideology of despair. It presupposes failure in two realms, urban school reform and teacher education, and suggests, I think erroneously, that the schooling of poor minority students can be improved without simultaneously changing urban schools or the relations between urban schools and the communities they are supposed to serve.

TTT's goal of trying to bring schools, communities, and liberal arts faculty into partnership contrasts sharply with Haberman's plan, and its aim of reconfiguring relationships among education's constituencies would lead to the kinds of changes in teacher preparation that Haberman dismisses as impossible. TTT's call for parity was ambitious 30 years ago and seems even more daunting in this era in which political conservatism dominates policy decisions. However TTT's objective of parity is a critical target, even if teacher educators fall short of success. Even modest attempts to reconfigure linkages among education's constituencies can yield valuable changes that reinvigorate urban teachers, novice and veteran alike, who struggle to give each child a high quality education. Another interesting change is that liberal arts faculty who were themselves active in social movements during the 1960s and 1970s may hear teacher educators' ideas about collaboration in teacher preparation differently from the professoriate of 30 years ago.

THE PEDAGOGICAL ORIENTATION OF URBAN TEACHER PREPARATION

Prospective urban teachers need first to understand that they will confront considerable institutional pressure to behave in ways that contradict teaching's moral purposes, and then to be given the skills to resist these influences. As a study following teachers through student teaching and their first year concluded:

> the most pervasive and powerful factor in determining the level of institutional constraints in all of the schools was *technical control* exerted through the timing of instruction, the curriculum and curricular materials, and the architecture of the school. . . . However as with any other form of attempted institutional control, technical control does not constitute an irresistible pressure for teacher conformity. Even beginning teachers can manage to avoid or redirect elements of technical control if they have personal goals and the political skills to realize these. (Zeichner et al., 1987, p. 54)

Programs that prepare urban teachers should make them knowledgeable about the social, political, and institutional constraints they will confront, imbue them with a commitment to reach every child, and give them a sufficiently strong pedagogical foundation so that they can begin their careers with at least modest success in fulfilling their moral purposes. But we are unrealistic to expect that most teachers, even those educated in an exemplary fashion, will be able to struggle over a lifetime of teaching for the ideal we have encouraged them to take as their own, if schools and society do not change in ways that support their undertaking.

Arguing against the change agent strategy does not contradict the idea that urban teachers are critical players in school reform. On the contrary, if teachers want to see work conditions improved, they themselves must step forward and initiate the change (Moore Johnson, 1989). However, the obligation to become active in school reform is a political duty of citizenship for teachers, who have a unique responsibility to contribute to debate about education and to lead school reform. Individual teachers can act on this civic duty in many ways, including leadership in school-site reform as well as activity in professional organizations. Nevertheless, unlike some progressive educators who conflate teachers' political and pedagogical responsibilities, I think these two realms should remain distinct and in constant tension with one another.

As citizens, teachers have a responsibility to advocate their point of view as clearly and forcefully as necessary to produce the social changes they believe are needed. As teachers, they must help their students think for themselves. Blurring these two roles distorts both: In school the teacher's role is changed to propagandist; as citizens teachers are alleviated from the special responsibility to inform and participate in educational activities or social movements that will improve education.

When teacher educators insist that prospective teachers they educate become change agents, they obscure the essential separation in their own political and pedagogical functions because they insist that teacher candidates adopt their political ideas about school reform. As an example of the problems this creates, might not prospective teachers agree with Foster's teachers that they fulfill their duty as teachers best by limiting their focus to their students' academic welfare, broadly defined? Do programs of teacher preparation have a right to insist that all teachers define their political responsibilities in the same way? Liston and Zeichner (1991) observe that although how teacher candidates

> choose to act as teachers and citizens is a matter that we cannot (and do not wish to) control in any final way, we can create in our teacher education programs educational situations that represent our commitment to certain values . . . (p. 35)

I agree with Liston and Zeichner's formulation of the problem and propose that we configure urban teacher preparation with the principle that each child deserves a high quality education and that teachers are guardians of this educational goal. This ideal gets to the heart of the ideological difference between effective and ineffective teachers in urban schools: a belief that poor children of color are capable of learning and are not to blame for schooling's failures. The ideal is stated in pedagogical terms, but it grows from a worldview that is politically progressive because it places responsibility for school failure on social arrangements.

Many teacher candidates hold conservative political views that contradict the political framework underlying this ideal, but they have chosen to become teachers because they want to help children, so the ideal fits their moral schema, and they take it as their own. Thus, in the course of their teacher preparation they can acquire progressive attitudes about education while retaining their politically conservative opinions about much else in the world outside of schools.

Precisely because most urban schools exert powerful pressures to conform to practices that are in conflict with the ideal of reaching each child, teacher educators need to help create institutional supports for the kind of teaching we demand of the teachers we prepare. The tension in holding two sharply contradictory sets of beliefs cannot persist for long in most people, and without structural support for their pedagogical radicalism, idealistic teachers can become profoundly demoralized. As a result, they may well reject their pedagogical idealism or urban teaching all together.

Programs that prepare urban teachers have a dual role: teaching them how to educate all children well and modeling collaboration among education's constituencies. If urban teacher preparation tries to accomplish both of these goals, urban teachers will have a greater chance of creating classrooms that show students, parents, and citizens how poor children of color succeed in school.

REFERENCES

Ball, D. L., Cohen, D. K., Peterson, P. L., & Wilson, S. M. (1994a, April). *Understanding state efforts to reform teaching and learning: The progress of instructional reform in schools for disadvantaged children.* Paper presented at the meeting of the American Educational Research Association, New Orleans, LA.

Ball, D. L., Cohen, D. K., Peterson, P. L., & Wilson, S. M. (1994b, April). *Understanding state efforts to reform teaching and learning: School districts and state instructional policy.* Paper presented at the meeting of the American Educational Research Association, New Orleans, LA.

Brophy, J. (1992, April). Probing the subtleties of subject-matter teaching. *Educational Leadership,* pp. 4-8.

Bryk, A. S., & Thum, Y. M. (1989, Fall). The effects of high school organization on dropping out: An exploratory investigation. *American Educational Research Journal,* pp. 353- 385.

Bullough, R. V., Jr., Knowles, G. J., & Crown, N. A. (1989, Winter). Teacher self-concept and student culture in the first year of teaching. *Teachers College Record,* pp. 209-233.

Carlson, D. (1992). *Teachers and crisis. Urban school reform and teachers' work culture.* New York: Routledge.

Cole, A. L. (1992, Winter). Teacher development in the workplace: Rethinking the appropriation of professional relationships. *Teachers College Record,* pp. 365-381.

Cornbleth, C., & Ellsworth, J. (1994, Spring). Teachers in teacher education: Clinical faculty roles and relationships. *American Educational Research Journal,* pp. 49-70.

Elmore, R. F. (1992, April). Why restructuring alone won't improve teaching. *Educational Leadership,* pp. 44-48.

Fine, M. (1986, Spring). Why urban adolescents drop into and out of public high school. *Teachers College Record,* pp. 393-409.

Fine, M. (1991). *Framing dropouts.* Albany: SUNY Press.

Fordham, S., & Ogbu, J. U. (1986, Fall). Black students' school success: Coping with the burden of "acting white." *The Urban Review,* pp. 176-206.

Foster, M. (1992). The politics of race: Through the eyes of African-American teachers. In K. Weiler & C. Mitchell (Eds.), *What schools can do. Critical pedagogy and practice* (pp. 177- 202). Albany: SUNY Press.

Foster, M. (1994, Spring). The role of community and culture in school reform efforts: Examining the views of African-American teachers. *Educational Foundations,* pp. 5-26.

Freedman, S., Jackson, J., & Boles, K. (1982). *The effects of the institutional structure of schools on teachers* (ERIC ED 234-047).

Fullan, M. (1993, March). Why teachers must become change agents. *Educational Leadership*, pp. 12-17.

Grant, C. A. (1989, June). Urban teachers: Their new colleagues and curriculum. *Phi Delta Kappan*, pp. 764-770.

Haberman, M. (1994, January 24–February 6). Redefining "best and brightest." *These Times*, pp. 26-27.

Haberman, M. (1995, June). Selecting "star" teachers for children and youth in urban poverty. *Phi Delta Kappan*, pp. 777-781.

Hawley, W. D. (1990, April). *It's harder than you think: Two decades of lessons from a restructured school.* Paper presented at the meeting of the American Educational Research Association, Chicago.

Kaestle, C. (1973). *The evolution of an urban school system.* Cambridge: Harvard University Press.

Kennedy, M. M. (1991, November). Some surprising findings on how teachers learn. *Educational Leadership*, pp. 14-17.

Labaree, D. F. (1992, Summer). Power, knowledge, and the rationalization of teaching: A genealogy of the movement to professionalize teaching. *Teachers College Record*, pp. 123-154.

LeCompte, M. D., & Dworkin, A. G. (1991). *Giving up on school. School dropouts and teacher burnouts.* Newbury Park, CA: Corwin Press.

Liston, D. P., & Zeichner, K. M. (1991). *Teacher education and the social conditions of schooling.* New York: Routledge.

Marantz Cohen, R. (1994, Winter). The ordeal of change: A true story of high school reform. *Teachers College Record*, pp. 148-166.

Marsh, D. (1975, Summer). An evaluation of the sixth cycle Teacher Corps graduates. *Journal of Teacher Education*, pp. 139-140.

McLaughlin, M. W., & Talbert, J. E. (1990). The contexts in question: The secondary school workplace. In M. W. McLaughlin, J. E. Talbert, & N. Bascia (Eds.), *The contexts of teaching in secondary schools* (pp. 1-14). New York: Teachers College.

Moore Johnson, S. (1989). Schoolwork and its reform. In J. Hannaway & R. Crowsor (Eds.), *The politics of reforming school administration* (pp. 95-112). New York: Falmer.

Ogbu, J. U. (1989). The individual in collective adaptation: A framework for focusing on academic underperformance and dropping out among involuntary minorities. In L. Weis, E. Farrar, & H. C. Petrie (Eds.), *Dropouts from school* (pp. 181-204). Albany: SUNY Press.

Phelan, P., & Davidson, A. L. (1993). *Renegotiating cultural diversity in American schools.* New York: Teachers College Press.

RAND Institute on Education and Training. (1995, February). *Student performance and the changing American family* [Policy brief RB 8011]. Santa Monica, CA: Author.

Rogers, D. (1968). *110 Livingston Street: Politics and bureaucracy in the New York City schools.* New York: Random House.

Seashore Louis, K., & Miles, M. B. (1990). *Improving the urban high school.* New York: Teachers College Press.

The teacher corps concept: A Journal interview [with Richard Graham]. (1975, Summer). *Journal of Teacher Education*, pp. 112–118.

Weiner, L. (1993). *Preparing teachers for urban schools. Lessons from thirty years of school reform.* New York: Teachers College Press.

Zeichner, K. M., Tabachnick, R. B., & Densmore, K. (1987). Individual, institutional, and cultural influences on the development of teachers' craft knowledge. In J. Calderhead (Ed.), *Exploring teachers' thinking* (pp. 21-59). London: Cassell Educational Ltd.

Zimpher, N. L. (1989, November–December). The RATE project: A profile of teacher education students. *Journal of Teacher Education*, pp. 27-30.

7

Urban Schools and Teaching: An Illusion of Education

Fred Yeo
Southeast Missouri State University
Barry Kanpol
St. Joseph's University

Much of the current Left literature on schools, in particular the critical theorists in education, argue that instead of education in U.S. schools, there is merely the carefully crafted "illusion of education" in an age of "democratic decline" (McLaren, 1994). This is particularly true in those miasmic institutions located in our urban centers euphemistically referred to as schools. Furthermore, having read fairly extensively on inner-city research and experienced for ourselves the conditions in such schools (Kanpol, 1992; Yeo, 1995), we are forced to the ugly conclusion that Kozol's (1991) descriptions in *Savage Inequalities* are not only correct, but increasingly so in the years since the book was published. It is perhaps justifiable then that the mood and language of critical theorists is one of increasing despair. The sad truth, it seems, is that there really is little hope for inner-city schools; no way for them to begin to match their more affluent contestors for cultural, political, and financial capital, despite the multicultural, diversity, and "school choice" panaceas that have gripped higher education and now teachers in our public schools. Even the often touted series of educational and governmental "interventions" into families and/or communities of difference (e.g., Hispanics, African Americans, Southeast Asians, etc.) under the guise of instilling values oriented toward assimilationist educational "success" are increasingly coming under fire (Valdes, 1996). Critical and other liberal theorists in education have been increasingly writing and theorizing concerning the conditions and results of urban education (Fine, 1991; Haymes, 1995; Heath & McLaughlin, 1993; Lomotey, 1990; Weiner, 1993; Yeo, 1996) and in particular the interplay in urban schools between race, class, and gender disparities (Sleeter & McLaren, 1995). However, seemingly lost within this literature is a push to seriously (and pragmatically) understand how one may actively configure pedagogy and curriculum to support critical democratic values within ostensibly dead-end urban school climates.

With this in mind, it is our intent to structure around a narration of one of our experiences in an inner-city school, a democratic educational platform that suggests ways to move beyond the despair and hopelessness that informs inner-city realities, yet without losing sight of them at the same time. Although this platform is seemingly technical and contradictory to so much of critical pedagogy's aversion to the practical, it still conforms to critical educational theory's outcry for democratic school institutions within borders created to understand differences (Giroux, 1992). We take the stand, however, that despite postmodernism's outcry against singular reality or one truth, steps have to be taken to incorporate difference and multiple realities into some form of comprehensive framework for a democratic ideal to have any chance of survival, particularly in the inner-city urban school milieu. In short, we risk reductionistically arguing for a democratic platform in the face of postmodern difference, multiple identity, and multifarious subjectivity, realizing that this attempt can only be partial and sporadic. On the other hand, what we do propose should not be taken as formulaic. Our conclusion suggests that teacher education departments around the country must take a more proactive stance in outlining democratic principles for in- and preservice teachers.

In the following narrative, although we realize the reader will perceive other than as it was written or contextualized, we hope that the sites of both potential and transformative praxis are viewed within a sense of possibility.

One caveat regarding this chapter that should be understood, however, is that of the ethical danger of writing about the experiences of a group to which one did not and cannot belong. Because we proceed to do so, there is the concern that it will be used to reinforce the very perspectives that we critique, or that it will be misunderstood. There is a tremendous risk being a White, male "authority" writing about groups to which we cannot claim membership. As bell hooks (1989) has trenchantly noted, as long as our authority is constituted by either the absence of the voices of the individuals whose experiences we seek to address, or the dismissal of those voices as unimportant, the subject–object dichotomy is maintained and alienation is reinforced.

> Scholars who write about an ethnic group to which they do not belong rarely discuss in the introductions the ethical issues of their race privilege, or what motivates them, or why they feel their perspective is important. (hooks, 1989, p. 44)

In a manner akin to "witnessing" then, this narrative articulates the anger and frustration of one of us and the students at the conditions in which they, their families, and teachers are socially triaged. It derives of the subjective and the understanding of those who are silent within its borders, however, the assertion is made that their voices are interwoven between the lines of text; one need only listen. Where their voices can speak louder, they do.

Finally, although the chapter has been written by the two of us as a joint effort, the narrative is in the first person of one of the author's representing his experiences and understandings.

NARRATIVE PRESENTED[1]

A short drive up Martin King Boulevard in South Los Angeles presents a stark contrast to the usual popular and/or media images of this city—beaches, palm trees, movies, and Beverly Hills. This is Watts; a terrain of nightmarish images within an atmosphere of ugly xenophobia, palpable tension, and violence bearing witness to the consequences of the lethal linkage of economic decline, cultural decay, and political lethargy in U.S. life. It is populated in increasing numbers and diversity by those people particularly burdened with lifelong poverty and soul-devastating despair, who live beyond the pale of the "American Dream." It represents the place that mainstream America perceives and mediates as a "jungle" populated by those on the margins (Haymes, 1995). Scattered within America's urban ghettos and barrios are those sites casually termed *inner-city* schools. Schools whose dehumanizing conditions should be a national embarrassment, except that they exist within a national accord of silence. They bear witness to our national response (or lack of one) to the increasing impoverishment of this country's urban minority populations.

Driving to my teaching job each morning, I pass from a world of clean, quiet residential streets and corner shops to one of graffiti, ever-present police cars, boarded-up shops, and the ruins from 1965. Walking onto school grounds was to be immersed in a sea of black and brown faces, of shouts, epithets and obscenities, of a sweaty brownian motion of bodies dressed in L.A. Laker jackets and red bandannas. To walk down the hallways is to be jostled and heckled amidst broken lockers, a litter of paper, and pieces of refuse. The windows in my room are broken, the door needs painting to cover gang signs and references to sex and drugs, light fixtures are broken, desks have taped up legs or are balanced on a stack of books, and the stucco walls are adorned with faded charts falling off as the tape wears out.

---

[1]In this narrative Fred Yeo was Barry Kanpol's student teacher in California in 1988 and continued to teach at the school site for 4 years. A more expanded version of this research appears in *Inner City Schools, Multiculturalism and Teacher Education: The Search for New Connections*, New York: Garland Press (1996).

It is 8:15 a.m., first period, Monday morning at Washington Middle School,[2] in the ghetto; the site of the movie *Boyz in the Hood*. Located in south central Los Angeles, the area known as Watts; the kids just called it the "Hood." Bounded by freeways dividing the area from the more prosperous neighborhoods, it is the interwoven territory of the Crips, the Bloods, and the Pirus. The landscape around the school consists of small World War II-era houses; boarded-up buildings; run-down stores; graffiti; burned-out hulks of long gone enterprises; liquor stores; and the quiet, tense, clots of men (young and old) sipping from cheap bottles of liquor, watching, staring, and waiting.

At the school, I taught eighth-grade science, math, and social studies. I coached the girls' sports and argued with the principal over the yearbook, school newspaper, and how many classes without a teacher I will have to bring over to Room 24. I was 40 years old, fresh out of a teacher education program where I had taken the usual courses in methodology; strategies; assessment models, and curriculum. I learned how to construct lesson plans, assertive discipline schedules, unit plans, tests, and reading assignments. I entered a world where much of the language was unfamiliar, where teachers and administrators hid behind closed doors and students placed great importance on colors of clothing, "dissing" the teachers and each other, and avoiding schoolwork. Lesson plans were spurious and techniques of classroom management were drowned in the sheer volume of fights, obscene language, and constant talk. Nothing had prepared me for classes where assigned homework was never done; test-taking was a farce in the presence of the shouting of answers; essays were generally unreadable, nonsensical, and obscene; and my attempts at dialogue floundered in the face of a street language in which I was the illiterate.

The science text was more than 30 years old and we had only enough for half the students. There was little science equipment, and what did exist was often unserviceable. The "stockroom" had been a place for teachers to meet and drink during the day; or so the bottles littering the room suggested. The seventh-grade science teacher said there had not been any monies to spend on science in the 10 years that she was at the school. There were no field trips, no overhead projectors, no audiovisual equipment, no maps, no chalk, no pencils or paper or physical education equipment . . . just the students.

I became immersed in the daily administration of what was termed the *Basic Skills Curriculum*, which consisted of a prepackaged course designed by the state for urban schools (see Carlson chapter 1, this volume). Most of the material was either ill-suited for kids well behind grade level or was missing significant materials (I was informed that the district did not have enough money to purchase whole packages). I found other classrooms were structured with the same plethora of packaged tests and frustrated teachers who routinely yelled at students to "shut up" and had devised means to lighten the load by sending kids elsewhere, anywhere. I listened to the PA announcements to "work

[2]Not the actual name of the school.

hard, follow directions, be on time, stay on task, so as to graduate and get a job." I learned from students that there weren't any jobs, except on the street selling "crack" and "snow." As I talked more with the students, I discovered that school literally had little meaning in their lives. I heard teachers rail against the gangs, and the students describe how joining meant survival in the "Hood." Many students would denounce what they called "banging" to a teacher, and walk away slapping palms with each other. There was a constant student angst about gang activities, especially the omnipresent "drive-bys"; it was a regular occurrence for students to come to school mourning friends and/or relatives killed in this insanity.

I talked at first about oceans, chemistry, and geology, and then began to listen about lives of abuse, hunger, and only knowing a few square blocks of squalid streets. I wondered why my students refused to stop talking to each other during tests, until I realized they walked, talked, and lived in a group world, so tests and exercises became group-oriented as we redefined what "cheatin" meant. I learned gang signs and how to speak "street"; they learned about white folks. I found out that many could only read at the second-grade level. They were 4 or 5 years behind in math skills, and in some cases these skills were non-existent. I found that most did not live with their biological parents, and many of those who did live with their mothers had fathers who were in jail or who were deceased.

After deciding not to join the numbers of teachers who had already quit that semester (I was the fourth teacher in 2 months for these children), I jettisoned the paraphernalia of teacher education, and instead used humor, self-deprecation, listening, and began to identify students and their personal histories, voices and cultures. Because this took a great deal of class time, I discarded "sponges," lesson plans, and assertive discipline. I questioned students about their language, the streets, and sexual attitudes. I learned about red shoelaces and scarves, dreadlocks, the "hood" and mastered the art of "baggin." I answered questions about what it was like to be White and old (40!). We talked about pollution and population and whether it applied to Blacks or were these inventions of the "Man," meaning Whites. Interestingly, many of these students had already learned that White was oppressive, although many had never seen a White person except for myself or on television. We formed groups to go outside and see who or what lived on the school grounds, bet on which type of clouds and weather would occur tomorrow, and rapped about stars and planets. I asked my students what they wanted to know about a science topic and went from their questions (no lesson plans, besides the principal never looked at them, much less visited the class).

As I increasingly realized that I simply did not comprehend much of what was happening around me, I struggled to understand the contradictions between the administration's rhetoric and the students' reactions; and the contradictions within the curriculum and instructional practices demanded by the administration versus the experiences related to me by students and parents. I came to wonder how it is that this environment could produce educated citizens for a democracy that did not seem to value them, educated or not. Without knowing anything about research, urban educational theories or history, multiculturalism or critical theories of education, I began to explore both the pain and joy that seemed to construct these children's lives. I wanted to understand why there were so few school supplies; why there were few job prospects and yet the administration continued to hammer out the equation of obey–study–rules–diploma = jobs; why so many of them came to school hungry; why their test scores were so uniformly low—and were the tests relevant; why sixth-graders got pregnant and seventh-graders acted jealous of it; why there was so much anger that constantly throughout the day exploded into fights; and a myriad of other questions that were to frame my daily interactions at the school. I asked questions of students and parents about their lives, their language, and their perceptions. I asked questions of visiting community service folks, and stayed overnight at students' homes and began to understand that there are different realities, ways of making sense of the world and that the school's knowledge and practices offered little to help these children understand the world in which they lived or the one the school rhetoric posed that it readied them for. Very little of what the school preached or taught was significantly relevant to my students in a world delineated by race, poverty, and social violence.

One might argue that reading and math literacy should be important to everyone as a basis for an equal chance at "success" at the "American Dream," however, this school did not or could not teach those skills. If students were poor readers (many were four to six grade levels behind), they were behaviorally managed in the classroom or ordered to show up for detention, where supposedly they would be tutored. There were no literacy programs at the school, no tutors in reading or math, and those few teachers who did attempt to work with students were inundated with the problems. By comparison to other districts and communities who, although in reasonable proximity, had more funds, better schools, more teachers, higher levels of equipment and materials, one had to question why this district and its schools were underfunded, dilapidated, and yet filled to overflowing with underprivileged youth. It became painfully clear that in this place, "equal opportunity" was not synonymous with having a just opportunity. I came increasingly to understand that these children and their school were subject to a brutal economic and social stigmatization that seemed to be racially construed and as to which most Americans could not be concerned about.

One factor that constructed the daily life at the school are the contradictions replete in the rhetoric and practices of teachers and administrators. One of the most profound contradictions was the dichotomy between the verities of students' lives and the rhetoric of teachers and administrators arguing that schooling and education would equal careers and jobs, even in the face of 65% to 75% community unemployment. In reaction to these contradictions, the students generally rejected the staff messages that society and education were neutral and equal opportunity was theirs for the price of studying and following teacher directions. An example of this rejection of rhetoric contradiction often occurred in assemblies where the principal brought in paid speakers (usually from the already slim budget of some other category, such as physical education equipment, supplies, or textbook funds) to tell students to study hard, follow the rules, be quiet and obey teachers to get As and a "Cadillac job"; angry students could be heard:

"There ain't no jobs fo Blacks in Dodge, man!"

Sometimes the administration's rhetorical contradictions were even more marked; one afternoon after a day of fights, "misbehavior," and of the three teachers fleeing (quitting), the principal came on the PA and announced to the school that students should be good and obey the school codes: "If you want to be free, you have to always obey and follow our rules." The students responded with laughter, disdain, and rude comments, clearly aware of and rejecting the contradictions of the message; I could only agree and we spent the rest of the science class period talking about rules, who makes them and why. This was often the kind of moment when the students would ask me about Whites, racism, and why their schools were so poor as compared with suburban schools they had visited during sports activities.

One of the major contradictions and sources of conflict arose out of the content and structure of the curriculum. The course schedule had been in place for approximately 20 years without change, with only two electives, computers and home economics. The balance of the schedule was labeled as *The Core* and consisted of math, english, social studies and science. Because not all students could take the electives, the counselor scheduled most of each grade level to repeat at least one class each day; usually math. Within any given core class, the curriculum was derived from the Basic Skills Plan. The package was linked to a text (which we never had) and consisted of a number of daily lesson plans, and postchapter tests for evaluation. The school year was linked to the plan by date and chapter, and resource teachers would collect an evaluation form for each chapter from the teacher showing the tabulated results (evidencing student learning evaluation), which would be collated and passed to the principal and then to the district. The teachers generally adhered to the packaged lesson plans, taught to the postunit tests, and used the chapter worksheets for daily lessons. The students filled in the worksheets, did little homework, and rarely used a text or other activity. All of the packages were state and district mandated and stressed in their Purpose Statements that these packages were for low-achieving schools and were to teach basic skills to students for the purpose of preparing them for vocational skills translatable to post-high school jobs. Jobs had long since left the community and a local 70% plus unemployment rate existed (see Carlson, chapter 1 in this volume, on the rationales and implications of this "skills" program).

The culmination of the contradictions was in the annual festival of CAT tests; state-mandated knowledge tests given to schools all over the state. This was the big event for the administration and district. Assemblies were held to exhort students to do their best, follow directions, and "prove to the rest of the country that we're Number One in the USA!" During that week students could get breakfast at school, and the PA announcements were entirely about the tests. Preparatory exams were given by teachers every day in class for 2 weeks prior; all other lessons were placed on hold for the duration. These tests used a style of English my students had rarely heard and were unfamiliar with, and tested reading, writing, and math skills the students were simply not prepared to handle. The resulting test data, although still in the lower 20 percentile of the state, was heralded by the principal as showing that the school was improving the student's education, and our school was lauded in local news media. The real results were available for all to see—the drop-out rate among students by the end of high school still ran in excess of 50%—the drop-out rate for teachers was around 250% over any given year, and the test scores really did not significantly change from year to year.

These schools are framed within communities where the jobless rate for males is around 75%; the apartheid-like economics of the ghetto translates into high crime where 50% of black males will have been arrested at least once by age 15, unremitting poverty, dilapidated housing projects, rampant alcohol and drug addiction, proliferating liquor stores and crack houses, and gangs. Within America's inner cities exist millions of humans whose lives consist of pain, hunger, poverty, crime, and misery; given relief only periodically by glimpses of the "Dream," often contextualized within the historic Black hope of education. Nowhere in the ghetto is this more problematic than in urban schools, where hopes and dreams of generational and racial betterment meet the "peculiar institution" of urban education.

To put it bluntly, racial segregation and racialized education of children are bad enough, but when the hellish conditions of inner-city schools are added, despair, hopelessness, and tragedy become the order of the day. Kozol (1991) described in depth the brutality of urban school conditions and the irrelevance of an education caught within tattered excuses for school rooms packed with 40 or more students or the decrepit conditions that allow schools to not have school nurses, but to have guns and knives, broken chalkboards, incessant anger, and hostility.

In order to offer discussion for amelioration of the conditions, practices, and failures or urban schools, we must face that which passes for education in them—the state mandates that position the funding, curriculum, and/or pedagogy, and the ongoing urban travesty against democratic ideals, is to face what Bell (1992) called the "faces at the bottom of the well; the maintenance in American society of racism" (p. 12). In other words, it is simply not enough to critique current social and cultural inequities in this country and their justificatory ideologies. It is not enough to note the abysmal educational conditions and opportunities in inner-city schools. We must at the same time, grapple with the need to ameliorate the daily situations that urban teachers struggle in and with; we need to offer a different curriculum and pedagogy that they can fit into the seams and fractures of the administrative massif in which they work. We need to offer a counterhegemonic program that borders on the essential in its radicalism and construct it so as to make sense for them and ultimately their students.

THE MOVE TO A DEMOCRATIC PARADIGM

> We must infuse our definition of politics with a common sense of ethics and spirituality which challenges the structures of oppression, and privilege within the dominant social order . . . as a critical project which transforms the larger society. (Marable, 1992, p. 258)

With Marable's statement in mind, the last 20 years or so have witnessed an outcry (at least within the halls of academia) by Left educators over race, class, and gender disparities, centered around a paradigmatic war on what counts as true knowledge. Behaviorism and/or Positivism has been severely criticized for its objectivistic bias and stereotypical deterministic assumptions. In this view, equal educational opportunity deterministically translates into equality and IQ results naturally and predictably lead to high achievement. In the very despair of the inner-city experiences, in the faces at the bottom of the well, the veracity of these assumptions must be questioned—here they are quite simply and unequivocally a lie!

More theoretical movements both within and out of the education field have sought to solve the urban dilemma. Critical theorists are now well aware of the concept of voice (Giroux & McLaren, 1986), the concept of *not naming* and *silencing* (Fine, 1991), or of various multicultural concepts that have at least attempted to challenge educators to rethink public schooling, perhaps even in inner-city schools to reconstitute their educational philosophy. For example, the move by reading education to a holistic approach (or constructivism) to reading is guided by a holistic, or more phenomenological understanding of how students deconstruct meaning from texts. Clearly, the move to understand the whole child is a more liberal and humanistic approach to education in general. It is a move in the direction against deterministic forms of knowledge. Its guiding philosophy is that everyone is different, has different experiences, and thus texts must be construed differently. We have always contended that this form of pedagogy, guided by this philosophy, is good when it builds self-esteem and challenges positivistic truths. However, we are critical of the holistic philosophy or the educational phenomenological literature in general, when there is a patent avoidance of the more critically loaded race, class, and gender configurations, subjectivities, and identities that could inform a holistic or humanistic philosophy. Without the inclusion of these critical elements, especially as practiced within urban schools, the holistic–humanist approach would be and is one more of many ancillary compensatory programs that ultimately prove to be irrelevant and nondemocratic.

Critical theorists both in and out of the education field argue that democracy is more than understanding the whole child. A tenet of democracy must include the "critical" component of a teaching–learning process. That is, if schools are to be democratic institutions, they must seriously incorporate what has been described elsewhere as a "democratic imaginary" (Kanpol, 1992) into school practices. Here, the common purpose of schooling is to pursue the undoing of oppressive, alienating, and subordinating conditions centered around race, class, and gender issues. This is a lot to expect in the face of Kozol's glaring narratives and the narrative presented in this chapter! Yet, we argue, the holistic experience, although certainly not reductionist, and certainly incorporative of understanding different experiences, is not enough to propel the democratic teaching–learning process into challenging the oppression that students and teachers face, particularly in inner-city schools. In light of these comments, we present some principles of the holistic–constructivist approach as it has been patterned into school reformulations of curriculum (Stainback & Stainback, 1992) set against what we believe to be a more critical democratic teaching and learning process. We do so with the knowledge that the transitionary philosophy to a critical democratic position must be scrutinized for both its strengths and weakness in the face of theoretical and practical insights!

PRINCIPLES OF THE HOLISTIC–CONSTRUCTIVIST TEACHING–LEARNING PROCESS VERSUS PRINCIPLES OF A CRITICAL DEMOCRATIC TEACHING–LEARNING PROCESS

Within the holistic (or humanist–constructivist) approach, the whole of the learned experience is presumed to be synergistic, in that the whole educational experience for any child is presumed somehow to be greater than the sum of its parts. In contrast, within a more critical stance, the whole learned experience is divided by parts reflected on as a part of different social experiences understood through the multiple identities that we bring to any experience. It is not enough to presume to understand the experience of a Latino in and out of the classroom, but gender, family history, environment, social class position, and so forth, all connote the different understandings that the student will use to interpret the school experience. In other words, the holistic approach is too narrow.

Within this view, the learner's spiral of knowledge is self-regulating and self-preserving without taking into consideration his or her experience, although we argue that the learner's spiral of knowledge self-regulates and self-preserves as it directly relates only to personal experiences and the learning process. Put differently, in a holistic view, even an avante garde style of assessment such as portfolio management presumes that the student learns or can learn all that the teacher provides. We argue that this view still fails to understand the effect of experiential limits to learning.

Again with a holistic approach, it is presumed open-ended that all people are learners actively searching for and constructing new meanings without taking into account any parameters or borders to that search and construction. It is our belief that all learners search for and conduct personal meanings and experiences as related to and bordered by their experiences within the institutional and social structures that connect them to their personal identities and experiences of race, class, and gender, to name only a few.

A holistic assessment model is predicated on an assumption that the best predictor of how someone will learn is what he or she already knows, which, although superficially true, is not expansive enough—it remains as a picture in time, it is static and presumes students are also. Instead, we offer that learning prediction is never complete, as experience and knowledge is an ongoing, changing process, and in a constant state of flux. The constructivist posits that learning proceeds from whole to part to whole in a well-defined, predictable pattern, however we would contend that learning is rarely so linear or determined. Instead, learning is defined by its incomplete nature as a whole as experience is always meaning-negotiated in a dialectical process of inquiry that is nonthreatening and nonauthoritarian.

In a constructivist setting, errors are seen as critical to learning, however, they are still seen as student errors. However, in a more critical stance, errors relate both to learning and the socialization process of values such as competition, success, and team work. In other words, errors become less errors and more opportunities for tangential learning sequences. In a like manner, holistic principles argue, to some extent rightfully so, that learners learn best from experience in which they are passionately involved, however, passion and/or an affective curriculum is insufficient if not linked to learners' dispositional interests mixed with normative judgment, democratically negotiated between higher school authorities, teachers, parent groups, and student representatives.

Holistically, there is an assumption that experiences can be extrinsically ordered, in that it is argued that teachers can and should orchestrate educational experiences so that they are connected to the learner's present knowledge and interest. However, again we want to take the position that it is the individual who orchestrates the understanding and utilization of his or her own experience, the teacher can negotiate settings and/or atmospheres that allow the learner to construct his or her own experience.

Within the constructivist or holist–humanistic approach, it is presumed and argued that learners will learn best from any experience in which they are passionately involved—the notion of motivation and relevance that teacher educators love to enjoin incipient teachers to incorporate in lesson plans! What has been gained instead from critical multiculturalism is that students (and teachers) learn best through engagement of their dispositional interests mixed with power-sharing democratic arrangements between all parties involved in the institutionalized educational process.

DEMOCRACY WITHIN DIFFERENCE AND INNER-CITY REALITIES

The discussion contrasting holistic and democratic learning principles suggests a movement away from predetermined behavioristic outcomes. Moreover, the practice of democracy accounts for understanding difference in its multiplicities. With identity subjectively formed and historically constructed, there can be no generalizations of experience, only personal and very general cultural particularities. The prior narrative also suggests that similarities and differences can intertwine within experience, particularly where the players can begin to empathetically and affectively understand their own deskilling. In the earlier narrative, one of the authors as the figurative new teacher was deskilled by the teacher education department he completed his teaching certification with; pointedly kept ignorant of the cognitive and affective knowledge to cope with inner-city realities. His students were also deskilled by the white middle class knowledge and ideologies incessantly thrown at them without any reference to a curriculum that particularizes their social milieu. Thus, it seems to us that understanding points of similarities and differences is both a personal and public matter.

One way to perceive the narrative is to note that over time, a normative criteria guided a curriculum based on the feminist notions (Gilligan, 1982) of attachment, care, and nurture, and superseded a "success at all costs," "be-the-best-we-can-be," ideology that was the ongoing message of the administration at the school and within the teacher education process. Democratic teaching, or a critical educational agenda, in the inner-city, as amplified by the narrative, means making connections to the institutional and social structures within which the school is a part (note Weiner's arguments to exactly this point in chapter 6). The social structures of authority, individualism, and competition, as well as mundane curriculum must be constantly challenged. Meaning-making within this particular context was ongoing, and always in process of democratic deconstruction.

With this in mind, authority, although important, does not translate to authoritarianism. The dialectical process between teacher and student is nonauthoritarian. Only when one's voice (the oppression and cultural grammar—norms and values) was heard and validated could a democratic process even begin to challenge these students' and the teacher's subordination, oppression, and alienation, at least within the parameters of the narrative.

Democracy in process is necessarily about trial and error. One of us as a new teacher (as does any new teacher) walked into this school armed with a bag of teacher education assumptions for classroom management and teaching methodology. Through trial and error both he and his students had to negotiate a path of what we describe as "social error making." The nonauthoritarian position outlined here suggests teachers can negotiate (but only through trial and error) an understanding of one's own and others' race, class, and gender, and how that can construct an educational experience for both that has mutual meaning-making. This may guide the teacher–student learning style. Understanding the "whole" child that is more democratic in nature in this process is about the in-depth structural comprehension of race, class, gender as related to hegemonic ideological constructions of value structures—socially defined criteria on what counts as male, female, success, competition, nurture, machismo, cooperation, esteem, respect, tolerance, and so on.

Democracy can be negotiated when learning includes a curriculum that takes into account a child's interest and identity. Without that, teachers again assume an autocratic position of power, dictated by the state-mandated curriculum and sourced within fear and disrespect. This does not suggest throwing state-mandated curricular into the garbage can, but does suggest considering understanding and disseminating curricular from multiple realities, identities, subjectivities, races, classes, and genders! Only then, will student learning in the inner city better occur—although we must personally admit to a continuing struggle with the question of "to what end?" given the overall nature of U.S. society into which these and similar students will move; that is, will such an education redistinguish from being the "faces at the bottom of the well" (Bell, 1992, p. 12)?

To summarize, our argument is that the holistic and/or constructivist learning paradigm is not enough in and of itself for inner-city schools to challenge oppressive structures and create what we described earlier, as a democratic imaginary. Holistic learning is simply not politically or morally conscious enough for the more democratic and politically loaded platform we have advocated. A new democratic paradigmatic learning process must be negotiated to begin to challenge inner-city school realities. What this means for teacher education programs becomes the focus of our conclusion.

CONCLUSION—A TEACHER EDUCATION CHALLENGE

Teacher education departments have been handed the responsibility of educating potential teachers for the classroom. This has historically meant preparing teachers to teach for the workforce. The racial and sexual undertones in such an education are in disagreement with kinds of teacher preparation needed for teachers to become critical change agents. What is suggested here is that, presently, teacher education departments do little or nothing to foster a liberative education for their students, thus leaving teachers to become emancipated or further dominated on their own (i.e., by "trial and error"). Teacher education seemingly does little more than prepare the potential teacher with a set of strategies to conquer discipline problems, prepare lesson plans with clearly defined behavioral objectives and the like.

Caught within a "technocratic rationality" mind-set, teacher education in the United States has objectified curriculum (what works best for one group will for another), prepare professionals who are in control, autonomous, and managerial. As the narrative suggests, a teacher needs to possess the feminist qualities that foster attachment (Lyons, 1983), spirituality (Purpel, 1989), community (Shapiro, 1990), and democracy (Giroux & McLaren, 1986; Goodman, 1989). It is not enough for teacher education to instruct their clientele on dress, writing clear behavior objectives, and having a stringent discipline plan for all groups, but instead it has become necessary to help education students be the kind of teacher that is akin to a cultural worker struggling for democracy in the inner city.

For us, the theme for challenging the stereotypical consciousness of technocratic rationality in teacher education departments and to better equip students with tools for working democratically within schools is to posit a democratic moral and political philosophy grounded in critical practice. We attempt, in part, an outline that would suggest such a democratic agenda:

1. Program approval within teacher certification programs must include multicultural courses that do not simply teach about different cultural learning styles. These courses must be fused with field trips to inner-city schools as well as with the practical teaching component to foster an understanding of different inner-city "theoretical" realities.

2. Social foundations courses must rigorously attempt to present students with the historical construction of the U.S. school system that will open the possibilities for student critique of such a system. These courses must both affirm student historical identities, yet challenge their hegemonic foundations as well. Within these courses, exposure to the philosophical stances of Dewey (1933), Friere (1973), and Giroux (1993), laced with feminist (e.g., Britzman, 1991; Stone, 1994) and "liberation theologists readings" (Purpel, 1989; West, 1993) will alert students to the moral and ethical nature of the school's and students' roles as teachers for democratic change.

3. Teacher strategy courses must coincide with the endeavor discussed here. That is, multiple strategies for multiple cultures must be both taught theoretically, and practiced in the field. Thus, traditional educational psychology cannot suffice for inner-city realities. Researchers such as Piaget, Bloom, and Thorndike must be critiqued even within methods courses for their weaknesses and vast generalizations.

4. Teaching traditional lesson and unit plans, as well as traditional forms of other methods, such as induction, set, sponges, discipline plans, and so on are fine only if critiqued and prospective teachers are familiarized with the need to simultaneously reflect critically on their and others asserted procedures. Furthermore, students must understand the arbitrariness of these traditional exemplars; that it is within the flux between alternatives that interpretations and meaning making occurs. As viewed by many critical researchers (Carlson, 1989; Fine, 1991; Giroux, 1992; McLaren, 1994), traditional teacher education methods rarely work in the heart of the inner city.

5. Student teaching experiences must reflect the philosophical position of the department. That is, although it is advantageous to send students to middle or upper social class school districts, it is only beneficial if this is contrasted with inner-city experiences. Within their student teaching, students must be encouraged to both view multiple realities, connect theory to practice, as well as be bold in their teaching. We fully realize the difficulty of students being bold in student teaching, however, students can only be bold if their department supports their efforts to attempt to teach to difference, similarity within difference and to a democratic imaginary.

6. Beginning teachers must be grounded in the understanding that theirs must effectively be a collaborative effort, that it must connect to institutional hierarchies and concerns, that teachers and administrators already in-situ are not necessarily the enemy, that although these folks may be resistant to change, such resistance can represent possibility for critical dialogue. Above all, teacher-education students must be taught to work within the present structure and value system without becoming incorporation.

The courses mentioned here must also be infused with guest speakers on the ramifications of social class structure, tracking and educational reforms (such as Outcomes Based Education). Students must be exposed in multiple ways to socially critique, such as through popular culture (movies such as *Grand Canyon, Boyz' in the Hood, Dangerous Minds, Stand and Deliver, Pump up the Volume and Dead Poet's Society*, etc.). For these courses to be compellingly interdisciplinarian, teacher education department members must be open to the possibility that other perspectives are equally valid and offer insight and experience in negotiating alternatives to their students.

In summary, although the above six points are a simple beginning, we also realize that apart from course work, teacher education departments would have to be interdisciplinary in nature, openly democratic, visionary, intellectual, and critical of policy in the most stringent and democratic ways. If professors in education are to seriously challenge students' consciousness, we too have to make shifts in the way we operate in our own departments. We have to challenge our own thought processes—be critical and open of our own biases, oppression, alienation, and subordination.

We are afraid that without the challenge that we have outlined first, teacher-education departments are not about infusing democracy into schools, but rather pass on a message: "We are autocratic, do it our way and you will succeed." This message with its presumptions must quite simply cease as the preemptive rationale of teacher education programs; instead, they must be about histories and experiences and the valuing of sensitivity and democratic idealism. Neither traditionally positivistic education or teacher education currently do much to offset the miasmic conditions or human results of inner-city schools. We firmly and assertively believe that it is past time for educators to take a public and institutional stance to argue for a teaching process in urban schools that is democratic and liberatory.

REFERENCES

Bell, D. (1992). *Faces at the bottom of the well*. New York: Basic Books.

Britzman, D. (1991). *Practice makes practice*. Albany: State University of New York Press.

Carlson, D. (1989). Managing the urban school crisis: Recent trends in curricular reform. *Journal of Education, 171*(3), 89-108.

Dewey, J. (1933). *The curriculum and the child*. Chicago: University of Chicago Press.

Fine, M. (1991). *Framing dropouts*. Albany: State University of New York Press.

Freire, P. (1973). *Education for critical consciousness*. New York: The Continuum Press.

Gilligan, C. (1982). *In a different voice: Psychological theory and women's development*. Cambridge, MA: Harvard University Press.

Giroux, H. (1993). *Living dangerously*. New York: Lang.

Giroux, H. (1992). *Border crossings*: New York: Routledge.

Giroux, H., & McLaren, P. (1986). Teacher education and the politics of engagement: The case for democratic schooling. *Harvard Educational Review, 56*(3), 213-238.

Goodman, J. (1989). Education for critical democracy. *Journal of Education, 171*(2), 88-116.

Haymes, S. (1995). *Race, culture and the city: A pedagogy for black urban struggle*. Albany: State University of New York Press.

Heath, S., & McLaughlin, M. (Eds.). (1993). *Identity & inner-city youth: Beyond ethnicity and gender*. New York: Teachers College Press.

hooks, b. (1989). *Talking back: Thinking feminist, thinking black*. Boston, MA: South End Press.

Kanpol, B. (1992). *Towards a theory and practice of teacher cultural politics.* Norwood, NJ: Ablex.

Kanpol, B., & McLaren, P. (Ed.). (1995). *Critical multiculturalism: Uncommon voices in a common struggle.* Boston, MA: Bergin & Garvey.

Kozol, J. (1991). *Savage inequalities.* New York: Crown.

Lomotey, K. (Ed.). (1990). *Going to school: The African American experience.* Albany: State University of New York Press.

Lyons, N. (1983). Two perspectives: On self, relationships and morality. *Harvard Educational Review, 53*(2), 125-143.

Marable, M. (1992). *The crisis of color and democracy.* Monroe, ME: Common Courage Press.

McLaren, P. (1994). *Life in schools.* New York: Longman.

Purpel, D. (1989). *The moral and spiritual crisis in education.* Boston, MA: Bergin & Garvey.

Shapiro, S. (1990). *Between capitalism and democracy.* Boston, MA: Bergin & Garvey.

Sleeter, C., & McLaren, P. (Ed.). (1995). *Multicultural education, critical pedagogy, and the politics of difference.* Albany: State University of New York Press.

Stainback, W., & Stainback, S. (1992). *Controversial issues confronting special education: Divergent perspectives.* New York: Allyn & Bacon.

Stone, L. (Ed.). (1994). *The education feminism reader.* Boston, MA: Bergin and Garvey.

Valdes, G. (1996). *Con Respeto: Bridging the distances between culturally diverse families and schools.* New York: Teachers College Press.

Weiner, L. (1993). *Preparing teachers for urban schools: Lessons from thirty years of school reform.* New York: Teachers College Press.

West, C. (1993). *Prophetic thought in postmodern times.* Monroe, ME: Common Courage Press.

Yeo, F. (1992). The inner-city school: A conflict in rhetoric. *Critical Pedagogy Networker, 5*(3), 1-4.

Yeo, F. (1995). The conflicts of difference in an inner city school: Experiencing boundaries in the ghetto. In B. Kanpol & P. McLaren (Eds.), *Critical multiculturalism: Uncommon voices in a common struggle* (pp. 197-215). Boston, MA: Bergin & Garvey.

Yeo, F. (1996). *Inner city schools, multiculturalism and teacher education: The search for new connections.* New York: Garland.

8

Curriculum and Pedagogy in Inner-City Schools: An Analysis of the Rationales for Failure

Fred Yeo
Southeast Missouri State University

The schools of America's urban centers have become publicly, and within educational narratives, notoriously familiar through popularized descriptions of bankrupt districts, burgeoning populations of minorities and immigrants, overcrowded classrooms, pandemic drug and alcohol abuse, gang violence, and impoverished communities malignant with anger and frustration waiting for a spark (e.g. Los Angles, April 30, 1992). One quarter of America's children live in poverty, which represents an increase of more than one third since 1970 (Coontz, 1995). Of these children 80% are in ghettos (Marable, 1992). The national drop-out rate for secondary schools is in the low 20s, but is 65% to 75% in urban schools. In Chicago's ghetto schools, only 8% of a ninth-grade class will graduate reading at grade level, only 15% will even graduate (Fine, 1991), and these constitute mere exemplars of a national malignancy. Many urban children come to school hungry, abused, and/or poorly clothed; from communities distinguished by ruined buildings, boarded-up shops, proliferating liquor stores, random violence, pent-up anger and the dehumanizing marginalization of unemployment, poverty, and self-inflicted crimes. They constitute what McLaren (1991) referred to as a complex of deterritorialized realities of nightmare metropolises and small towns that have lost their soul, where everyday life consists of living narratives of exile and victimage.

The urban school has been well documented and repetitively publicized.[1] Political and educational rhetoric contain constant references to the miasmic conditions of social, economic, and educational failure in urban communities and have for 30 years; so why do the conditions persist? In this chapter, I argue that it is because throughout those years our educational institutions have consistently failed to connect schools' and their urban environment or to move beyond their ideological maintenance of what Omi and Winant (1986) referred to as a system of social meanings and stereotypes of racial ideology that is a permanent feature of U.S. culture. Our society has assiduously underwritten and maintained various pernicious educational approaches in urban schools, even in light of persistent failure. In this chapter, I describe the cultural politics that configures inner-city schools and community, and the national–cultural paradigms that construct the "peculiar institution"[2] of inner-city education, as well as the diversity-based educational practices currently propounded as curricular solutions to inner-city school issues. Finally, I suggest an educational alternative intended to unlock and engage the human and cultural potential currently marginalized in ghetto schools.

All too often, urban schools are perceived as if they exist in a communal vacuum, as disembodied entities without history or location. Thus, to begin to understand these schools and their clientele, we must relink what educational schemes fail to and engage the communities in which these schools are located.

THE INNER CITY: COMMUNITY AND SCHOOLS

The economic relations of the ghetto to white America closely parallel those between third-world nations and the industrially advanced countries. (Tabb, 1970, cited in Marable, 1983, p. 53)

Central to the inner-city school milieu are the economics of the ghetto and its consequent human deprivation. In the 1960s, center cities reflected traditional working-class situations; mainly blue-collar White and Black with a growing influx of unskilled labor (Wilson, 1987). This changed in the 1970s due to the twin effects of civil rights legislation and an expanding national economy. As Whites and middle-class Blacks relocated to the suburbs, so too did the factories, industries, and relevant businesses; "White flight" was joined by

---

[1]Similar descriptions of urban education, statistics, and calls for programs were heard in the 1960s (e.g., Frost & Hawkes, 1970; Miller & Woock, 1970).

[2]Peculiar institution is a term used to describe the institution of slavery in the ante-bellum South. This term is used by several writers, particularly bell hooks and Manning Marable to describe inner-city conditions and/or schools.

"Black flight" removing mainstream social systems (Glasgow, 1980; Wilson, 1987). As hooks and West (1991) said, "we have always had to deal with traumatization, but we had buffers. We had Black civil society, Black family, Black churches, Black schools, and so forth. What market forces have done in the last twenty-five years is to thoroughly weaken those institutions of Black civil society" (p. 97).

The result has been a dramatic increase in unemployment and poverty in the inner cities, crime and crack have become the new urban slavery (Marable, 1992). The residents of these "third world " cities have come to be labeled as the *underclass* (Wilson, 1987); collectively described as the long-term poor, the hostile street gangs, the hustlers and conmen, and the traumatized (homeless, the drunks, and the mentally ill; Gollnick & Chinn, 1990). In the current political rubric, the underclass is to blame for its own conditions; to be poor is to be stigmatized, attributed personal qualities of laziness, dishonesty, loose morals, and criminal aggression (Gollnick & Chinn, 1990).[3]

Additionally, the endemic societal and institutional racism within the dominant, White, Euro-American culture aimed at deculturalizing people of color provides social justification for the lack of political response to these conditions. The invisible walls of the urban ghetto have been erected by White society, or at least by those who maintain political, economic, and social power to perpetuate powerlessness.

> The dark ghettoes are social, political, educational, and—above all—economic colonies. Their inhabitants are subject peoples, victims of the greed, cruelty, insensitivity, guilt, and fear of their masters. (Clark, 1965, cited in Massey & Denton, 1993, p. 3)

The current formulation of racism in this country stems from the dominant ideology that aligns itself with particular capitalistic virtues, such as meritocracy and individualism encapsulated within an understanding of ethnicity that questions the exclusion of racialized Others at the same time as it guarantees it. This has hegemonized racism within historically mediated meritocratic paradigms, resulting in underclass segregation, and the promulgation of cultural and/or family value deficiency rationales to explain racism's results. This hegemonizing ideology interprets race as part of that system of meritocratic hierarchializing whereby we determine status and distribution of social benefits. Derived out of Western rationalism, it presumes that all members of society start at the same level and any differences that occur are a result of individual efforts or a lack thereof. This ideology fails to acknowledge the impact of oppressive socioeconomic conditions on subordinate groups. The belief result

---

[3]From 1975 to 1985, in the five largest U.S. cities, the number of poverty areas increased by 161% (Wilson, 1987). The jobless rate for Black males in the inner cities rose to around 75% (Glasgow, 1980).

interprets social problems such as poverty whereby the members of a minority group must be inferior to Whites, or they would be doing as well as Whites (or at least the ones that are acknowledged; Gollnick & Chinn, 1990). The sociocultural result of this ideologically based racial-oriented meritocracy is that the dominant culture has become largely indifferent or even hostile to the deepening poverty and despair affecting a growing population of African-Americans, Latinos, and Native Americans in our nation's cities (Giroux, 1992).

Although state and federal bureaucracies have legislated to eliminate racial discrimination and educational textbooks claim that equal opportunity abounds and segregation has been expunged from our society (e.g., Hessong & Weeks, 1991), ignored is the issue that minority groups in the inner cities simply do not have nor are they allowed availability to the "equal" job, residence, medical, or educational market. They are limited by transportation, skills, education, literacy, connections, and so on. As Glasgow (1980) pointed out, the underclass entrapment of poor Blacks is furthered by their lack of connections with institutions that act as feeder systems to the labor market. Equally ignored is the maintenance of residential segregation institutionalized by Whites that continues today and shows little signs of change (Massey & Denton, 1993). As Massey and Denton so aptly described, the ghetto is part of U.S. society, maintained by the institutions and cultural practices that are deeply embedded in the structures of U.S. life. As conditions in the ghetto have worsened and as poor Blacks, Hispanics, and others, have adapted to the deteriorating environment, "the ghetto has assumed even greater importance as an institutional tool for isolating the by-products of racial oppression; crime, drugs, violence, illiteracy, poverty, despair and their growing social and economic costs" (Massey & Denton, 1993, p. 217).

The "cultural ecology" theory formulated by Ogbu (1988a, 1988b, 1990) attempted to explain the socioeconomic implications of U.S. endemic racism through a typology that distinguishes subordinate minorities (those in oppressive power relations)from other minorities through three categories; autonomous minorities are part of the dominant culture (usually racially White), but are not truly subordinated; immigrant minorities are those who have in general come voluntarily, tend to measure success against their origin and although subject to discrimination and/or racism, have not internalized the effects; the Caste-like minority is ascribed particular racial attributes that leave few options for mobility. They are involuntarily structured within society through slavery or conquest and have often internalized their permanent inferiority, albeit paradoxically along with resistant and/or oppositional strategies. They face a "job ceiling," which circumscribes occupational, educational, and economic opportunities and consigns them to jobs at the lowest level of status, power, and income (the ubiquitous "labor surplus pool"); or to outright public welfare dependency (Ogbu, 1988a, 1990). This ceiling has caused the social evolution of "survival strategies," such as seeking (as does the Black middle class) to comply with dominant ideologies in conventional society and jobs, or in oppositional strategies seen in every inner city—the "street economy," the nonconventional economic and cultural adaptations to the job ceiling. (Ogbu, 1990)

Whether one agrees with Ogbu's somewhat structuralist approach, the implications from his analysis are that "survival" strategies, particularly as evolved in the inner cities, incorporate knowledge, attitudes, and skills that are not compatible with education's predominantly White, middle-class paradigms of learning and behavior. Such strategies are learned by even young children and are played out at the school site. According to Ogbu's research in urban schools, subordinate minorities usually react to political and social silencing and devaluation by forming oppositional cultural frames of reference, which often includes the development of identity patterns that they experience not merely as different but more particularly as in opposition to the social system of their dominators—"White oppressors" (Ogbu, 1988a, p. 176). Although this discussion on economics, sociopolitical, and racist problematics may seem esoteric to inner-city schools, the connotations for urban education are critical to understanding its dynamics.

> The oppositional cultural frame of reference becomes particularly important in the school context because blacks generally equate school learning with white culture. It is believed that such learning can only result in giving up black culture. (Ogbu, 1988a, p. 177)

URBAN SCHOOLS

In like manner to the inner cities from which they derive, urban schools are configured by a matrix of forces; economic, social, political, the pernicious effects of what McCarthy (1992) termed the synchronicity of racism, sexism, and classism, the state's hegemonic inflections and the oppositional and cultural understandings of the schools' clientele. The understandings formed by the students, parents' and teachers' internalization of and/or opposition to dominant educational purposes becomes particularly evident in the experiential and ideological conflict between school staff and students (Yeo, 1992, 1995).

Minority oppositional cultural references and behaviors are deeply rooted in the conflicting impulses by which ghetto residents perceive educational practices. Within the African-American culture there is a paradoxical conflict; historically they have fought for education and literacy as oppositional to slavery and "Jim Crow" and many of the older generation still see education as a way out of the ghetto, although parents will often admit that their encounters with schools have resulted too often in destroyed aspirations and failure (Glasgow, 1980; Heath & McLaughlin, 1993; Ogbu, 1990; Weiner, 1993; Weis, 1989). The lives of parents, adult relatives, older siblings, and neighbors demonstrate the utter failure of education to bring good jobs or end Black job-lessness and poverty (Berry & Asamen, 1989; Ogbu, 1988a, 1990). As Fine (1991) noted, low-income youth, weave their experiential understandings through what they long to be true, but don't believe—that education will bring with it economic mobility. "These adolescents live in communities in which the rhetoric that stresses education as the route to mobility is subverted by daily evidence to the contrary" (Fine, 1991, p. 106).

> When a principal spends $500 deleting the P.E. dept's entire budget (for equipment, of which there was none!) for a speaker (a cousin) to tell students to study hard and obey teachers to get A's and a "Cadillac job"; students could be heard—"That man's fulla boosheet, dere ain't no fuckin jobs fo niggers, man!"—"shit man, my homie's gettin me a Cad for heppin ta move da blow [crack]!"—"My brother gradeated from the 'Two' (a local high school) wid a four-o and he cain't get no job!"; these comments (along with many others) from "A" students![4]

One result of the irrelevance and distrust of schools in the inner city is evidenced in the tragic cycle of failure and adolescent dropping out. Among Black and Hispanic students, the drop-out rate exceeds 55%, and for Black males it approximates 72% nationwide (Comer & Haynes, 1990). Latino students drop out of school at a rate higher than any other group, in some places, 80% (Nieto, 1992). One obvious reason is the condition of the school: run-down buildings, graffiti, broken doors, windows and desks, untrained teachers, texts that are 20 years old and older, omnipresent security guards, and inept administrators. Much of this is a direct result of fiscal retrenchment by federal and state governments; monies targeted to at-risk districts have been reduced significantly and allocation regulations dropped. This results in such anomalies as a near bankrupt district purchasing a helicopter for the superintendent, district chauffeurs making more than the highest paid teacher, expensive, catered receptions being hosted by schools for district administrators, and district office staffs bloated by nepotism. Yet urban districts routinely cancel field trips, academic departments go unfunded for years, new texts mandated by the state go unpurchased, and teachers burn out under class loads of 45 or more students per class.[5]

Although not negating the previously discussed societal bases for these conditions, the dominant ideologies and educational motifs also construct more immediate school-site reasons; the irrelevance of the school's practices to students' lives and knowledge, the disconnection between the teachers and students, and the curricular approach administratively mandated in the classroom. Fine

[4]Comments by students during an assembly overheard by the author who was at the time a middle school teacher in south Los Angeles.
[5]For additional description of the conditions of inner-city schools and of the lives of the students and teachers who survive within them, see Kozol (1991).

(1991) noted appropriately that urban schools that serve low-income students are organized in ways that offer sparse educational expenditures to children based on race/ethnicity, social class and community. Although the urban school curriculum privileges notions of individualism, competition, mobility, meritocracy, it simultaneously silences discussions of social class, race, gender, and sexual arrangements (Fine, 1991).

This dichotomy is played out under a mandated packaged curricular approach termed "basic skills," promulgated by state and federal agencies and corporate interests, so as to ensure that urban students receive at least minimum literacy and computational skills to enable them to enter the workforce (Carlson, 1989) of nonexistent jobs. Ironically, many inner-city districts are too poor to purchase the materials and even where available, the "official" version becomes quickly distorted. The packages are used to facilitate teacher standardization necessitated by faculty turn over, side track disruptive relations between teachers and students, and assist principals to promote "increases" in test scores. As a result, the schools are perceived within the inner-city community as repressive in the overuse of rigid tracking schemes and isolated from the community. Parents and students distrust and resent the use of discipline derived of schools' view that "ghetto kids" are unable to handle freedom or innovative classroom experiences. This is exacerbated by the feeling of being betrayed by Black teachers whose structure and control emphasis is felt as a non-Black distancing (Glasgow, 1980). Students are prepared to pass tests and time, for jobs that do not exist in the inner city, and are constantly battered with the dissonance of school rhetoric and customs that contradict what they know.

Additionally, there is a tension between middle-class teachers and administrators who do not live in the community and underclass parents and students; the first preferring disconnection from the latter. One problem for urban administrators in attempting connection with the community is that urban parents, of a number of minority groups, see what they understand to be an inferior education perpetuated on their children through curriculum and teaching approaches that they suspect are White-originated (e.g., biased tests, tracking, texts, counseling, etc.; Ogbu, 1990). The emphasis in the basic skills program is on competition, individualism, and meritocracy, which runs contra to the value system of the Black community which emphasizes holism, group orientation and self-effacement (Fordham, 1986, 1988; McLaren, 1989; Nieto, 1992; Ogbu, 1988a). The results are massive dropouts, illiteracy and school rhetoric attempting to justify the failure of promulgating a White, Euro-western education on Hispanics, Asians, and African Americans by blaming its clientele.

However, as if finally acknowledging that urban schools and educational practices are disconnected from students' experience and communities, multicultural education has been touted as a paradigm of change for inner-city schools; as a panacea for educational failure. The next section examines the variations of multicultural education, either as in use or as proposed to be emplaced in inner-city schools.

MULTICULTURALISM AS AN EDUCATIONAL DISCOURSE

Sleeter (1989, 1991) and Sleeter and Grant (1987, 1989) distinguished several approaches to multicultural education. Although these styles are in general constructed through the lens of the dominant culture, as is discussed later, they tend to be polyphonic in addressing, at some level, cultural differences. The primary approaches all utilize the language of multiculturalism, but are coded within mainstream values (e.g., assimilation, meritocracy, and individualism) while being conditioned by deficiency theories. The following discussion briefly describes the major usages of multiculturalism in urban education.

Assimilation. Typical for most English as a second language, bilingual, and compensatory programs, assimilation conceptualizes empowerment as the development of the skills and capabilities needed to succeed in schools and society (Sleeter, 1991; Sleeter & Grant, 1993). It endeavors to mainstream "deficient" students through acculturation within the assumption (and rhetoric) that once students acquire such skills, they will succeed without regard to race, ethnicity, or mother culture. This approach is both pervasive and a continued failure in inner-city schools and is the source for a great deal of anguish as teachers implore students to obtain good grades so they can "make it." It often relies on teacher justifications of failure such as "you can't save them all," and administrative admonishments to "study hard so that you can get a job," which is contradicted by student experience (Yeo, 1992, 1996). The approach is problematic because it denigrates student language and culture in favor of White Euro-American values and attempts to convey skills for social mobility to the immobilized. One of the defining ironies of inner-city teaching is the administrative use of the rhetoric of obedience and skills made irrelevant by students' experiential understanding of the lack of local employment and rejection by the broader society (Yeo, 1995).

Human Relations. Human relations emphasizes sensitivity training, self-esteem, and teaching that "we are all the same" despite differences. It advocates interpersonal relations without interrogating differences within cultural constructs. Human relations does not raise issues of how social and institutional racism and sexism silences and masks cultural communication. It advocates a "color-blind" pedagogy, harmony, and interpersonal relations without interrogating how those arise differently within cultural constructs (Nieto, 1992). In inner-city schools, most administrative and teacher rhetoric is couched in the language of this scheme and is the terrain of constant conflict with the students "street" rhetoric (Yeo, 1992). Similar to those who employ the assimilation approach, practitioners of human relations place great emphasis on cultural artifacts, overt customs (dress, foods, holidays, etc.), and behaviors. This approach places tremendous significance on the espousal and generation of feel-good educational methodology, both within and outside urban schools. An entire industry has grown up around providing schools with sensitivity materials—lesson plans, films, training sessions, workshops, and conferences. In inner-city schools, this approach is popular with teachers and administrators as it echoes pervasive community religious connections and values. Many classrooms and school libraries are surfeited with materials garnered from various community organizations (usually outside of the ghetto), film strips, and tapes (that usually cannot be used because of the lack of equipment) and there are even speakers who will come to schools to speak about harmony and "gettin along." These messages usually fail as frustrated educators attempt to disconnect students from "street" knowledge and behaviors, which are continually represented as being unacceptable (Yeo, 1992). Exhortations to resolve problems by talking seems irrelevant in the face of lives of violence, guns in the school, and turf battles within the hallways. Students regard such "teacher talk" as irrelevant and/or lacking "machismo." Much of the administrative and teacher rhetoric is couched in the language of this scheme (as well as the imperatives of individualism in the first approach) and is subjected to constant challenge by the students' own street rhetoric (Yeo, 1996).

Single Group Studies. As in Black studies, Chicano studies, and women's studies, single group studies are rare in inner-city education. It is usually subsumed within chapters of standardized American history texts or found in a lone title by a Black author within a literature class. The approach attempts to foster cultural pluralism by teaching courses about history, experience, and culture of distinct ethnic, gender, and/or social class groups (although less of the latter). It typically emphasizes ethnic division (e.g., Black studies, Chicano studies, and heterosexual genderization through women's studies. Additionally, because the tendency within this approach is to emphasize only ethnicity or gender (not usually any combination), it ignores multiple forms of diversity and oppression (Sleeter & Grant, 1987) as well as differences within the labeled groups.

The more "radical" approaches to multiculturalism (as discussed by Sleeter & Grant, 1993) are virtually unknown in urban schools. Their goal is to use multiculturalism to empower collective action by students to delegitimize the structure and oppressions of school and society, although how this is to be accomplished pedagogically is unclear, nor are there clear connections between educational praxis and the urban community. These approaches call for curricular reform on the basis of diversity, alternative lifestyles, culture, and social justice, yet still lie within the framework of the dominant educational value system (Sleeter & Grant, 1987) in their emphasis on individualism, meritocracy, and positivistic approaches to knowledge and education. There is also virtually no reference to the nonsynchronous nature of sexism, racism, or classism.

The first two models are the more common approaches found in urban schools. Primarily assimilationist along mainstream cultural valuations, they pay "lip-service" to diversity, often in the form of celebratory functions, such as "Martin Luther King Week," "Black History Month," or "Cinco De Mayo." Student experience and culture is delegitimized in favor of dominant cultural capital, and serves the purpose of demonstrating to school clientele that the schools are not isolated or indifferent to the community. The results are assemblies about Martin Luther King or performances of the "Mexican Hat Dance." There are lists of Black "heroes," although the conflicts in which they participated are masked and their respective critiques of U.S. society are silenced. The exigencies of life in the ghetto or barrio are not discussed, nor are connections made from past oppressions (slavery) to those of today, such as poverty, racism, and ethnocentrism (Macedo, 1995; Nieto, 1992; Sleeter & Grant, 1993).

What is not acknowledged in the main two approaches is that children bring different historical and cultural experiences and knowledge to school, which is evidenced in diverse motivational patterns, language, meanings, and skills. Ultimately, although acknowledging that cultural, or at least ethnic/racial, differences do exist, teachers tend to act as if the first step is to convert all children to replicas of White, middle-class suburban children. "A Euro-American-centered consciousness has therefore remained the basis of curriculum development and instruction in the public schools" (Boateng, 1990, p. 75). Although voicing diversity concerns, programs of assimilation under the guise of multiculturalism promote the deculturalization of African-American children to Euro-American norms creating academic and social alienation (Boateng, 1990). This is equally true in the assimilation programs that promote linguistic chauvinism for Hispanic and Native American students (Ruiz, 1991).

Within the educational literature, the primary alternative to the mainstream is the radical or Left conception that collective and critical pedagogy can translate to social action. It recognizes that multicultural education must be pervasive, rather than supplemental, and that Eurocentric education cannot be changed by simply adding units or lessons here and there about African Americans, Native Americans, Mexicans, or women. Yet, this approach is equally problematic within the confines of inner-city schools because of its basic assumptions that such "reconstructive multiculturalism" can effect a political project within education such that an infusion of diversity and "celebration of difference" into the schools will connect to change in the greater society (Weiner, 1993).

In the next section, I examine this (reconstructionist) approach in more depth and suggest an alternative that connects inner city classrooms, critical pedagogy, and the community.

RECONSTRUCTIVE MULTICULTURALISM AND THE INNER CITY

The goals for reconstructive multiculturalism promote:

(1) the value of cultural diversity, (2) human rights and mutual respect; (3) knowledge of the historical realities of U.S. society, racism, sexism and poverty; (4) social justice; and (5) equity in the distribution of income. (Gollnick & Chinn, 1990, p. 272)

As Sleeter and Grant (1993) noted, this approach has also been termed *emancipatory pedagogy, transformative education, culturally responsive teaching, critical multiculturalism*, and other similar titles used by various authors to describe a socially reconstructive multiculturalist conceptualization. One major problem with this notion of multiculturalism is that it is still quintessentially mainstream liberal in that it speaks to the importance of a plural, integrated, and democratic society; but with this notion of diversity comes a transparent norm constructed by the dominant "host society" that ultimately values consensus and harmony at the expense of difference and the other (McLaren, 1992), which goes unquestioned by the reconstructionists;

Difference is still defined within liberal strands of meaning, which often translate into the smoothing over of supposedly irreconcilable and permanently divisive identity politics revolving around race, gender, ethnicity and nationality - This form of liberal multiculturalism is what the politics of assimilation is all about. (McLaren, 1991, p. 26)

Thus, the critical flaw in this educational motif is the reluctance to confront the issue of whiteness as a paradigmatic issue. Although an improvement over traditional or assimilationist multiculturalism, because it attempts to connect schooling to students' lived experience, knowledge, and voice, the reconstructive model tends to be reproductive by conceptualizing the political and pedagogical struggle over race, gender, ethnicity, and difference without connection to students' actual lives and communities. In fact, some critical multiculturalists are unsure of how much weight to even grant students' experience for fear of essentialization and reductiveness (McLaren, 1995). Critical multiculturalists, while acknowledging the slipperiness of identity, all too often frame discussions of inner-city schools and students within a constant of ethnicity. Recent anthropological research demonstrates that inner-city youth generally use other identity signifiers than ethnicity and that one of the assumptions made by "cultural workers" in urban communities that results in their irrelevance to inner-city adolescents is the reliance on and essentializing of ethnic identity (see K. Anijar, chapter 2 in this volume, regarding the imposition of ethnicity from the outside (Heath & McLaughlin, 1993):

These young people . . . see notions of "ethnic identity" as anachronistic symbols of another generation and political agenda. . . . For today's youth, ethnicity comprises not the primary identity but an additional layer of identity that youth can adopt . . . ethnicity signals only one part of a broader social identity. (p. 222)

This "radical" approach suggests that schools become the base for radical and liberatory changes in the greater society. Yet it constructs as many questions as answers: "How will the adoption of a multicultural curriculum and pedagogy reconstruct the dominant values of the school, of the social system?" "How will its project end ingrained structural and institutional racism, parochialism, and class stratification?" "If the reconstructionists' political project is for a more just and democratic society, how will a multicultural curriculum in its most liberatory sense produce such pervasive societal change, particularly one grounded in inner-city schools?" If not intended for urban schools, then it must be castigated as being as equally irrelevant as the other models. Unfortunately, these questions, in large part, go unanswered, thereby disconnecting the theory from praxis and replicating educational irrelevance, at least in urban educational settings.

One of the possible reasons that the radical literature has not connected multiculturalism to inner-city schools is because they are patently a poor base from which to reconstruct U.S. society. It is difficult to suggest with a straight face that the reconstruction of the dominant ideologies of this country will be derived of the ghettos and barrios. Multiculturalism still espouses a liberal notion of integration of others; that the goal of education is to construct a democratic society for all—a scheme of integration with somehow the dominant White, Euro-centered power structure becoming convinced to share or diminish its hegemony. The goal of integration is rarely questioned, except by the minorities, and their political voice continues to be silenced even by those who claim to be interested.

If applied to inner-city education, one problem with the radical project to change society by changing the practices of education is that it places the burden for the democratic nature of our society, or a change thereof, on the backs of those with the least power and means to effect that change (Weiner, 1993). The logic of the proposition seems problematic, albeit attractive. That teachers and students can emancipatorily effect systemic change within schools and the larger society solely through the inculcation of a critical pedagogy of liberatory emancipation begs the question of the derivation of the critical teachers, sympathetic administrators, lightening of the burden in urban schools of huge class sizes, insufficient or nonexistent resources and willingness of predominantly White, middle-class teachers to accept the inherent premises. It is difficult enough to convince middle-class minority teachers to allow students space to critique (Yeo, 1992) without considering the improbability of generating systemic social change from these sites. Given the research that suggests that exposure to multicultural education and/or urban school classrooms is less than successful in changing the ontological and ideological perspectives of preservice and current teachers (Sleeter, 1991), from whence will derive the impulses and creativity for such change? It is certainly doubtful that the state that is profoundly wedded to a technocratic, instrumental educational process and already racializes its distribution of educational resources will accede to assisting—nor can we realistically be any more hopeful as to some future critical multicultural impulse from teacher education. It is equally doubtful that a society that already demonizes the urban as a jungle (Haymes, 1995) and inner-city youth as alien Darkmen will be sympathetic to the ideological incorporation of an urban derived emancipatory multiculturalism.

If we hypothesize somehow isolating the minority student from the ghetto or barrio, and spend years inculcating the values inherent within this multiculturalist project, what can we speculate on his or her matriculation from high school? We have not ensured that more such students can enter college in this time of higher educational cutbacks, nor will we have changed the basic market system that he or she will enter, whose valuing of an educated minority is paradigmatically denigrative within the dynamics of racialized job ceilings. Without changing the environment to which inner-city students must return each afternoon, we have not accomplished a project of change, only raised a fallacious hope and increased the irrelevance of their educational system. To "make schooling for democracy a reality" means little in the face of grinding poverty, the pervasiveness of drug and alcohol abuse, and massive unemployment. Assuming that we can replace the present curriculum and pedagogical practices in inner-city schools with meaningful, relevant, and connected multicultural education, such that students become engaged in the classroom, we must still cope with the question of the project. If it is to prepare students with skills for jobs in the ghetto (which is problematic), we have accomplished little more than the "Basic Skills" approach. If the goal is the world of dominant White society, we have merely adopted the ends of the assimilationists. If it is to effect change in society as a whole, the implications are equally problematic.

A second problem with this "vision" is its potential hubris; Carlson (1989) noted that the urban schools are distrusted and resented by their communities because they are perceived as disconnected and isolated. Yet minority parents and students perceive education as a basis for their childrens' future. Even the poorest student will assert that it is important to "gets my education!" Black Americans have fought for the right to determine their education throughout their history, and if that future is seen as being successful within or without the urban scene, we are in danger of denigrating the very vision we claim to honor and "celebrate" by virtue of our privileged White radicalism. To disconnect their education from a culturally historical perception in favor of a critical social reconstruction that is not part of their vision runs the risk of being arrogantly disconnected and irrelevant to the communities about which we claim concern.

Within the meliorist strand of multiculturalism, schools are perceived as being agentic for the reconstruction of society. The assimilationist and the sensitivity trainer would remake ethnic minority students into White clones, which is impossible, and the results are there to see in the drop-out rates and school failures. The radical multiculturalist would remake ethnic minority students into the reconstructionists of society, without regard for whether they or their schools can form the political and economic power to do so, or even desire to do so; both camps are also basically integrationist, since neither takes into consideration whether a particular ethnic minority group wants community with others (Peller, 1992); it is simply presumed and is thereby silencing. It is this very assumption of a kind of righteousness of knowing and knowledge that dooms the Left reconstructionist, critical or not. The seeds of arrogance are the fruits of irrelevance. Until we can learn to work with, and perhaps even subordinate to, those we would help, we risk the same failures Welch (1990) critiqued in *A Feminist Ethic of Risk*.

This critique should not be interpreted to suggest that education, even within the borders of the inner city, is not or could not be important, nor that multiculturalism would not be an effective vehicle for a more limited and/or localized vision of change. Instead of the panacea for all ills, a multiculturalized curriculum and pedagogy that recognizes, interrogates, and affirms the voices and experiences of these students and their communities could play a significant role in revitalizing the energies of the citizens of these communities.

The problem lies with both ends of the multicultural spectrum presuming the ability of schools to change broader, White-dominated society. If it is the urban environment to which most of our inner-city students must return, then schools must target their endeavors to assisting students with that life. Education should be viewed with less importance for its social change potentiality and more for its own experiences. For example, it is questionable what an eighth-grade Black kid from Watts is ever going to do with a knowledge of geology or English literature, but we can convey a sense of Black culture and history, of how and what being Black in America means, instead of attempting to remake him or her White or burdening with the responsibility to change the totality of society. We should be helping that student to understand the experiences he or she copes with daily, including within school. It becomes vital to convey how historically communities have created their own spaces and economies through collective questioning of dominant cultural ideologies and practices.

In so far as the larger society is concerned, we should help students understand its ideology, racism, genderism, and classism, and the history of social change, such that they can understand the power of coalitions, consensus, and structured confrontations with dominant groups; existentially something inner-city youth already know through the nuances of lives spent compromising with street demands. Rather than tasking them with changing society in toto, I suggest that schools would be more efficacious helping students learn how to (re)construct their communities while interacting with those of others.

The focus needs to be on the linkage between school and community, for change of both. The lessons of cooperation, constructive confrontation, realization of the factors of one's social and cultural history, and the coming to understand the structures of power within the greater society could be the capital for connecting the schools to the communities for the betterment of both. Reconstructive multiculturalism would be well advised to view integration as less of a goal than community engagement, community empowerment as the purpose of education rather than some wider national cultural revival.

To task schools with relevancy for their own clientele seems both more meaningful and hopeful than the implication that they should be responsible for the reconstruction of a White society to which they are virtually invisible and irrelevant. This is what minority writers mean when they speak about;

> ... a pedagogy that reinforces intra-ethnic solidarity and pride without promoting inter-ethnic antagonisms . . . while at the same time providing strategies for coalitions with other groups with similar needs and interests. (Lomotey, 1990, p. 78)

CONCLUSION

This chapter has been intended to connect the actualities of urban environments and inner-city schools with a much touted educational practice—multiculturalism—and to suggest that as well-meaning as each of its interpretations sound, they suffer from flawed understandings as to an inner-city clientele. These run from the assimilationist denial of the special identities of students and their cultures and languages to the reconstructionists' vision of societal re-creation arising from education. In simple terms, all interpretations of multiculturalism as currently propounded suffer from irrelevancy as to the nature of education and community as found in America's ghettos and barrios, because each fails to connect the two.

Those multiculturalisms currently attempted in inner-city schools, giving too little credence to the potentials of education, founder in the face of student and community rejection and distrust. The radical notions, however, presume too much power to the disenfranchised of the inner cities. In all fairness, the radicals do not attempt generally to connect multicultural education to inner-city schools, perhaps for that very reason, but thereby condemn by denial.

Yet, as discussed, I believe that a critical pedagogy of multiculturalism has the potential to transform the curriculum and pedagogical practices of inner city schools for the betterment of both the schools and their communities. This belief is derived from the conviction that currently inner city schools are reflective of the communities in which they lie and constitute a breeding ground for continued frustration, anger and self and communal violence. Current educational paradigms merely fuel its continued propagation; in order to change the perceptions and involvement of students and community, we must change what it is that these schools do.

Inner-city education in and of itself cannot produce more funds or resources, but it can perform more relevantly with what it has. To do that requires a change of the goals, methods, and concerns of these schools, as well as their institutionalized hierarchy that is often possible (if not realized) through the local community. One potential paradigm for that change is multiculturalism of a more democratic and connected format.

This brings us back to where we began with the inner-city school, and Fine's (1991) typification of the place of urban schools within our social system, which bears quoting at length:

> Public schools have historically managed social contradictions by sorting and tossing bodies of students, and by obscuring evidence of those discarded. But, the bodies of those discarded in the 1990s are not represented as the products of urban decay, but framed instead as the causes of crumbling urban economies, crime, inadequate housing, unemployment, drug abuse and racial/class discrimination . . . they document vividly why *educators must pursue the restructuring of public schools.* (p. 229)

Fine captured the essence of the inner city and its educational institutions; they are about discarded bodies and the triaging of society. If we truly desire to effect a change for the better in these conditions, then business as usual in ghetto schools must cease, and attempts framed to engage students, staff, and communities in different operative connections. What we have been doing simply does not work for the majority of inner-city youths or adults, we need to accept that as Black, Native and Hispanic Americans already have, and alter the way we look at education in the inner city. This may well mean reinterpreting the way we perceive both the people and the institutions of our urban centers and educating others similarly:

> We have to change our own mind . . . We've got to change our minds about each other. We have to see each other with new eyes. (hooks, citing Malcolm X, 1992, p. 9)

REFERENCES

Berry, G., & Asamen, J. (1989). *Black students.* Newbury Park, CA: Sage.
Boateng, F. (1990). Combating deculturalization of the African American child in the public school: A multicultural approach. In K. Lomotey (Ed.),

Going to school: The African American experience (pp. 73-84). Albany: State University of New York Press.

Carlson, D. (1989). Managing the urban school crisis: Recent trends in curricular reform. *Journal of Education, 171*(3).

Comer, J., & Haynes, N. (1990). Helping Black children succeed: The significance of some social factors. In K. Lomotey (Ed.), *Going to school: The African American experience*. Albany: State University of New York Press.

Coontz, S. (1995, March). The American family and the nostalgia trap. *Phi Delta Kappan*, pp. K1-K20.

Fine, M. (1991). *Framing drop-outs*. Albany: State University of New York Press.

Fordham, S. (1988). Racelessness as a factor in Black students' school success. *Harvard Educational Review, 58*(1).

Fordham, S., & Ogbu, J. (1986). Black students' school success: Coping with the "burden of acting white." *Urban Review, 18*(3), 176-206.

Frost, J., & Hawkes, G. (1970). *The disadvantaged child*. Boston: Houghton Mifflin.

Giroux, H. (1992). *Border crossings: Cultural workers and the politics of education*. New York: Routledge, Chapman & Hall.

Glasgow, D. (1980). *The black underclass*. San Francisco: Jossey-Bass.

Gollnick, D., & Chinn, P. (1990). *Multicultural education in a pluralistic society* (3rd ed.). New York: MacMillan.

Haymes, S. (1995). *Race, culture and the city: A pedagogy for black urban struggle*. Albany: State University of New York Press.

Heath, S., & McLaughlin, M. (Ed.). (1993). *Identity & inner-city youth: Beyond ethnicity and gender*. New York: Teachers College Press.

Hessong, R., & Weeks, T. (1991). *Introduction to the foundations of education* (2nd ed.). New York: Prentice Hall.

hooks, b., & West, C. (1991). *Breaking bread: Insurgent black intellectual life*. Boston: South End Press.

hooks, b. (1992). *Black looks: Race and representation*. Boston: South End Press.

Kozol, J. (1991). *Savage inequalities: Children in America's schools*. New York: Crown.

Lomotey, K. (Ed.). (1990). *Going to school: The African American experience*. Albany: State University of new York Press.

Macedo, D. (1995). Literacy for stupification: The pedagogy of the big lies. In C. Sleeter & P. McLaren (Eds.), *Multicultural education, critical pedagogy, and the politics of difference* (pp. 71-104). Albany: State University of New York Press

Marable, M. (1983). *How capitalism underdeveloped black America*. Boston: South End Press.

164   Yeo

Marable, M. (1992). *The crisis of color and democracy.* Monroe, ME: Common Courage Press.
Massey, D., & Denton, N. (1993). *American apartheid: Segregation and the making of the underclass.* Cambridge, MA: Harvard University Press.
McCarthy, C. (1992). *Race and curriculum: Social inequality and the theories and politics of difference in contemporary research on schooling.* Washington, DC: Falmer Press.
McLaren, P. (1989). *Life in schools.* New York: Longman.
McLaren, P. (1991). Critical pedagogy, multiculturalism, and the politics of risk and resistance: A reply to Kelly and Portelli. *Journal of Education, 173*(3), 29-59.
McLaren, P. (1995). White terror and oppositional agency: Towards a critical multiculturalism. In C. Sleeter & P. McLaren (Eds.), *Multicultural education, critical pedagogy, and the politics of difference* (pp. 33-70). Albany: State University of New York Press.
Miller, H., & Woock, R. (1970). *Social foundations of urban education.* Hinsdale, IL: Dryden.
Nieto, S. (1992). *Affirming diversity: The sociopolitical context of multicultural education.* New York: Longman Publishing.
Ogbu, J. (1988a). Class stratification, racial stratification and schooling. In L. Weis (Ed.), *Race, class and schooling* (pp. 163-182). New York: State University of New York Press.
Ogbu, J.U. (1988b, May). *Minority youth's school success.* Address presented at the Conference Advancing Effective Teaching for At-Risk Youth, Johns Hopkins University, Baltimore.
Ogbu, J. (1990). Literacy and schooling in subordinate cultures: The case of Black Americans. In K. Lomotey (Ed.), *Going to school: The African American experience* (pp. 113-134). Albany: State University of New York Press.
Omi, M., & Winant, H. (1986). *Racial formation in the United States.* New York: Routledge & Kegan Paul.
Peller, G. (1992). Race against integration. *Tikkun, 6*(1).
Ruiz, R. (1991). The empowerment of language minority students. In C. Sleeter (Ed.), *Empowerment through multicultural education* (pp. 217-228). Albany: State University of New York Press.
Sleeter, C. (1989) Multicultural education as a form of resistance to oppression. *Journal of Education, 171*(3).
Sleeter, C. (Ed.). (1991). *Empowerment through multicultural education.* Albany: State University of New York Press.
Sleeter, C., & Grant, C. (1987). An analysis of multicultural education in the United States. *Harvard Educational Review, 57*(4).
Sleeter, C., & Grant, C. (1989). *Turning on learning: Five approaches for multicultural teaching plans for race, class, gender & disability.* New York: Merrill-MacMillan.

Sleeter, C., & Grant, C. (1993). *Making choices for multicultural education* (2nd ed.). New York: Merrill.

Tabb, W. (1983). *The political economy of the black ghetto.* New York: W.W. Norton.

Weiner, L. (1993). *Preparing teachers for urban schools: Lessons from thirty years of school reform.* New York: Teachers College Press.

Weis, L. (1988). *Class, race, & gender in American education.* Albany: State University of New York Press.

Welch, S. (1990). *A feminist ethic of risk.* Minneapolis, MN: Fortress Press.

Wilson, W. (1987). *The truly disadvantaged.* Chicago: University of Chicago Press.

Yeo, F. (1992, August). The inner-city school: A conflict in rhetoric. *Critical Pedagogy Networker, 5*(3).

Yeo, F. (1995). Conflicts of difference in an inner city school: Experiencing border crossings in the ghetto. In B. Kanpol & P. McLaren (Eds.), *Critical multiculturalism: Uncommon voices in a common struggle* (pp. 197-215). Westport, CT: Bergin & Garvey.

Yeo, F. (1996). *Inner city schools, Multiculturalism and teacher education: The search for new connections.* New York: Garland.

9

Urban People's Knowledge and Voice: A Challenge to the Hegemony of Learning Settings and Situations

Daniele Flannery
Pennsylvania State University, Harrisburg

Urban areas generally receive little attention from the press, elected officials, or policymakers (Heath & McLaughlin, 1993) unless civil disturbances (e.g., Los Angeles), drug wars, or youth gangs temporarily move public concern to focus on them. However, such attention is fleeting. When attention is directed to an urban area it is usually focused on the future generation (Health & McLaughlin, 1993)—on the education of urban youth in schools, as if urban youth existed in a vacuum from the adult world and the community at large, and as if schools were the only place where urban youth engage in learning. Extant urban education literature mirrors this same faulty focus. It typically studies children who live in urban areas and focuses on the elementary and secondary schools, implying that it is only within these settings that learning occurs. This, despite the admonition by the Carnegie Council on Adolescent Development (1992) that educators need to give special attention to out-of-school experiences of young people.

Missing either in the sporadic public concern or in the urban education literature is concern about the learning of the adult population in urban areas. What little writing about adults does occur, is primarily about young adults, most of whom have just left adolescence. This literature usually focuses on adolescent and/or adult transitions to employment (Anisef & Axelrod, 1993), literacy education (Fitzsimmons, 1991), or basic urban worker education programs

(Perin & Greenberg, 1994). In each case, the notion of education is limited to more formalized settings, usually as an adjunct to schools, and limits its concerns to basic educational and/or vocational skills.

As an adult educator concerned with the teaching–learning exchanges of adults, I argue that not only has the learning of urban adults been ignored (an exception being the historical studies in Ravitch & Goodenow, 1981), but the settings for that learning have been reduced to those legitimized and controlled by the larger society (i.e., institutional settings). I argue here that urban education is much more extensive than either youth education or education in formal school settings, and in order to understand urban communities, we must begin to take into account the informal educational sites that engage both urban adults and adolescents. Although there is an increasing number of mainstream and left research accounts of the education, of youth, the education of urban adults is a missing area of concern within educational research. This is equally true for those whose research approach is quantitative, as well as ethnographic.

In any milieu, adults have a right to success—economic, social, personal, and political. Adults continue to learn throughout their lifetimes, and have a right to continual learning and education. Adult education is part of the process by which health information, housing rights, employment training and updating, social service offerings, community development, and political awareness are obtained, and public opinion formed. Adults are a large part of any community's members, and the extended or immediate family members among whom the children live, and from whom they learn how to "make it" in the community, as well as on the "street." In urban areas in particular, "levels of linguistic and cultural diversity, the visibility of extreme poverty, the conflicts evident in daily transactions" (Coulby, Jones, & Harris, 1992, p. 4) exist. Urban adults often live with the same conditions as urban youth. They face inferior housing, questionable protective services, unpredictable jobs and sporadic human services, and generally poor health. So how do they engage in learning to survive and live?

Persons concerned with the learning of adults and children must begin to acknowledge that learning takes place in formal, nonformal, and informal ways (Coombs, 1973) with most adult learning taking place outside of formal educational settings. Much adult learning takes place in nonformal learning settings (Coombs, 1973). In nonformal settings, learning is planned for, but learning is not the primary purpose of the agency or group or even of the interactions between providers and community members. Museums, labor unions, state unemployment offices, a campaign for AIDS awareness at the local Spanish community center, medical clinics, religious education, educational efforts by the library mobile, are examples of nonformal learning sites. Most adult learning is informal learning—in natural or accidental learning settings (Coombs, 1973), such as getting information from a neighbor, learning something from a TV show or during a Kwaanza celebration. Much of it is also bound up in culturally determined exchanges between persons of different generations.

Although much "adult education" may be informed through personal contacts and the exchange of experimental and generational information, a significant amount of adult learning occurs through culturally determined adaptation to institutional contacts and programs.

The area of study of urban adult learners and of various kinds of learning provides vast, yet untapped, opportunities for the study of urban education that this chapter argues is of vital importance to both the understanding of learning in urban communities and enhancing the lives of its citizens.

CHAPTER PURPOSE

The general purpose of this chapter is to share one study that focused on adult teaching–learning in an urban setting, specifically regarding health education. The meaning of health care was left open so the narratives that follow demonstrate the Puerto Rican women's self-understanding of the education (informal and nonformal) they received from doctors, nurses, or health educators. Health provided an apt context for the study because health-related issues affect all persons, regardless of class, race, ethnicity, age, and so forth, and because health-related learning in urban areas tends to occur in informal, nonformal, and formal settings. Additionally, health issues (e.g., HIV, Aids, teen pregnancy, drug use) are currently at the forefront of urban health agendas, thereby facilitating contact with possible research subjects. In particular, because urban areas are made up of minicommunities, each with their own culture, and because learning is "intimately related" to the culture in which the learner lives (Jarvis, 1987), this chapter focuses on an urban community of Puerto Rican adults.

Puerto Ricans comprise the largest numbers of Latino/as the Northeastern United States (Pennsylvania Governor's Advisory Commission on Latino Affairs, 1991). The largest percentage of Puerto Ricans outside of New York live in the Pennsylvania urban city in which this study took place. Furthermore, Puerto Ricans have the worst health status of all Latino groups (Schur, Bernstein, & Berk, 1987) suffering from alcoholism and alcohol-related liver disease, diseases of the lungs, stomach cancer, and HIV disease and Aids. Women's voices were gathered as the primary narrative, because as primary caregivers of family members (Lotito, 1988), Puerto Rican women tend to possess greater knowledge about health information than do Puerto Rican men, and women make the most contributions to the health needs of their families (Barrow, 1982). Importantly, too, the health status of Puerto Rican women is compromised more often than that of men because of health problems of a reproductive nature (Novello, 1991). Puerto Rican women experience higher birthrates than the general population and have high numbers of premarital births, with 21% of all births to Puerto Rican women being to adolescents (Giminez, 1989). The infant mortality rate for Puerto Ricans is 8.6%, the highest among Latino groups (Hutchins & Walch, 1989). Despite these figures, Puerto Rican women receive the least amount of prenatal care of all Latino groups, and only 12% of Latino women receive prenatal care at all as compared to 57% of Euro-American women (De La Rosa, 1989).

The health care system itself presents serious problems for Puerto Ricans. These include lack of private health insurance (Novello, 1991), lack of quality health care (Radecki & Bernstein, 1989), lack of consideration of ethnic identity factors (Zambrana, 1991), and importantly, lack of emphasis on transmission of health information (Kaluzny, 1991) or for our purpose, what we might term health education. Problematically, a prevalent attitude among health care educators is that Latino individuals are not interested in health information (Giachello, 1985). Non-compliant is the term frequently used by many in the health system toward those persons who do not appear to carry out the wishes of that system. This labeling is particularly used to describe minority women, such as the subjects here. In this sense, it mirrors the attitudes of many teachers and school administrators toward urban parents (Grant, 1995; Ogbu, 1990).

Most urban education studies, however conscientious, have been through the lens of the outsider. Critical theorists in education have stressed the importance of giving people voice (McLaren, 1989), but, however much the idea has been advocated to give voice to people and to their own text, all too often in the case of urban (and in particular, urban women), it has been omitted. The concept of voice is integrally related to women's empowerment and emancipation. One's voice is one's knowledge, the meanings one makes of life (Gilligan, 1982; Giroux, 1988; Lutrell, 1989; McLaren, 1989), one's values and ideologies, the history and experiences of life (Belenky, Clinchy, Goldberger, & Tarule, 1986; McLaren, 1989). One's voice is used to "interpret and articulate experience" (McLaren, 1989, p. 230) and underlies decision making. Voice is the means through which people can interact with others, make themselves "heard" (Belenky et al., 1986), and be "active participants in the world" (McLaren, 1989). However, not all individuals or groups are given voice. In our society, to be given voice is to be acknowledged and legitimized within relationships of power, to be recognized as existing, and to be valued as having a unique perspective to offer to the world, despite one's different social status. Ironically, what we in urban education must come to live with and acknowledge is that because the dominant society does not deign to give voice does not mean that people's voices do not exist. On the contrary, all people have voice and knowledge, and whether they choose to share their community knowledge or decide to ignore the voice of those in power in the society is a matter of their choice. This, as is seen here, is nowhere more true than the understandings and reactions of Puerto Rican women to health care information and education.

This chapter fills in what is missing, it allows the "voice" of the others (the urban Puerto Rican women) as "insiders," to share with us, the "outsiders" their voice, their knowledge, their text, their values, and in what manner and ways education–learning is credible to them. The concept of *education–learning* used in this chapter is "premised on the assumption that education is a kind of exchange between people: the process by which knowledge, skills, attitudes, values, and beliefs are passed back and forth from individual to individual and from group to group" (Lagemann, 1981, p. 141). While acknowledging that education–learning occurs in formal, nonformal, and informal ways and settings, I have chosen to investigate the primarily informal education the interviewees experience as to health information exchanges and the varying ways it is legitimated, and how that information and its sources are interpreted. The specific purpose of this chapter then is to give voice to Puerto Rican Women living in an urban area to learn about their teaching and learning exchanges with regard to areas of health knowledge, information, and learning. Through this study, as we gain insight into these adult women's learning, we may also gain questions to ask about the learning of adults of both genders as well as of urban Puerto Rican children's learning.

PUERTO RICAN WOMEN PARTICIPANTS

The women who participated specifically identified themselves as being Puerto Rican, able to speak English, and as adults. The women's definitions of what constitutes a female adult in the Puerto Rican community was often denoted in their discussions by such remarks as "when she marries," "when she proves herself," "when she has a baby" (teenager or not, married or not). Culturally, there are also gender issues with regard to this determination that might be referenced as positive as to women, but problematic as to males. Although the woman is acknowledged as an adult by the community, her status is simultaneously diminished by Puerto Rican males "who seek to marry a virgin."

A community gatekeeper made the initial contacts with the first three women. Gatekeepers are those persons empowered by the community to decide who is trustworthy enough to have access to the community (Goetz & LeCompte, 1984). Successive participants were referred by previous participants. Ultimately, 21 women were willing to participate in the research.

Women's stories were collected in face-to-face interviews, using an audiotape. Because the purpose of this study was to allow the Puerto Rican women to describe their values, knowledge, and teaching–learning exchanges with regard to their experiences of health knowledge, information, and learning, the opening broad guide questions included: "Tell me the most important things you know about your health" "Where do you find out information about health?" "To whom do you listen for health suggestions?" "What kinds of health-related questions do you have?"; "Tell me about the clinic where you get health services." Other questions were developed during interviews to encourage participants to relate their unique personal experiences. For example, if a woman said that her mother taught her everything about home remedies, the investigator would further explore this by asking her to describe a situation in which this occurred.

The interviews took place at the time and place of convenience to the participants, primarily in small homes, apartments, or public housing facilities. All were decorated with Puerto Rican memorabilia and photographs of children and other family members, and Spanish music radio was on in many of the homes. All of the women offered the interviewer liquid refreshment during the interview. Children, if present, were instructed by the women to go and play or to be quiet. The length of each interview was 1 to 2 hours. The women hugged and kissed the interviewer when she left the home. The importance of the Puerto Rican environment for the interviews, the gracious offering of refreshments, the personal sharing and hug at the end of the interview are lived examples of important cultural characteristics of warmth and hospitality talked about by the Puerto Rican women during the interviews as essential to Puerto Rican identity and as necessary to learning environments and situations. This last is crucial in constructing participants' reactions to and interpretations of their medical experiences, as well as their receptivity to any informational exchange. The trustworthiness of this study was ensured through constant checks with participants, supported by visits to the clinics, health resources, and Botanicas (shops providing healing herbs) mentioned by the participants.

All of the women's narratives were embedded in the context of what it is to be Puerto Rican, a Puerto Rican woman, and how these influence Puerto Rican women's health-related learning. As the women spoke they shared their most important Puerto Rican values. Integrally connected to these values, three learning themes emerged: traditional knowledge, contextual knowledge, and trust knowledge. It must be noted that throughout this chapter health-related learning may be channeled through informal, nonformal, and formal learning settings. In the narratives, women cite exchanges between friends, folk-learning handed down through generations, visits to clinics with information by nurses aids, nurse educators, or doctors, billboards, and classes such as Lamaze.

IDENTITY AND VALUES

Objective and subjective components of being Puerto Rican appeared in all conversations: the use of the Spanish language, connections with family and communal roots, the placing of social emphasis on personal friendliness, communication patterns, the importance of family, and women's caregiver activities. Examples of this were previously noted as in the offering of drink and a concern for the interviewer's comfort. A vital pride in Puerto Rican identity and its connection with the self and with the everyday was woven throughout the narratives.

Puerto Rican identity is integral to us and a valuable component of our identity.

It's part of my tree . . . part of who I am. It's a base where I start, a foundation.

You don't want to forget where you're from and your roots and everything. And to me, you know, those are my roots and I don't want to forget that. That's very important to me.

The women painted a collage of important Puerto Rican identity facets, including hospitality, the Spanish language, communication value, and the emphasis on family. One of the women's most cherished values is the hospitality shown to others, referred to by one participant as representing culturally "our warmth and welcoming."

I feel very, very proud because, maybe our culture . . . you know, most people that I know, they find something nice in us.

Our way to be—it's like we're friendly, among us. Even though (we) might be shy, most of the people they are like that, friendly, generous, we have that in our treatment.

In the main, Puerto Rican culture is an oral culture built around certain communication values. First, the use of the Spanish language is valued, and being articulate in Spanish is often a source of pride.

I'm very proud of my language. I mean, Spanish language is very rich. . . You know, we have a word for every single thing . . . not like the American language, the English language.

Next, as an oral culture where word of mouth is important, there are established common networking techniques where information is spread among family and friends.

We share that stuff. It's crazy, but we're Spanish people. All my friends are Spanish . . . I tell them stuff, like they know already, because I guess it's a tradition of Spanish people.

We find out that someone has something, that this person is sick by word of mouth . . . knowing how everybody's doing. Everybody's health...that's how we find out how everybody's doing, by word of mouth.

Confidentiality of oral communication is important to Puerto Ricans, and many times information is discussed in a round-about way so the person being spoken about is not exposed, or so the actual topic to be discussed is couched in the hospitality expected of all exchanges.

> Like my mother, when she calls her mother, she doesn't call directly to tell her that she's sick; just to say hi and stuff. In the conversation, she will say, "Oh, I'm not feeling better" and then she goes what is she taking and all this stuff. So that's basically when she says, "Well, do this. You'll feel better."

Family values and family closeness are a most essential part of being Puerto Rican. The Puerto Rican family is a large network of people that includes family of origin, immediate family, extended family, and close friends. Within the concept of the extended family exists relationships that, although not actually of a blood relation, are considered within the boundaries of family. There is an understanding of "family" among Puerto Ricans similar to the "fictive kinship" concept among African Americans about which Fordham (1988) wrote.

> When you say family, I always think of the whole, the cousins, aunts, uncles, and everybody else.

> Family closeness is paramount to us in all matters. Family is a source of support and also a vital source of information during times of crisis.

> Family is very close and we stick very close, even your aunts, uncles, and we have this big family gathering all the time. And to me, family is very important and we are close to our families.

> It's important, it's good. Like a tragedy happens it's good to have family around. They give you a lot of support. It's better having people around than being lonely. So it's real important to me.

> If I think it's a serious illness, I call my aunt and ask for her advice. That's my first choice, she'll give me the advice or what she thinks. I rather hear it from her than from a piece of paper.

In the Puerto Rican culture, women have the responsibility of the bulk of caregiving tasks within the family network. Among those tasks are those related to health. In fact, Puerto Rican women have been referred to as the diagnosticians (Harwood, 1981) and managers of the health care of significant others (Weisman, 1987).

My mother, she's important. I think that for the emotional role, she is the most important in the family.

My mother always took care of us . . . between my husband and I, when he gets sick, I very much take care of him and when I get sick, I'm still up and about trying to do whatever I can. And it's not because he demands that of me, but just because I feel that that's what I am supposed to do. I know that, but I still do it. And that's what I've seen all my life, also.

HEALTH-RELATED LEARNING

The women's voices about their health-related learning were strong and unified. They, without naming it as such, challenged the hegemony so prevalent in health-related institutions, so practiced by doctors, nurses, health educators, and others involved in formal, nonformal, or even informal health education. They were clear that their Puerto Rican values, knowledge, history, and community were their first and primary bases for constructing their learning and for new learning experiences. They determine the rules of discourse. As I noted earlier, this culturally derived learning is expressed in three themes: traditional, contextual, and trust knowledge.

Traditional Knowledge

Puerto Rican beliefs come first in any health-related learning. As in any culture, the Puerto Rican community has a long tradition of health beliefs, remedies, and ceremonies for a return to health. As noted earlier, the role and power of health caretaker is clearly a gendered one, passed down through generations of women, and accepted as such in the Puerto Rican community.

We have our own traditions, beliefs and remedies for our health.

To begin with, it is the women who have the responsibility of taking care of the sick.

Sources for our health well-being include family members, primarily women, such as our grandmothers, mothers, sisters, and other female relatives and friends.

I don't think that they (doctors) are really interested in what people use as far as home remedies or any medicinal things within the home. I don't think it matters to them. They're the authority and they tell you what to use.

Many, if not most of these sources, verbally relay information about health that assists the women in caring for family members through self-care activities in the home. Self-care activities include: ethnic-specific home remedies, word of mouth about treatments, and over-the-counter medications that are known in the community to work. Some of these include chicken soup and teas made from boiling certain leaves, roots, or other substances.

> My mother learned (home remedies) from her mother and eventually I'm learning from my mother. It's a chain. They learn from their mothers.

> We do it because it's a tradition . . . they're traditional things passed down . . . if it's traditionally passed down and your mom said it works, it works!

Importantly, information about a treatment received via word of mouth from an expert family source, such as a grandmother, mother, or sister is considered highly valid, genuine, and trusted information. As is discussed further in the third learning theme, more validity is given to the Puerto Rican women's voices in health issues than to physicians, clinics, and so forth.

> I think, like the doctors—they study and study and study, so what they say could be true, but I always think somebody that has gone through the experience and knows her true feelings and it's true. My aunt, she has the age and she's been through a lot of experiences . . . I would rather ask her.

Contextual Knowledge

Puerto Rican cultural values, mentioned earlier as important to Puerto Rican ethnic identity, must be integrally present in the health-related learning setting in order for the Puerto Rican women to choose to learn or to value the information that they receive.

> That comes in the way that they (doctors) treat you. If they treat you with confidentiality and in a good manner and good attention in what you are telling them. So that helps a lot to open your mind and to express everything that you have, that will help.

The use of the Spanish language was emphasized as a mechanism by which to promote learning.

> I think if you have a doctor that sits with a Puerto Rican woman and explains everything very clearly, in Spanish if need be, you know, and they feel comfortable with the person, they'll come back.

It is a relief when you see somebody that speaks Spanish in these places, of yes, it is, because you feel like there's one of your people there. As long as they are Hispanics you feel more comfortable. Because you know you're going to get better service. Because of the language.

A lot of Puerto Rican women's health care and information was received via interpreter. Even if they wanted to ask questions, they did not speak the language. For some even though they know how to speak English, they feel more comfortable when they find a Hispanic place for them to go. Participants emphasized that time and explanations enhance learning situations.

He (doctor) was very, very nice with me and he also explain everything . . . the way that he was explaining to me was so nice and he also draw some pictures and he started showing me pictures and explaining this way and that and this is what is going on.

They would sit down and they would speak with you on how well you're doing. They used to sit down with you, "Are you doing OK?" They would explain all that to you and they would take the time with you in the room.

The women talked at length about the importance of personal warmth, friendliness, and hospitality that increased opportunities for learning in health care settings.

It's a small-town kind of idea, where the doctor knew the whole family and could talk about anything that was happening in the family. Puerto Ricans are still very much small town. That's the type of lifestyle they feel most comfortable with. If you have a doctor that can relate to that, make them feel comfortable in the office, they'll come back.

I met a nurse at the clinic which, oh, she was so good to me. When I came here that I didn't know what to do, where to go, and I called this place and she was helping me so much and she was giving me comfort and she is very special. A very, very good person. She was leading me to places where I could go and get some more help if I needed it. She was the key for me. That's why I didn't feel ashamed or I didn't feel intimidated of going. Because I knew that she was there and would do what was good for me.

They also gave examples of contextual barriers to learning.

We don't understand those medical terms. I feel dumb. Because, you know the doctor or nurse'll be talking and you don't know if they're thinking, are you dumb or something. You don't know. So when they use those medical terms, like some of us are afraid to ask, well, "What do you mean?" Times

I'll just say, "yeah, I understand—and I don't understand one word, but when I leave the office it's like, I don't know. Do they think I'm dumb?

A final contextual aspect had to do with the space/place at large, the feeling of the setting.

(Re: community educators:) There couldn't be a language barrier there. They'd have to be able to sit down and speak to them in their own language. They'd have to understand the family type of idea. You know, it would be the type of place where anybody in the family could go and maybe that educator knew everyone in the family. "How's your Uncle John" and "How's your cousin, or whatever, that kind of thing. It makes a Puerto Rican feel right at home and this person knows a lot of their family. Bringing the conversation down to their home level instead of it being just on a health level.

Just comfortable, . . . like put some toys for the kids and stuff.

Homey, comfortable couches. It would look like a home, like anybody's home. People would dress in regular clothes.

. . . Spanish music and Spanish pictures and Spanish colors.

Trust Knowledge

The presence of Puerto Rican cultural values influence the levels of trust in the health-providing source. Some sources are trusted; others are not. People and sources are trusted in different degrees with trusted sources ranging from most trusted to least trusted. Puerto Rican people who exemplify Puerto Rican values are the most trusted.

Within our own culture, certain people may be more trusted than others depending on their status in the culture. For example, women have been the keepers of the health traditions and remedies. Their status as trusted on health issues will be higher than men's status.

We give trust to our local Spanish radio station, to Spanish churches and to our neighbors.

After Puerto Ricans, non-Puerto Rican people or contexts (e.g., clinics, schools) are trustworthy and reliable if they exemplify Puerto Rican values. These include experiences with some health care providers, such as nurses and physicians, as well as non-Puerto Rican friends.

So this doctor, even when he sees us on the street, you know, "Hi, how are you doing?" He's not necessarily involved in the Hispanic community. I've never seen him in the Hispanic community, but he knows this family very well. And this doctor could make the family comfortable enough with him so that the whole family came and he is their family doctor. He doesn't speak Spanish, but somehow he has made the family feel welcome in his practice which is very important to us as Puerto Ricans.

There are people and learning settings who are not trusted. Puerto Ricans, even family members may have lost the Puerto Rican women's trust because they have gone against Puerto Rican values. This can happen, for example, when mothers, fathers, and other Puerto Rican caregivers abandon children, or when alcoholism, drug abuse, or other social problems result in a lack of dependence on people for nurturance and care, or for reliable health information.

I hardly ever saw her (mother) . . . she was always in the streets . . . because of me the house was clean, because of me I did everything and I think I never had anybody to help me. She was not there for me.

She (mother) wanted to be up and down the streets and parties and everything . . . she had a teenage daughter that she should be asking if I needed help. Not a friend or an aunt, just her, and I never had her with me.

Health care settings, educators, doctors, and nurses who do not demonstrate Puerto Rican values (i.e., "they aren't friendly, don't take time to ask about your family . . . are not hospitable and warm"), are not trusted as sources of knowledge, and therefore, not a source of learning.

Don't look down at me, make me comfortable . . . and you can do any diagnosis and we might come to you that one time, but we may not come back again. If I don't feel welcome, there's no way I'm coming back. That's very important.

There's some kind of lack of feeling like they (Puerto Rican women) belong. You're talking about people who love to just, they're very family-oriented, they're very, you know, you just get down to earth with them and you just talk at their level and I don't know that doctors do that all the time.

I just find them (health care providers) to be ignorant, that's all. It's like they're there to help you in one way. And they're not. The sooner I get everybody out of the office, the sooner I can go home. I don't like that.

You go in, you sit for 2 hours in there and then you're out in 5 minutes. And I wasn't any more satisfied when I went in than I was when I came out. You don't feel any ease at all, at all.

There is no Spanish-speaking person. And I told them, I think that is horrible because I'll tell you what; When my mom was in there, the majority were Puerto Rican people . . . and it's a shame that there isn't any Spanish-speaking people in there to help out. It really is.

There are also sources and people who begin as neutral with regard to trust. If Puerto Rican women do not get the health information they are looking for, they find creative ways to obtain it. Ways that are more self-directed in nature. These activities include using resources such as Spanish radio, the Spanish center, books, magazines, television programs, health-related books, supermarket pamphlets, and women's magazines. The sources are trusted as long as they do not go against Puerto Rican traditional knowledge or values.

I see a lot of it (health information) on TV and you hear from radios, you hear from TVs, so I just kind of comprehend off of that.

A lot of people that don't know English listen to a Spanish TV station, cause sometimes they give a medical.

There's a Spanish radio station. Everybody finds any information you want to hear on it . . . Spanish people listen to that radio station a lot. Any information you want, that is given there, they will all know about it.

A lot of people here can't read; they're illiterate. They listen to radio and TV for health information.

I think *McCall's* magazine—they will have a section on health and I like to read.

In summary, what we have learned from this brief consideration of one group of urban peoples, a group of urban Puerto Rican women, is first that they have a set of ethnic values that are the core of their lives. They have their own historically rich knowledge base with regard to health-related learning and they have an established hierarchy of trust in would-be teachers based again on Puerto Rican values. Second, these Puerto Rican women resist the dominant health-related learning efforts if they are treated as voiceless. Third, learning is purposefully rejected by these Puerto Rican women when their knowledge is ignored, when the physical and emotional environment in health care settings, the delivery of health information, and the content of health information is contrary to their ethnic values and priorities, and when they cannot trust the knowl-edge-sharers because they do not embody the Puerto Rican values the women cherish.

In point of fact, the health care system fails these women because, in addition to slim health resources, it ignores their voice, their knowledge, and the knowledge of previous generations; it insults them by offending their cultural values and imposing its own culture on them (Westburg, 1989). The health community is mystified by the increasing spread of disease (e.g., AIDS) in the Puerto Rican community, despite its efforts. It arrogantly continues labeling the community as *non-compliant*. What health care system educators and practi-tioners fail to realize is that the community is very committed to its own health traditions and values. Once health lessens its own arrogance and engages in the culture of the people it is to serve, it will find this group of Puerto Rican women willing to engage in mutual exchange.

DISCUSSION AND CONCLUSION

The lessons from the voices of these Puerto Rican women should not be dis-counted by any urban educator. Adult urban education, whether conducted through human services organizations (governmental or private), schools, churches, and neighborhood and community organizations must take into account and include the context of the culture involved. Adult educators in for-mal, nonformal, and informal learning settings need to develop a better under-standing of cultural factors in order to facilitate connections with learners. DeGruttola (1985) argued that "no learning takes place unless there is some real connection between the subject as learner and the object in the environment" (p. 67). Cross (1982) categorized factors that prevent participation in learning situa-tions as situational, institutional, and dispositional barriers. In this study, the Puerto Rican women described what happens when barriers exist that negate their ethnic identity. Therefore, it is imperative that all adult educators consider the context of the actors' culturally framed lived experiences. In this case, some of the ways adult educators and health care staff can augment their knowledge base of Puerto Rican knowledge and values include use of the Spanish lan-guage; understanding and openness to the health knowledge already in the com-munity; understanding the levels of trust required in the culture and those that are established within the context of gender differences; creation of a friendly, personable learning environment commensurate with the values of the culture; and providing culturally respectful and culturally appropriate health and other kinds of services and information.

The use of the Spanish language enhances learning situations particu-larly in any setting where it is usual for these Puerto Rican women to feel dis-comfort (e.g., welfare offices while enrolling for adult basic education classes, health care settings, etc.). Furthermore, as Monrroy (1983) stated, "most persons under stress will revert to their first language" (p. 137). It is imperative that urban educators learn and use the Spanish language if language is as important to the enhancement of learning situations as it was with these Puerto Rican women.

It was essential for health care providers to establish personal, friendly relationships with Puerto Rican women. An expression of interest in the women as individuals and their families created positive learning opportunities. The development and utilization of empathy by education and health care providers is critical to the creation of positive learning situations. As Coulehan (1992) stated:

> Empathy is the skill of understanding accurately what the patient says and feels and communicating that understanding to the patient. . . . If empathy is lacking, one might ask the right questions, but the patient might not have the comfort or trust required to volunteer important information. (p. 364)

Therefore, empathy demonstrated by health care providers and educators will communicate attention, interest, comfort, and understanding to these Puerto Rican women and will create more meaningful learning situations for them.

The women in this study demanded that their cultural health knowledge be accepted, which represents a demand to be given our own voice that we each formulate (Flannery, 1992). Based on their community knowledge, additional knowledge would be offered and connected to what they had already experienced. However, many times this information, if forthcoming at all, was presented to them in terms that were confusing, ignoring, or going against their cultural knowledge. Hornsey (1982) argued that "much of the relevant health knowledge and information is presented in ways that are not immediately acceptable, accessible, and interesting. The language and imagery are almost invariably directed towards middle-class people" (p. 65). Therefore, in order to communicate health information successfully, health care providers must present health information in terms that are understandable to the learners involved. Also, for Puerto Rican women, this means that the cultural factors described earlier must be taken into consideration. Because the family is a critical component of Puerto Rican ethnic identity, the inclusion of family members is important for the creation of trusting, interactive learning. Furthermore, it is critical for health care providers to possess an understanding of the Puerto Rican woman as the primary caretaker in the family unit. As such, she must be able to understand all health information that is passed on to ill family members. Finally, because ethnic-specific remedies are a critical part of Puerto Rican connections to roots, it is imperative for health care providers to have a knowledge and understanding of the place these remedies hold in the context of Puerto Rican women's lives.

IMPLICATIONS FOR FURTHER RESEARCH

First, this research must be extended to other urban adult populations and learning settings. Second, there is room for research to explore the many facets of learning in urban areas—formal, nonformal, and informal. Third, urban education research must be willing to take a serious look at the situated knowledge of the communities that make up the urban area. In regard to this study, research is needed to discover more culturally respectful ways of delivering health information to Puerto Rican women and to all Puerto Ricans. In this study, the conclusion is that health education, health care, and cultural identity are inextricably interwoven and must be addressed at the community level where individuals live and work. With a larger community view, urban education must look at the interconnectedness between all urban peoples and education. Ultimately, it is hoped that the knowledge gained from this study will contribute to the improvement of health education efforts specifically for Puerto Ricans, and that many more and broader studies will be conducted from the vantage point of adult education to probe the meanings of learning when people are and are not given voice.

What can be said about urban education from this narrative on health learning by Puerto Rican women? First, like formal school education, health approaches are geared to the dominant culture. Through the hegemonic understandings of minority communities and the differential resources to be found therein, the resulting public health care is at best poor, and at worst deleterious to the local people. As a result, poor health conditions are maintained and the local, urban (often racially determined) ethnic culture is blamed for what is described as noncompliance. How many times are children in urban schools expected to fail, and blamed for "not getting it"? Second, in this case, urban Puerto Rican women were voiceless; they were disenfranchised as health-knowers—their traditional knowledge ignored. In the health settings—as in the urban schools and other areas of urban education—the body of knowledge deemed worth knowing (curriculum) and the methods used to transfer that knowledge are often alien to the Puerto Rican culture. This fact is not new, just arrogantly ignored. Resnick (1991), Director of the Learning Research and Development Center at the University of Pittsburgh, demanded that the educational community "rethink what we mean by learning." The new thrust of cognitive science— that learning is deeply embedded in culture and community—is leading toward some "profoundly disturbing" questions about how learning takes place. Writing specifically of Puerto Rican education, Wolinsky et al. (1990) challenged a need to understand the relationships of ethnic factors and health-related learning since 1990. Too, educational efforts in all venues have continued to be criticized as being planned by, and directed toward, the learning styles of Euro-American middle-class adults (Giachello, 1985; Hornsey, 1982; Lotito, 1988; Malgady, Rogler, & Costantino, 1987; White, 1978).

Lets face it, in all areas of urban education, adult and youth, formal, non-formal, and informal, traditional knowledge, contextual knowledge, and trust knowledge are being ignored or rejected. Either the product or the processes of learning, or both, are an affront to the local urban cultures. To assume learning is not possible is haughty and a blatant rejection of what we see around us. How is it that urban people know well what their elected officials are doing? How is it that urban youth can create and remember poignant and on-target poetry and rap? How is it that urban women know how to perform safe abortions for their own people? How is it the Puerto Rican women of this narrative had passed on effective remedies for certain illnesses?

We—the real outsiders—have to face the issues: First, what is most important—that learning occur or that the learning occur the way the dominant people want it to occur? Second, whose knowledge is of most worth—or can multiple knowledge promote and enhance learning? Third, are we so insecure that our values (e.g. efficiency, distance, sterility in health centers—or in schools) must dominate over community mores (e.g., for the Puerto Rican women—staff time to be interested in others, Spanish art and language, chairs in a circle to promote community, building on the remedies of the community first, understanding that the women are the community keepers and legitimizers of health-related information and behavior)? Finally, Apple's (1993) definition of *power* as the "capacity to act and do so effectively" "connected to a people acting democratically and collectively in the open, for the best ideals" (p. 202) as exemplified by the narratives of the Puerto Rican women blows our steely attempts to preserve hegemony to bits. People's power is being used. As with the Puerto Rican women, so too the students in urban schools do act collectively and in the open when it comes to learning. They learn what is important for them to learn, as they decide it, and let outsiders go on mumbling our canons. The problem is that by clinging to our own hegemony and ignoring the traditional knowledge, the contextual knowledge, and the trust knowledge in the urban communities we are failing at the teaching–learning exchange. We have failed to improve infant mortality rates, and the spread of HIV and AIDS in the urban communities. We have failed to improve literacy rates, graduation rates, and employment rates in the urban communities. What is left to do but face ourselves naked and ask ourselves, "Are we committed to real teaching–learning or are we committed to go on enacting a farce of real domination?"

REFERENCES

Anisef, P., & Axelrod, P. (Eds.). (1993). *Transitions: Schooling and employment in Canada.* Lewiston, NY: Thompson Educational.

Apple, M. W. (1993). Between moral regulation and democracy: The cultural contradictions of the text. In C. Lankshear & P.L. McLaren (Eds.), *Critical literacy: Politics, praxis and the postmodern* (pp. 193-216). Albany: State University of New York Press.

Barrow, N. (1982). Women in the front line of health care. *Convergence, 15*(2), 82-88.

Belenky, M. F., Clinchy, B. McV., Goldberger, N. R., & Tarule, J. M. (1986). *Women's ways of knowing: The development of self, voice and mind.* New York: Basic Books.

Carnegie Council on Adolescent Development. (1992). *A matter of time: Risk and opportunity in the non-school hours.* New York: Carnegie Corporation of New York.

Coombs, P. (1973). *New path to learning.* New York: International Council for Education and Development.

Coulby, D., Jones, C., & Harris, D. (1992). *Urban education: World yearbook of education.* London: Kogan Page.

Coulehan, J. (1992). Teaching the patient's story. *Qualitative Health Research, 2*(3), 358-366.

Cross, P. (1982). *Adults as learners.* San Francisco: Jossey-Bass.

DeGruttola, R. (1985). Culture and ethnicity as consciousness. *Equity and Choice, 1*(3), 63-64.

De La Rosa, M. (1989). Health care needs of Hispanic Americans and the responsiveness of the health care system. *Health and Social Work, 14*(2), 104-113.

Fitzsimmons, K. (1991). African-American women who persist in literacy programs: An exploratory study. *Urban Review, 23*(4), 231-250.

Flannery, D. D. (1992). Towards an understanding and implementation of culturally diverse learning styles. *Community Education Journal, 19*(4), 10-12.

Fordham, S. (1988). Racelessness as a factor in black students' school success. *Harvard Educational Review, 58*(1).

Giachello, A. (1985). Hispanics and health care. In P. Cafferty & W. McCready (Eds.), *Hispanics in the United States* (pp. 159-194). New Brunswick, NJ: Transaction.

Gilligan, C. (1982). *In a different voice: Psychological theory and women's development.* Cambridge, MA: Harvard University Press.

Giminez, M. (1989). Latino/"Hispanic": Who needs a name? *International Journal of Health Services, 19*(3), 557-571.

Giroux, H. A. (1988). Border pedagogy in the age of postmodernism. *Journal of Education 170*(3), 162-181.

Goetz, J., & LeCompte, M. (1984). *Ethnography and qualitative design in educational research.* New York: Academic Press.

Grant, C. (Ed.). (1995). *Educating for diversity: An anthology of multicultural voices.* Boston: Allyn & Bacon.

Harwood, A. (1981). *Ethnicity and medical care.* Cambridge, MA: Harvard University Press.

Heath, S. B., & McLaughlin, M. W. (Eds.). (1993). *Identity and inner-city youth.* New York: Teachers College Press, Columbia University.

Hornsey, E. (1982). Promoting health education through adult education: Some British experiences. *Convergence, 15*(2), 60-69.

Hutchins, V., & Walch, C. (1989). Meeting minority health needs through special MCH projects. *Public Health Reports, 104*(6), 621-626.

Jarvis, P. (1987). *Adult learning in the social context.* London: Croom-Helm.

Kaluzny, A. (1991). Implementation of prevention of chronic disease: Theory and application. In H. Hibbard, P. Nutting, & M. Grady (Eds.), *Primary care research: Theory and methods* (pp. 197- 202). Rockville, MD: Department of Health and Human Services.

Lagemann, E. C. (1981). Education as exchange: A perspective derived from women's history. In D. Ravitch & R. K. Goodenow (Eds.), *Educating an urban people: The New York City experience* (pp. 141-153). New York: Teachers College Press.

Lotito, B. (1988). *Entre nostros: Communicating with the Hispanic client.* New York: Newbury House.

Lutrell, W. (1989). Working-class women's ways of knowing: Effects of gender, race and class. *Sociology of Education, 62*, 33-46.

McLaren, P. (1989). *Life in schools.* New York: Longman.

Malgady, R., Rogler, L., & Costantino, G. (1987). Ethnocultural and linguistic bias in mental health evaluation of Hispanics. *American Psychologist, 42*(3), 235-245.

Monrroy, L. (1983). Nursing care of Raza/Latina patients. In M. Orque, B. Bloch, & L. Monrroy (Eds.), *Ethnic nursing care* (pp. 116-148). St. Louis: C.V. Mosby.

Novello, A. (1991). Hispanic health: Time for data, time for action. *Journal of the American Medical Association, 265*(2), 253-255.

Ogbu, J. (1990). Literacy and schooling in subordinate cultures: The case of Black Americans. In K. Lomotey (Ed.), *Going to school: The African American experience*, Albany: State University of New York Press.

Pennsylvania Governor's Advisory Commission on Latino Affairs. (1991). *Latinos in Pennsylvania. Summary Report and Recommendations.* Harrisburg: Author.

Perin, D., & Greenberg, D. (1994). Understanding dropout in an urban worker education program: Retention patterns, demographics, student perceptions, and reasons given for early departure. *Urban Education, 29*(2), 169-187.

Radecki, S., & Bernstein, G. (1989). Use of clinic versus private family planning care by low-income women: Access, cost, and patient satisfaction. *American Journal of Public Health, 79*(6), 692-697.

Ravitch, D., & Goodenow, R. K. (1981). *Educating an urban people: The New York City experience.* New York: Teacher's College Press, Columbia University.

Resnick, L. (1991, February 6). *Report on educational research.* Washington, DC: U.S. Department of Education.

Schur, C., Bernstein, A., & Berk, M. (1987). The importance of distinguishing Hispanic subpopulations in the use of medical care. *Medical Care, 25*(7), 627-641.

Weisman, C. (1987). Communication between women and their health providers: Research findings and unanswered questions. *Public Health Reports, 102* (Supp.), 147-151.

Westburg, J. (1989). Patient education for Hispanic Americans. *Patient Education and Counseling, 13*(2), 143-160.

White, N. (1978). Ethnicity, culture, and cultural pluralism. *Ethnic and Racial Studies, 1*(2), 139-153.

Wolinsky, F., Aguirre, B., Fann, L., Keith, V., Arnold, C., Niederhauer, J., & Dietrich, K. (1990). Ethnic differences in the demand for physician and hospital utilization among older adults in major American cities: Conspicuous evidence of considerable inequalities. *The Milbank Quarterly, 67*(3-4), 412-449.

Zambrana, R. (1991). Cross-cultural methodological strategies in the study of low income racial ethnic populations. In H. Hibbard, P. Nutting, & M. Grady (Eds.), *Primary care research: Theory and methods* (pp. 221-228). AHCPR Conference Proceedings. Rockville, MD: Dept. of Health and Human Services.

10

Can Critical Pedagogy Work in the Inner City?:A Conversation With Peter McLaren

Barry Kanpol
St. Joseph's University
Peter McLaren
University of California, Los Angeles

It is not uncommon, as some critical theorists in education may agree, that many of our foundations students are often both shocked and dismayed at what the inner-city realities of teaching encompass. Other students, it could be argued, do not particularly care for the plight of inner-city schools simply because a teaching job awaits them in a surrounding middle- to upper middle-class suburb, where much of the life style may already be comfortable and may feel safe to them.

My students often complain, and rightly so, that they cannot understand the poverty, oppression, and alienation facing inner-city clientele. They also argue, again correctly, that if I as an instructor have not taught in the inner cities I cannot preach a message of hope and possibility that is offered by critical pedagogy as a field of knowledge within the critical theory tradition. Faced with this dilemma daily, I often argue that it is my social responsibility to bring to light the oppression, alienation, and subordination of minorities in the inner city. Not to do so would actually exacerbate my own students' alienation, subordination, and oppression as well as my own, simply by not dealing with the reality of the inner city. As an instructor who cares to open eyes to educators, albeit in a "critical" manner, the use of texts becomes paramount.

McLaren's now well-reputed book, *Life in Schools,* has received much acclaim for the insights that critical pedagogy offers. However, even after reading McLaren's work, my students are angry and often frustrated with him. Why, I ask, are they upset with McLaren for leaving his post to better himself? It has often struck me that we can always shove the blame of poverty and hopelessness elsewhere. Why not blame the victim again? Thus, my students' response to McLaren's work is hegemonically constructed so as to maintain distance from the real conditions of poverty, alienation, and oppression. Knowing this, I have over the years expressed an interest for my students to share personally their concerns with McLaren. Take it out on him, not me, I argue! Unfortunately, they are at first mainly concerned with why McLaren left his elementary teaching post. It is my job as a critical educator to direct my students' questions to the more pressing issues that critical pedagogy renders, as related to the inner city as well as other educational interests. What follows is a phone conversation with McLaren and one of my Master Level classes.

A CONVERSATION

Barry: Hello Peter. We have 14 female and 2 male students here this evening. We have a list of questions. We have read *Life in Schools.* People are concerned. I will ask the first question and we'll go from there, Okay?

Peter: I hope this interview goes better than the one I did for television in Hollywood a few weeks ago. I was asked to debate southern California's answer to Rush Limbaugh—a frightening individual named Dennis Praeger. The topic was multiculturalism. The producers refused to air the show, claiming I sounded too literate for a television audience. Okay. Let's see how it goes.

Barry: Peter, very broadly put, how would you give us an understanding of critical pedagogy?

Peter: First of all, let me underscore the idea that critical pedagogy cannot be talked about in a singular sense; rather we need to refer to critical pedagogies in the plural. To talk of critical pedagogy in the singular is to suggest some overarching unitary cohesiveness. A master narrative perhaps. Many people who write about and practice critical pedagogy have different points of emphasis epistemologically, ethically, ontologically, and politically. Yet despite this they share a concern for how race, gender, and class play themselves out in the social and cultural logic of schooling. They seek social justice and social transformation. Other things shared in common would be an intense desire to create greater equity, conditions of access, economic justice, democratic policy initiatives, reform efforts, and decision making. Lamentably, some people are domesticating critical pedagogy and what I think are its most radical messages, characteristics, and practices. My own position, for instance, has shifted from a progressivist position to one that is more and more in concert with some of the positions developed variously within a neo-Marxist framework. I have been moving more and more to the Left. And so, I often look at somebody who is doing critical pedagogy, for instance, and ask why he or she thinks it's critical pedagogy. Often I get the reply: "Yes, I'm practicing critical pedagogy because I'm using a whole-language approach to teaching reading." Somebody may justify that that is critical pedagogy simply because it employs a progressive methodology like whole language. One has to be a little bit cautious in viewing and assessing whether something is really critical pedagogy. I'm not arguing that there is an authentic pristine form of critical pedagogy, because there are multiple ways of defining the term and engaging in its politics and practices. I have spoken to people who claim to be doing critical pedagogy but within my axiomatic use of the term are not doing critical pedagogy at all. They are domesticating its critical impulses, turning radical moments of challenging class exploitation and racism into sitting students in circles and inviting them to "feel good" about themselves in some Do-It-Yourself version of pulling yourself up out of whatever mess you're in.

Student: I teach first grade in Harrisburg. My question is: With respect to your own experiences and knowledge and identity as an educator in the United States, are there comparative systems throughout the world?

Peter: This question is so difficult to answer. I am not a comparativist in education and so I don't do empirically grounded cross-cultural studies and even if I did, I think I'd be at great pains to satisfy you with an answer to that. I can only speak out of my own social, cultural, and political location as an educator who has taught in Canada and the United States and who has lectured briefly throughout Latin America, Europe, and Southeast Asia. I have been affected by my family, my peers, religious traditions, and people with whom I come into contact. Right now, for instance, in California I'm learning a great deal from students from Chicano communities who are trying to figure a way of doing a study of the L.A. high school walk outs. Prior to the vote on Proposition 187, students in L.A. were walking out in record numbers, the most in California's history, more than in the 1960s, but nobody is talking or writing about it. The media isn't covering it. So my location as a professor who lives in

L.A. is shifting my concerns. I think that, broadly speaking, you can say that there's exploitation in a global sense surrounding social relations of capitalist production and the cultural logic of capitalism. There now exist new forms of capitalism that are different to earlier species of capitalism. There is a growing logic of commodification and consumption that's effecting everyone and in a powerful way overdetermining our identities in similar ways even though we may be located in different cultures and countries.

Same Student: So, talk to us about global capitalism!

Peter: I think that capitalism exploits the needs of the many for the benefit of the few. The social relations of capitalist production has created an elite class, and a vastly larger class whose conditions of livelihood are rapidly diminishing. Multinational corporations carry a consumerist imperative creating desires in people for certain products that they do not need. Capitalism is predicated on profit and the extraction of surplus value. And while the industrial economy has shifted demonstrably to a service economy, its fundamental social relations of exploitation have not changed. Your question is a very complex but important question. But while global capitalism doesn't *determine* our identities, it *influences* our subjective formation in similar ways despite our geopolitical location.

Student: Why do you think that critical pedagogy can be successful as a political forum for teachers?

Peter: I don't know if it will be successful. I think it could be successful. I would certainly like it to be successful, and I'd like to keep some hope alive surrounding the success of critical pedagogy both nationally and globally. But to be honest, I'm not sure that it will be. I don't see many signs that it's ever going to become a major tool of analysis in educational research or a tool for teaching or a tool for conducting investigations in rural schools or inner city schools. There are very few classrooms where I think the conditions are right to practice critical pedagogy. I think that many people appropriate certain elements of critical pedagogy, for instance. People will read the literature, whether it's my literature, Paulo Freire's work or that of Barry Kanpol or Henry Giroux. Yet many teachers complain that they can't do this or that because they might lose their jobs. They worry that the community would never let them take a critical position on issues. It's a tricky business, critical pedagogy. Some people try to practice critical pedagogy in a clandestine fashion, without naming it as critical pedagogy. Others try to build alliances with other teachers and community members first, and then come out with a bang. You have to size up the territory for yourself. You just can't go out alone and take on the school establishment by yourself. You need to have support from other teachers, sometimes teacher unions, teacher federations, and other social movements and groups and constituencies and that are not always in place. So I think it's a really tough battle. Personally, all I can do is keep fighting for social justice. There aren't a lot of us. Barry is one. There may be less than a few hundred people that really do this around the country, who actually get out and share critical pedagogy with prospective teachers and practicing educators. We're just trying to survive where we are in our own university locations. And we hope that people are going to start taking this work seriously and not simply dismiss it as some kind of radical extremism. So I think that teachers pick and choose what they want given the contextual specificity of their own sociopolitical locations as educators and given the milieu of their teaching sites. And how successful it will be is really hard to say. Critical pedagogy offers no guarantees—there are no warranties that come with this because it is not a product or an appliance, but rather an attitude, a form of ethical commitment. It is a critical disposition. Its politics drives its methodology, not the other way around. Critical pedagogy, taken seriously, is a way to read the word and the world, as Paulo Freire would say. Unfortunately, where it does seem to prevail in school boards or in specific schools, it seems to be a kind of watered down version of the critical pedagogy I'm talking about in *Life in Schools*. And I guess that's better than nothing. But, I think there's a real fear that a lot of the work will simply become domesticated. Now, if it becomes domesticated then it actually becomes part of the system. So critical pedagogy could actually be so domesticated that it becomes almost a practice that actually increases the hegemony of the dominant culture. If you give the dominant culture a watered down version of critical pedagogy you could, in fact, eliminate critical pedagogy and strengthen the disease called global capitalism and its attendant viruses known as exploitation, sexism, racism, patriarchy and racial supremacy.

Student: Hello Dr. McLaren. How do you define success for students in schools from different areas.

Peter: Well that's a great question. I don't really define success in relativistic terms, such as if a person feels good about what she or he is doing. Success is not gauged by the expenditure of exuberance. I think that, generally speaking, the way that success has been analyzed and evaluated within mainstream educational discursive regimes speaks to a liberal-psychological model—you must feel good about yourself, and as long as you feel you are learning, no matter who you are, and as long as you can read and write, and maybe appreciate culture and can read the editorial page of a newspaper and form your own opinion—then that is success. That's generally what teachers say when defining success for their students in very basic terms as far as becoming functionally literate is concerned. I think success needs to be a little bit more than that. I think that success has to do with what Paulo Freire says is reading the word and the world. Success has to do more with critical literacy than functional literacy, than with merely educating students to adapt to the larger racist, sexist, and exploitative society. It means understanding how your desires, thoughts, and views—what I call your subjectivities—are formed so that you are able to understand how you are motivated to think what you think and do what you do and are able to understand that well enough so that you can raise the question: "What is it that this particular culture, community, society, country, continent, and world has made of me that I now would like to reject?" Who am I when I am going through one day of my life? You need to have a way of understanding how you've been formed. You need a critical vernacular in order to scaffold your lived experiences, in order to frame or critically situate your everyday quotidian events and practices, in order to critically analyze and interrogate the warp and woof of your mundane, ordinary consciousness and to find out that the ordinary consciousness is not so ordinary after all; it's a complex weave of numerous vectors of power, of competing discourses, of agonistic cultural practices, of prediscursive intelligences, of material relations linked to capitalism. So that success now becomes the means to decolonize your mind. I think what I'm trying to say is that you must have a language *for* the self as well as *of* the self, a language to be able to understand why you do what you do and think what you think, so then you can say: "How do I want to act and behave and what are the constraints that disable me and why does the culture motivate me to want things that aren't necessary or to ignore the pain and suffering of others?" We need to rethink the possibilities *of* and *for* the self, and to develop a critical social theory that will provide us with the tools necessary to accomplish this. What I am saying is that within the United States, cultural formations, institutional arrangements, discursive practices, and hierarchies of power linked to race, class, gender, and sexual relations mediate against the development of a critical consciousness. Educators need to challenge this situation.

Barry: Peter, given the multiple realities of Jane Finch Corridor and your experiences how could what you have said be placed?

Peter: Expand on that a bit more for me please, Barry.

Barry: How do you define multiple subjectivity, self, construction of self, and identity within the context of when you were teaching in the inner city?

Peter: I see what you mean. I think that I basically operated from what could be called, in Paulo Freire's terms, *naive consciousness*. It was not until I left the Jane Finch Corridor that I was able to really understand the limitations of my worldview, and the significance of those limitations as a form of motivated amnesia, an historical amnesia. I didn't possess a conceptual or ideational framework for the kind of decolonization I was referring to earlier. Not had I the intimate familiarity with the history of revolutionary struggle or with Marxian social theory that I needed in order to begin a project of self and social struggle, of active, critical mindfulness. The hedonistic, narcotic stupor that informs much of North American culture prevented me from fully realizing the limitations of my belief system and the limitations of the attitudes that I held. I really do believe that I hadn't fully understood how my whiteness, my maleness, my history as a working and then middle-class male had made me assume my own superiority about my culture that was basically working against the interests of the Jane Finch Corridor constituencies and economically disenfranchised people in general. In other words, I didn't fully locate myself in my own history in a critical way. I think I was a liberal teacher, in the diary section of *Life in Schools,* with the best of intentions, well meaning, not perhaps the greatest teacher in the world, but someone who was creative and tried and took risks and fell on my face many times and picked myself up to face yet another day. But I was somebody who didn't really understand the kids who I was teaching and the community I was serving and how their lives were structured and codified and semiotically and materially managed.

Student: Dr. McLaren, the way you tell that reminds me of *Dead Poet's Society*. What seemed to be a wonderful situation for kids turned out to work against them.

Peter: Yes, absolutely.

Student: It seems that you are portrayed as a hero by these kids and by the media representation you received for your work.

Peter: That's true. I don't like the label of hero—never have. I was seen as a White, blue-eyed crusader coming from the White suburbs to tackle the jumble of pathology that conservatives and some liberals associate with these inner-city kids. I was defined as the "James Dean of education"—the White rebel. And it was absolutely bizarre. I was glad that the dominant media didn't attack me as a complete flake, but at the same time, I was made into a hero or an anti-hero, which I found uncomfortable. I don't like that kind of attention. I prefer to work behind the scenes. The media needs to operate the way it does because it is operating within familiar media techno-narratives. How do you place this guy McLaren? They didn't want to place me as a social critic or as an intellectual, so I became a White *"To Sir With Love."* The irony of that period in my life is that although I have written and edited many books, never will my work get the national publicity that *Cries from the Corridor*, on which *Life in Schools* is based, received. And, yet that's my least important book as a critical educator. I know I'll never have the kind of audience that I had with *Cries from the Corridor*. It will always be much smaller and directed toward not the general public but educators, intellectuals, and school teachers, and that's a reality that I have to face and it is a very uncomfortable one. I'd prefer that *Critical Pedagogy and Predatory Culture* or *Revolutionary Multiculturalism* be read over *Cries in the Corridor*. But that will never happen.

Student: Hi Peter, I teach fourth grade I was wondering how you feel schools can challenge dominant stereotypes such as gender bias?

Peter: That's an excellent question. You know it's interesting because the notion of gender and gender bias has now become a part of the popular public discourse. There was something in the media on 20/20 that looked at gender bias while trying to suggest that there's more of a biological basis to gender differences and the biology is, in terms of influence, as important as culture. I think the biological determinism was certainly overstated in that program. But at least the debate is out there. That's one good thing. Perhaps it's being wrongly presented. In terms of what people are doing, I think there's a wonderful book that Shirley Steinberg and Joe Kincheloe have edited called *Kinderculture*. I've done a piece very critical of the Power Rangers. Other theorists have looked at The Simpsons, Beavis and Butthead, Barbie dolls and I'm sure there are many more critiques of gender within popular culture directed at educators of children. It is imperative that we continue to analyze how student subjectivities are formed in relation to gender. As a teacher, you need to challenge how the media construct gender bias. How they construct discourses of masculinity, femininity, citizenship, patriotism, civic duty, identity, love, compassion. You need to challenge dominant regimes of representation. You need to resignify, to re-enchant these discourses, and develop a willingness to dissent and become maladaptive to the White male-privileging hierarchies of power. Otherwise, it will be extremely difficult to challenge those media stereotypes in your classroom with your young students. Every teacher, I guess, has a specific way of achieving that, depending on the grade level. Maybe in kindergarten from encouraging young girls to play and explore and invent and take risks in the playground, to actual lessons in later grades where students are provided the space to talk about gender differences, to find alternatives to stereotypes, and to tease out contradictions. Just bringing to consciousness and engaging in dialogue about differences and similarities with your students will help challenge stereotypes. Teachers are much more creative than I am; just give them the idea, ask them "Why is this the case?" etc, and they take over and come up with the most innovative, transforming lessons you can imagine. My work just heats up the engine. It's the teachers and students who drive the car. I think the crucial thing for students is to come to an understanding that behavior can be different and if behavior can be different in different cultural contexts then maybe we can self-consciously change our behavior.

Barry: This leads me to the question: How it is possible for males to talk about gender issues? And what is feminism for teachers working in the field?

Peter: That's interesting. I think it's very difficult but not impossible for males to talk about the feminine. I think that we all have partial knowledge about these issues. Males speaking as feminists or about feminists always have to, I think, be critically conscious of their positionalities as males. That is to say, they have to reflect: "What is about my maleness that might be shaping my discussion of feminism?" "What is it about my history, for instance, as a White male, that shapes or limits my understanding of femininity?" "What are the contingencies surrounding my narrative forms of address, or that mediate my positionality or my own discourse as a feminist or as someone who wants to say something about feminism?" But I don't think it is impossible for males to talk about it. I mean, the notion of gender, of course, is malleable. And I think that gender as an essentialist identity is becoming contested today in many different arenas and especially among feminists such as Butler, Spivak, DeLauretis, Grosz, and hooks. For instance, cross-gender is being talked about. We have a proliferation of gender studies: gender and sexuality, class and gender, ethnicity and gender and studies about how gender influences our identities as females, Chicano/as, Asians, African Americans or Jews. We can't talk about gender in isolation from other aspects of our identity formation. In other words, we may be articulating our identities in ways in which class gets highlighted or inflected. In other contexts or situations, we might want to take into account gendered aspects of our identity. Or we may want to examine how race, class, and gender become discursively coarticulated in specific contexts. I'll give you an example. I'm part of the gay, lesbian and bisexual alliance at UCLA. I'm straight, but believe it's important to be a part of this alliance. Some of my friends said that I should really identify my location because my gay colleagues might assume that I am gay or bisexual and when they find out that I am straight there may be resentment because they may feel I was trying to deceive them. I approached one of the leaders of the alliance and he said that it's nobody's business but mine, but he thanked me for thinking about the possibility that I should raise this as an issue. These are the kinds of issues one has to deal with, placing oneself in one's own location and understanding other positionalities. This is precisely what it means to be a critical educator. What is your positionality, sexual orientation, social class position in relation to others? In the past, had I understood these kinds of issues better, had I narrated my identity and understood other narratives better, I would have been a better teacher and more critical! I can never speak as a female or a person *from* the inner city. But I *can* speak in solidarity *with* specific feminisms and other marginalized group positions. In fact, I would rage against any liberatory pedagogy that would discount me because I am White or male. Yet, at the same time, I need to be acutely sensitive to the history of White, male, heterosexual privilege. I need to know when to take a smaller role, when to be less present, when to give up power, when to share power, when to create power. I need to purge myself of White, male arrogance, to dismantle discursive and institutional structures of power that advantage my ability to enunciate my own voice and negotiate my day-to-day existential identity. I need to let go of my fear of the other, my fear of losing power, of losing advantage. My White student teachers in my classes here at UCLA find it difficult to do this. There is a real white backlash, a new species of xenophobia, of postmodern structures of self-indulgence, of a new hatred of the other: a real horrible situation nurtured here in southern California by Governor Pete Wilson and his hate-filled attacks on immigrants, on affirmative action, and by his views on militarizing the border with Mexico. And there's the racism of *The Bell Curve*. The battle is fierce. Republicans are fueling a species of hatred so horrific it's almost unbelievable.

Student: Dr. McLaren, I'm an English teacher in rural Pennsylvania. I have a question. In reading your book and *Savage Inequalities,* and also Kathleen Weiler's book, it strikes me that there's so much despair, as we look at what's happening in the inner cities. What kind of hope can you offer as a critical pedagogist? How can we look with more optimism toward the future?

Peter: That's one of the toughest questions to answer and I've been asked that question before and it's always one I feel bad about because it is the question I answer the least successfully from the perspective of the person asking that question. I get depressed a great deal and you know when you read the life histories of many critical theorists, there's suicide, despair, and insanity sometimes. And, I don't want to romanticize despair, but neither do I want to romanticize hope. I guess part of what drives me as a social theorist and as a critic and as a writer is the tremendous anger that I feel all the time, because I look around me and I say to myself that things don't have to be this way. They can be so much better. And, I know they can be an awful lot worse as well. But I'm not satisfied when people say to me, "Well, look Peter, we could be living right now in Bosnia, so feel better about your life, or you're not living in the West Bank, so relax a little bit." They're right, yet at the same time I feel so much pain. They call Los Angeles "Beirut by the Beach" and Los Angeles is my reality, and when I see the hatred felt by Whites and African Americans and Chicano/as toward each other, I tend to despair. When I see Republican virtue turned to cruel articulations of Latinophobia, I cringe. When I see Americans misidentifying free market capitalism with democracy, I recoil in horror. When I see Chicano students sitting together in high school lunchrooms, and Whites clustered together and African Americans hanging tight away from everyone else, I see a situation rooted in an imperialist, Euro-American capitalist logic that divides body from spirit, heart from mind, and divides people along racial, class, and gender lines. I'll give you an example. I was recently walking through the UCLA campus at midnight. Occasionally you can spot homeless people sleeping on campus. We go and eat lunch in our beautiful, well-equipped cafeterias and homeless people sometimes wander in. You can see a lot of annoyed students—it breaks their comfort zones. Suddenly, they are forced to recognize the "other" that they themselves have helped create, that we have created because of our greed, narcissism, Eurocentrism, our patriarchal wilderness, our corporate structures, our institutional practices, and our binary divisions that structure our subjectivities at the level of language and so on. I'm looking down from my sunlit office at a beautiful cappuccino bar, at the large umbrellas to protect people from the sun, and I'll probably go and have a cappuccino right after this interview and chat with my students who are wandering around looking gorgeous and tanned and basking in the sunlight. All of a sudden, a homeless person might appear and everyone will mutter: "Oh God." Here we are in an institution of higher learning that is supposed to cultivate some kind of social consciousness, some kind of compassion and yet I walk by the homeless believing that I can't do anything, and I give myself all the alibis necessary to dampen my guilt. Yet this kind of reality is starting to invade even these protective enclaves of our cities like university campuses. I think people are beginning to realize that the world outside this campus and the world inside this campus are very different places and we experience both of them in abstract, desocialized ways. If we can't in some way reach out to people sleeping on our benches in the campus—what's to suggest that we are going to do it in the real world, when we have all these everyday pressures on us? Why can't universities be sites where we can be a model community, where we can live up to the promise of democracy, where we can organize programs around social justice and take the campus into the communities and the schools, for instance? It's really hard for me to have this kind of hope. I mean—I anguish and I guess out of this anguish hope still dreams itself into existence. Hope is the hieroglyph written on the tablet we call freedom. Hope is grounded in agency, in desire, in the spaces of enunciation, in the possibility of me acknowledging you as more than a partial me, as more than a repressed mirror image, as more than a missing fullness I fill in with my own pathology. Rather, hope is the ability to love. I could say that on the one hand I feel hopeful that you are calling me right now, that there is a group of students who care enough about critical pedagogy to ask to spend time with me, but it is hope with a limit. It is a "hopefulness" that is always contingent and tampered by a knowledge of the real, a hopefulness that is always constrained by the outside. Hope and despair are always in dialectical tension and need each other in order that agency may be possible, that history may be possible, that possible futures rather than predetermined ones can shape us as we shape them. Yet are possible futures predetermined? To be imprisoned by such paradoxes is to miss their point: that of facing up to our responsibility to ourselves and to others, to our ontological vocation of becoming more fully human—which can never be realized as long as needless suffering exists. That we can be agents of liberation in the midst of unfreedom—that is freedom! I have to say I do have a sense of something larger than myself, a sense of spiritual givenness. I do believe that there is a force larger than and more encompassing than television or the media which, I think, metaphysically grounds our identity. My critical pedagogy is more faith-based than fear-based. We need to have faith in ourselves and faith in the power of commitment, compassion, and love. This is true, particularly of the inner city, much of which represents the poverty I have talked about. A critical pedagogy for those areas scrutinizes identities but as a leap of faith also invokes the powers of reason, of critical analysis, of theoretical investigations, of negative dialectics, of critical hermeneutics, of critical semiotics, and so on, in order to question the larger picture of social justice and what part teachers can play in this world for the cause of liberation, so often undermined by the material conditions of existence and the social relations reproduced under late capitalism.

Student: Hi. I teach a third grade classroom in what I consider an upper middle-class area. I had a hard time dealing with my first exposure to critical pedagogy. And with what you've talked about now and after I've read your book and *Savage Inequalities*, I can understand what's going on in these inner-city schools, but I was offended in the beginning that I was even told that due to my structural-functional background I was a part of the problem. Now that my eyes have been opened to more phenomenological and critical traditions, what can I do in these scenarios and situations?

Peter: I think that's good. I mean I really believe that we construct our realities. And, that this always occurs within certain constraints we brush up against, as Marx reminds us. We don't just simply invent our world, outside the existence of the real. I mean, if I try to leave my office right now and the door is closed, I'm going to smash my head and probably knock myself out. On the other hand, we need to recognize the constraints to our freedom that have become so camouflaged that we can't see them as part of the problem. How do the categories we use to construct our realities codetermine those very realities? How are we always already limited by the discourses that provide us with the "quilting points" of our identities? How do we mistake the effects of our experiences for the experiences themselves? How do we conflate our conception of the self and the discourses we have available for thinking about self, about agency, about action, about hope, about praxis? How is knowledge never pristine but always an effect—an effect created by the media in which it is expressed and by its reception by various actors who are always situated in various contexts. I do believe that we need to get a sense of how structures affect agency, and vise-versa, a sense of how what happens in a barrio in east L.A. fundamentally effects me in different ways, so that we are all connected. And, I don't mean this in a New Age kind of way. We are all connected not only through our own sense of traditions but we're also connected through our politics of dissent. We're all connected in a fundamental way. We all vitally depend on each other. And, I think that when we as North Americans recognize that when our benefits and standard of living, our lifestyle, our ability to engage and escape in leisure activities, in some way are connected to the urban ghettos and conditions in the Third World, so that our sense of material enjoyment is often at the expense of other communities who have suffered under imperialist assaults by Western capitalists and religions in order to give us this sense of enjoyment—we will have created the ground work for a critical pedagogy. If you study economics and you understand the politics of colonialism, the politics of materialism, the politics of scarcity, the politics of economic dependency, you begin to realize that our standard of living is directly connected to U.S. imperialism in Latin America and elsewhere. And, it's very hard sometimes to see that connection. You say, "Oh God, that has nothing to do with me," but it does. We all get the fallout from neo-liberal social poli-

202 Kanpol & McLaren

cies, from structural discrimination and structural racism; and look at
our histories of genocide. We are also suffering that now. We see
our history as a people in the L.A. uprising of 1992. It's really hard
sometimes to feel compassion or a sense of commitment to others
who are different. A more phenomenological kind of looking at the
world rather than a structural-functionalist way of looking at the
world can certainly help to deepen one's understanding of the complex webs of interdependency that inform our realities as subjects
and agents of history. But even from the perspective of phenomenol-
ogy it is difficult. We can have this compassion and feeling of wanting to create spaces of empowerment, yet we brush up against the
reality that our intentions and our good will just aren't enough to
undo these major structural oppressions. People will always look at
the world in very different kinds of oppositional ways as long as
social antagonisms continue to exist. People view the world differently because their standpoint is situated in different social relations,
some that privilege some groups over others in material and symbolic ways. And, "What can we do?" is a very difficult question. I'm
trying to wrestle with this question of diversity. When I did *Life in
Schools* and *Cries from the Corridor*, I thought we needed only a
diverse world with diverse voices. Then I realized that diversity in
and of itself isn't enough. Who is orchestrating and articulating the
nature of diversity? In the U.S., it's basically a hegemonic, patriarchal, White, heterosexist culture that constitutes the prevailing system of intelligibility and all these other views and perspectives are
simply added on so as they can join the voices already in place.
However, the hidden structure of this diversity, or the hidden tran-
script, is constituted by the social practices and social formations put
into place historically by Anglo, White, affluent males. It's so difficult to undo these webs of hegemonic articulations and antagonisms
even if, as social agents of change, we have great intentions.
Sometimes it means that as Whites we have to take a back seat.
Sometimes it means creating spaces for students to articulate their
frustrations. But, it's very difficult.
Student: I'm unclear as to the distinction between a liberal educator
and a radical educator. Can you make that distinction and contextu-
alize this for me from an inner-city school teacher's perspective?
Peter: For me, a liberal is somebody who feels that all we need to do
is to shift the resources a little bit more to those who lack them.
Liberals feel the need to inflect the culture and massage different
registers of that culture so that people have more access to resources.
A radical, on the other hand, suggests that liberals are simply working within the structures of exploitation of late capitalism and thereby consolidating those structures even as they like to posture about

the need for change, the need for empowerment, the need to take a stand against injustice. Liberals are simply creating more access or shifting the resources that are the result of capitalist exploitation. In other words, you are just moving the exploitation around and putting it in the hands of different groups. They simply shift exploitation to different sites. Radicals want not only to shift the sites of exploitation, but to cut exploitation at the joints and that makes for a deeper understanding of exploitation, domination, and oppression. Liberals talk about oppression subjectively, like, "Well I'm a White male and I lived with an alcoholic father and an abusive mother in an Appalachian community in a trailer park, so therefore I'm just as oppressed as the minorities." They play the game of who constitutes the greatest social victim. Liberals look at oppression in a subjective way—everyone is oppressed if they feel that they are, whereas radicals talk more about exploitation and the social relations of capitalist consumption and production. Exploitation has to do with use value, surplus value, with the basic exploitation of human labor under capitalism, the selling of one's labor. Capitalism is more difficult to define with the advent of flexible specialization and with a politics of conspicuous consumption and liberal individualism growing exponentially. But, the radical will say to the liberal: "Wait a second! Capitalism at its roots is problematic. It is premised on winners and losers." Look, if we all had the standard of living enjoyed by rich people in Westwood, L.A., the world could not sustain itself. If every family in the world had a refrigerator and a car, the world would unlikely be able to sustain that. So, capitalism is premised on winners and losers. The difficulty is this. We have been coached by Republicans and Democrats alike in this culture and country to see free market enterprise as synonymous with democracy. My argument is that an unbridled free market is actually antithetical to democracy. And, so I think we've grown up with both a liberal and certainly a Republican logic that suggests that we abolish tariffs and that we have this unbridled free global marketplace. Democracy will somehow be ushered in automatically since the effect is somehow guaranteed by the premise. That's absolutely preposterous if not morally dishonest. Capitalism is vicious and is predicated on certain winners and losers. To open critical pedagogy to inner-city possibilities we need to develop an ethics that will protect us from this type of Republican morality. By that I mean, we need to develop an ethics that will contest the totalizing mores and conventional narratives that inhibit the development of the ethical imagination, an imagination that dreams without hate, without fear, without repressing the other. With such an ethics we will be able to develop a philosophy of hope, of dreaming, imagining, one that is linked to critical pragmatism, a bringing together of thinking, doing, and becoming under the ethical imperative of freedom. So can we dream this dream together? Can we love each other collectively? Can we coexist beyond mere tolerance but as *compañeros y compañeras*? Can we love actively and act lovingly? Can we transform the act of knowing into knowing how to act, and with whom, under circumstances not of our own making? Can we scandalize traditional schooling by teaching for maladaption to the present order and the ills that plague our inner-city communities? We need to contest the discursive economy of power and authority that holds sway over mainstream teaching. Within the state-mandated terrain of how one should be educated, the official strategic discourse, lies the liberal-humanism pedagogy that licenses particular forms of representational strategies and forms of ethical address over others. Critical pedagogy has always been a counterofficial discourse, a strategy of displacement and subversion with its related set of counterauthoritative discourses. It has offered counterstatements to the regulatory forces that emerge within the webs of representational codes of postmodernity. It has revealed how a liberal consensus democracy actually masks the power relations upon which such a presumed consensus is premised. It has revealed how liberalism's commitment to multicultural diversity is such that diversity is turned into a privileging hierarchy that is grounded in white supremacist and capitalist patriarchy. Critical pedagogy teases out and attempts to explain the disjunctures between what is professed by the dominant regime of truth and what is implemented. As we negotiate our way through postmodern culture's structures of difference, does critical pedagogy seek to ground its vision in a transcendental ethics or vision of the future? A transcendental ethics can animate an other-worldliness and that's not necessarily desirable. I think criticalists can talk about a transcendental ethics when they refer to a contingent universalism—a vision larger than themselves but that is constantly engaged agonistically—that is, a narrative that inspires and gives direction but that resists closure, a kind of heterotopia that can put into critical relief the discursive practices that regulate our everyday. I want to invite all of you to come and visit me here in Los Angeles. Not just to taste the cappuccinos, but to feel the political pulse of the city. To see how the homeboys and homegirls negotiate sets of discourses that regulate their everyday lives. We need to understand just what "assets" the dominant systems of intelligibility and knowledge practices here at UCLA afford them. If we open up a space for political analysis, we'll see just how important cultural capital is when subordinate groups try to compete in a playing field that is anything but equal. Let's try to work on some ideas together—I'd like that. We need to create spaces together—hybrid spaces of possibility that are constructed when we cross borders and bring something to the spaces that we visit. I'm never left untouched by contact with others. The question is: "What is the form of contact that will take place?" Will it be reciprocal? Violent? Democratic? Imperialistic? Loving? Creative? But we'll never find out if we don't take the kinds of risks that call educators into the future.

CONCLUSION

As we read McLaren's responses to student questions, one thing is certain—one cannot do critical pedagogy in the inner city without making the larger connections to social surroundings. In McLaren's terms, this must necessarily be related to the effects of capitalism and systems of exploitation, alienation, and oppression. So, where does this all leave us? To what end do teachers who end up in the inner city use critical pedagogy? I would have to say that end must beg teachers to be cultural workers. That is, all aspects of the daily routines of teacher lives in the inner city must be connected systems of subordination, particularly on a microlevel for change to take place. Realities of the inner city breeds "despair" in most people who write about such schools. I argue that despair is only paralyzing, cynical, vicious, and harmful if taken to the extreme. That is, critical pedagogy must necessarily start its cause with deconstructing structures of despair—maybe as related to race, class, and gender inequities in the inner city. But hope can raise its head if critical pedagogists or what I term *critical cultural workers* in the inner city take one battle at a time. Let's look at these battles. Yes, McLaren is right. First, we must situate our own subjectivities before any such interrogation of the dominant culture can occur. Second, critical pedagogy in the inner city will entail cultural workers understanding the multiple dialects and the tension between those dialects and the accepted vernacular by the dominant culture. To do so would enable critical pedagogists to enter into the "Other" world, both in empathy as well as insincerity, with the intent to open the possibilities of the subordinated to both understand and survive within socially constructed subjectivities. Third, dominant values such as excessive competition, rampant individualism, and various humiliating stereotype can all be interrogated, not only in one-on-one situations, but through curriculum choice and dialogue over this choice. Fourth, the battle for the critical pedagogy must also lay itself out in front of the administration. Hierarchy that involves authoritarian regimes must be challenged in democratic fashion. Finally, that means finding support within the staff for a socially just cause.

I have only tipped the iceberg with these suggestions here. McLaren's personal voice often leaves students with some despair, but also some hope that there are concerned educators who care enough, who are passionate enough, who are even angry enough, to talk on behalf of the underprivileged, despite the privileged position critical theorists and my students often come from. It is the tension between despair and hope that McLaren's words ring in my student's ears. We all know that is not enough to repair the cancer of inner-city school realities. We all know that critical pedagogy within its multiplicities perhaps opens up only some possibilities, where it always seemed that even that was far off!

Author Index

T

Tabachnick, R. B., 119, 123, *127*
Tabb, W., 148, *165*
Talbert, J. E., 117, *126*
Tarule, J. M., 170, *185*
Taylor, B. O., 102, *111*
Thum, Y. M., 116, *125*
Tiger, L., 62, *70*
Tucker, W., 65, *70*

U

U.S. Bureau of Census, 85, *98*
U.S. Commission on Civil Rights, 91, *98*
U.S. Department of Education, 18, 24, *35*

V

Valdes, G., 130, *145*

W

Walch, C., 170, *186*
Weeks, T., 3, *13*, 150, *163*
Weiner, L., 3, *13*, 113, 118, *127*, 130, *145*, 151, 156, *165*
Weis, L., 151, *165*
Weisman, C., 174, *187*
Welch, S., 160, *165*

West, C., 3, *13*, 142, *145*, 149, *163*
Westburg, J., 181, *187*
White, J. L., 86, *98*
White, N., 183, *187*
Williams, R., 76, *81*
Williams, R. M., Jr., 85, *97*
Willie, C.V., 96, *98*
Willimen, P., 76, *81*
Willis, P., 76, 79, *81*
Wilson, B. L., 102, *112*
Wilson, S. M., 117, *125*
Wilson, W., 148, 149, *165*
Winant, H., 2, *13*, 148, *164*
Wolinsky, F., 183, *187*
Woock, R., 148, *164*

Y

Yeo, F., 3, 5, *13*, 129, 130, 131, *145*, 151, 154, 155, 158, *165*
Young, T., 27, 28, 32, *35*

Z

Zambrana, R., 170, *187*
Zeichner, K. M., 119, 120, 123, 124, *126*, *127*
Zimpher, N. L., 120, *127*

Subject Index